JOB STRESS AND BURNOUT

SAGE FOCUS EDITIONS

JOB STRESS AND BURNOUT
Research, Theory, and Intervention Perspectives

edited by
WHITON STEWART PAINE

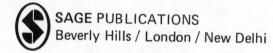
SAGE PUBLICATIONS
Beverly Hills / London / New Delhi

68278

158.7

For information address:

SAGE Publications, Inc.
275 South Beverly Drive
Beverly Hills, California 90212

SAGE Publications India Pvt. Ltd.
C-236 Defence Colony
New Delhi 110 024, India

SAGE Publications Ltd
28 Banner Street
London EC1Y 8QE, England

Printed in the United States of America

Library of Congress Cataloging in Publication Data
Main entry under title:

Job stress and burnout.

   (Sage focus editions; 54)
   Bibliography: p.
   Includes index.
   1. Burn out (Psychology) 2. Job stress. I. Paine, Whiton Stewart.
BF481.J55   1982   158.7   82-7339
ISBN 0-8039-1847-X
ISBN 0-8039-1848-8 (pbk.)

FIRST PRINTING

Contents

Acknowledgments

This volume is truly a joint effort, and it would be impossible to acknowledge all of those who made contributions during the last two years. Special thanks are due to the Sisters of Mercy of Southeast Pennsylvania and two of their institutions, Mercy Catholic Medical Center and Gwynedd Mercy College, cosponsors of the First National Conference on Burnout, which led to this book. They were joined by Cornell University, Crozer-Chester Medical Center, Eagleville Hospital and Rehabilitation Center, London House Management Consultants, the Medical College of Philadelphia, Syracuse University, the University of Maryland, and Villanova University in planning and carrying out that major effort.

Individual thanks are due to Alison McPherson, Nancy Rovin, and John F. Sherlock (fellow members of the Conference Committee) and to Madlyn McCoy, a casebook example of how to be an effective secretary without burning out. I also extend my respect and gratitude to the authors, who worked together so well and who gracefully undertook the major rewriting that resulted in this volume.

Finally, appreciation is due to Mercy Catholic Medical Center, whose ongoing support led to this volume.

Prologue

I've got the burnout blues
Everything is tense,
Feel too many stressors
Beating on my sense.

Watch my mind, it's racing
Back and forth it goes,
Damn it's hard to tapdance
Minus half your toes.

This endless flow of clients
Drowns me in their needs,
Hope, compassion, love are gone
As ire wounds my deeds.

Nights are just not restful
Days are nightmare bent,
Everything is dragging here
As energy is pent.

Success has been relentless
Pushing me past kin,
All those expectations
Have just done me in.

Policies, procedures
Weight my desk and life,
As bosses sit there screeching
Through me like a knife.

The people I do work with
Friends once in the past,
Now ambush me in corners
How long can this last?

9

Heart it keeps on pounding
Empty gut's aflame,
Cigarettes, coffee, booze and pills
Must keep me in the game.

Once I knew my passage
Running with the light,
Today I creep in darkness
Pausing, trapped in fright.

Most of life's a shambles
Work is but a joke,
Constantly I'm pushing
Time goes up in smoke.

At home, a spouse is waiting
Amazing they're still here,
One more crisis with this job
And they'll be gone, I fear.

Influenza stalks me
Despair I seek and find,
Sick days spare my body
Mental health days heal my mind.

Everything's a jumble
Values are askew,
No one's got my answer
This empty soul is new.

Got the burnout blues
So I just sit and stare,
Feel too many stressors
And no one seems to care.

—WSP

1

Overview
Burnout Stress Syndromes
and the 1980s

WHITON STEWART PAINE

"Job stress" and "burnout" have become two of the buzzwords of the 1980s. Already both are a bit shopworn, victims of too much media hype and of the attitude that "of course job stress and burnout are problems; they always have been." However, this volume and an increasing body of research suggest that the facile dismissal of these topics is both shortsighted and potentially dangerous. Burnout stress syndromes (BOSS), the consequences of high levels of job stress, personal frustration, and inadequate coping skills, have major personal, organizational, and social costs—and these costs are probably increasing. Understanding and intervening in these syndromes is the focus of this book.

Background of This Volume

Most new intellectual subfields develop in similar ways. They are started by creative individuals who become intrigued with a problem or a set of problems. Their initial work attracts others with similar concerns and interests. The area then grows through the professional literature, combined with such events as workshops, seminars, and conferences. Frequently there are one or more landmark meetings that begin to define the subfield and then events that attract wider audiences of practitioners interested in using the knowledge developed through research, theory, and past applications. The study of stress in the workplace has followed this pattern over the last fifteen years, culminating in the 1977 Occupational Stress Conference sponsored by the federal government.

Research on burnout developed largely independently of the occupational stress area. According to the publishers of Merriam-Webster's dictionaries, burnout was a concern in the fields of professional athletics and the performing arts in the 1930s. Present interest in the area grew out of the early work of Herbert Freudenberger and Christina Maslach. Their efforts, and the work of others they stimulated, led to the First National Conference on Burnout held in Philadelphia in November 1981.

The Philadelphia conference was unusual in that it deliberately attempted to accelerate the developmental process described above. It brought together the pioneers, new workers, and policy and decision makers who must decide how resources should be allocated to deal with the problem. The timing made sense for two reasons: We now know enough about job stress and burnout to justify a synthesis; we also have learned enough about failures in parallel areas to suggest how this area can be developed most fruitfully in the next decade. This book is one result of the conference.

Four general topics provided a structure for the conference and for this book. These topics were chosen because they both define significant literatures within the area and illuminate topics that require considerable additional work. Part I addresses some basic methodological and theoretical issues. Part II focuses on the necessity of treating the BOSS within a larger intellectual, social, institutional, and economic context. The most important practical issues involve the selection, utilization and evaluation of interventions. Thus, Part III deals with the many available interventions designed to strengthen the ability of individuals to deal with work stress. A separate area of importance concerns interventions at other levels, including techniques that impact on work environments and on entire organizations. These last topics have been a continuing concern to those studying work stress but have only recently begun to enter the literature on burnout.

One final point about the origins of this book: The following chapters are unusual in that they reflect a continuing dialogue between the authors on these topics. They shared outlines and drafts prior to writing the chapters you now hold. In their work they have attempted to summarize their own expertise and to extend that expertise into new and relevant areas. All of the chapters contain new insights; many represent major new contributions to the literature.

About the Contributors to This Volume

Almost every major pioneer in the burnout area is represented in this volume. The phenomenon was first formally differentiated by Herbert

Freudenberger, and Christina Maslach is the field's best-known methodologist. Jerry Edelwich and Archie Brodsky, Cary Cherniss, and Ayala Pines were responsible for four of the earliest generic books on the topic.

The remaining authors, who are experts in parallel areas, are cognizant of burnout and are applying their expertise to this new field. Constance Hoenk Shapiro analyzes the key role of supervision using insights drawn from social work, and Marybeth Shinn provides a detailed analysis of methodological issues. Jerome F.X. Carroll and William White conceptualize burnout in ecological terms in the late 1970s, and Robert Minnehan and Whiton Paine draw on similar skills to attempt the first analysis of economic and legal implications. Robert Golembiewski, a major figure in the area of organizational development, connects that area to burnout for the first time. Jack Wilder and Robert Plutchik, both experienced educators, use their curricular expertise in an analysis of professional education, and Nancy and Donald Tubesing draw on their psychology backgrounds to summarize the burgeoning area of stress management techniques. Finally, John-Henry Pfifferling and Fred Eckel, an anthropologist and a medical educator, respectively, raise some future concerns.

Along with an emphasis on competence, the list of authors also reflects an attempt at balance. It includes physicians, psychologists, social workers, practitioners, academics, males and females, a wide range of ages, and representatives of all sections of the country. The authors were also chosen because of their ability to write generically—to go beyond their backgrounds in one professional area and address the basic issues succinctly. Finally, most of the authors have past experience in responding to the application-oriented needs of decision makers because of their past work as consultants, writers, and trainers.

Topical Structure of This Book

The BOSS is complex. There are major differences between individuals in their responses to stress. Work environments are heterogeneous and have different stressors. Other differences exist between organizations, professional fields, and cultures. At times it almost appears that everything is potentially relevant to an understanding of the phenomenon, a point well made in Carroll and White's ecological analysis. However, a review of the literature, and of the literature in parallel areas, indicates that there are some major issues that need to be addressed immediately. The major ones discussed in the following chapters are:

(1) How can the field best progress?
    (a) by dealing with the severe definitional problems **(Maslach)**
    (b) by confronting potential problems in using research and other information for decisions **(Shinn)**
    (c) by answering the need for generic and specific limited models **(Carroll & White)**

(2) What is the overall context of the BOSS?
    (a) the historical, political, social, and economic trends **(Cherniss)**
    (b) the role of professional education in increasing or decreasing vulnerability to burnout **(Wilder & Plutchik)**
    (c) the relationship of burnout and job stress to the larger literature on stress in general **(Paine)**

(3) How can individuals be strengthened to deal with job stress and its effects?
    (a) through training **(Edelwich & Brodsky)**
    (b) through stress management techniques **(Tubesing & Tubesing)**
    (c) through counseling and psychotherapy **(Freudenberger)**

(4) How can organizations be changed to reduce stress?
    (a) through effective supervision **(Shapiro)**
    (b) through changes in the work environment **(Pines)**
    (c) through broader organizational change **(Golembiewski)**

These questions led to the division of this book into the four sections described earlier and, in greater detail, below.

Models and Methodology

Traditionally, scientific progress requires a close interdigitation of reliable and valid data with the development of models that explain those data, guide further research, and structure interventions. The burnout area is likely to follow the same well-worn path at an unusually rapid pace. Luckily, there are a variety of appropriate experimental designs and theoretical insights that can be drawn from parallel areas of the social and behavioral sciences. To list just a few examples, the potential utility of basic epidemiological theory (Kamis, 1980), social psychology (Maslach, 1977), facit analysis (Einsiedel, 1980), and job turnover **(Shinn)** have all been explored recently. The importation of potentially useful concepts and techniques should continue at a rapid rate until enough is known to support generally accepted models and, ultimately, theories.

Most of the chapters herein have major theoretical implications. For example, model builders must take into account the legal and economic implications summarized by **Robert Minnehan and Whiton Paine** and the historical, political, economic, and social factors discussed in Cary **Cherniss's** summary. The chapters on strengthening individuals and changing organizations reflect attempts to apply potentially useful concepts from other areas. In turn, all six would be strengthened if valid models of the burnout process were available to guide the selection of interventions.

The fundamental question of what should be included in a general model of burnout is addressed in **Carroll and White's** ecological chapter. This pioneering effort will, it is hoped, facilitate the development of comprehensive approaches to understanding the phenomenon.

Even if a generally agreed-upon generic model of the burnout process is developed in the next ten years, it will still have to be modified to meet the specialized needs of different organizations. Relatively crude but useful models need to be conceptualized to describe the burnout process (BOP) in specific situations and thus guide intervention decisions. These models can be developed at different levels, including:

(1) individuals analyzing their own responses to stress;
(2) work groups or teams;
(3) organizational subunits (emergency rooms, departments, plants, and so on);
(4) entire organizations;
(5) industries or human services areas;
(6) professions; and
(7) countries and cultures.

The first three levels are likely to generate the most specific models, but all will require the adaptation of available methodologies and the development of new approaches. All seven levels are discussed in Carroll and White's ecological analysis.

Methodology

Despite instrumentation problems, research studies are burgeoning. Typically, they are one-shot, correlational investigations of a limited set of variables with small populations. This is a natural area for dissertations and easily mounted studies, and the literature is already difficult to follow. One recent review analyzed the inadequacies of the fifty studies done through 1980 (Perlman & Hartman, in press), and the number has certainly tripled since then.

Christina **Maslach,** a pioneering methodologist in the area, developed the most widely used scale (Maslach & Jackson, 1981b) and published the first major research study (Maslach, 1976). Her article on the problem of defining burnout should be read carefully. Definitional problems exist at all levels of the phenomenon: individual, interpersonal, job, and organizational. Most available instrumentation focuses on self-report techniques (**Shinn**) and small groups of subjects. However, major studies are under way with large sample sizes to define the extent and characteristics of burnout in different populations.

Marybeth **Shinn** provides a useful guide to this increasingly large research literature. It is definitely a "buyer beware" situation, because research and evaluation results are likely to become a primary selling tool for a wide variety of competing theories and intervention efforts. The behavioral and social sciences have developed a variety of sophisticated methodological tools that are confusing to decision makers. Such terms as "multiple regression," "factor analysis," and "quasi-experimental design" can tend to confuse the basic issues of what was found and what it means. This is particularly true since many of the techniques, especially for computerized statistical analysis procedures, either are used inappropriately or yield outputs that are overinterpreted.

In addition, one of the challenges of the 1980s will be to integrate the rapidly developing literature on burnout into other, much larger, bodies of knowledge. In particular, workers in the general area of stress have not typically included burnout in their models or in their research. For example, the recent authoritative *Handbook on Stress and Anxiety* (Kutash, Schlesinger, & Associates, 1980) contains no reference to the BOSS and does not cite the work of the authors of this volume in its discussion of theory and intervention. Everly and Rosenfeld's 1982 guide for clinicians on treating the stress response is similarly limited. The burnout literature itself is weak in its utilization of the sophisticated theoretical and methodological tools that have been applied to the study of stress.

It seems clear that burnout is a stress syndrome (Sweeney, 1981). Thus, workers in the area must begin to use information on occupational stress more effectively (MacNeill, 1981), models such as learned helplessness and concepts such as life-stress events and hassles. At another level, practitioners must link the BOSS to the rapidly developing area of health promotion, wellness, holistic health, and disease prevention (**Pfifferling & Eckel**). The recognition that medical treatment has relatively little impact on the leading causes of death has shifted focus to lifestyle issues and the implications of individual choices on the physical and emotional impacts of stress. Stress management and burnout prevention must become a central ingredient in the recent emphasis on behavioral medicine and health psychology (**Pfifferling & Eckel**).

Ultimately, research and evaluation results will provide an important basis for selecting intervention techniques. At present such choices are difficult for many decision makers, in part because they tend to ignore wider issues of context and environment.

Burnout in Perspective

"Burnout" is not a term that has sprung magically into prominence. The noun dates back to the mid-1970s, but probably has many roots, including the psychiatric concept of patients who are burnt out. It also has many definitions (**Maslach**). The common aspect involves physical, emotional, spiritual, intellectual, and interpersonal exhaustion.

In order to understand the phenomenon, it is important to understand the context in which the BOSS has become a focus of attention. The problem is certainly as old as stressful work environments and professional frustration. It was a hidden problem because, until recently, professionals had multiple options for dealing with their developing exhaustion. Alternative jobs were comparatively easy to find, either within or outside their own organizations. Colleges and universities offered relatively inexpensive continuing training and credentials. Similarly, organizations provided more options and resources to aid burned-out workers or simply to facilitate their search for employment elsewhere. The most common organizational attitude was, "If you don't like it here, leave." Most did.

Cary **Cherniss** makes clear in his article that the environment in which professionals work has changed dramatically. Social, political, economic, intellectual, and professional trends have combined to increase stress and decrease alternatives. Unfortunately, these trends are likely to continue, and in some cases become stronger, over the next decade. Succinctly, it is not so rewarding to be a professional any longer, and it is often even less satisfying to move up and become a manager or an administrator. This sense of increasing dissatisfaction is compounded by an awareness of decreasing options.

Job mobility within and outside organizations has decreased dramatically, and there is developing recognition that the staff you have today is likely to be the staff you have next year or even five years from now. These and other factors must be understood because they are compounding the problem and will continue to do so in the next decade.

There are additional, practical contextual issues that must be resolved. The literature on the BOSS stresses the pervasive negative impacts of the problem. Actually, it is important to note that job stress is not uniformly negative. Some degree of stress is necessary to motivate job performance (Einsiedel, 1980) and to provide enough environmental stimulation to prevent boredom **(Pines)**. Burnout has also been useful in facilitating a desirable degree of staff turnover in human services, has helped fill enrollment rosters in some professional schools, and is a potent motivator for individual growth and change. It is already providing a decent livelihood for a wide variety of entrepreneurial professionals. There may also be other individual and organizational benefits as yet uncatalogued.

On a pragmatic level, **Robert Minnehan and Whiton Paine** have raised the basic question of burnout's bottom line. Despite its presumably high personal costs, it is unlikely that concern about the BOSS will result in the release of resources until its costs have been more clearly defined. This is a complex area, and Minnehan and Paine's preliminary analysis is thought-provoking and somewhat alarming. They suggest that the following four types of analyses are currently feasible and likely to become more important as valid and reliable data on the BOSS become available.

First, we need to develop procedures for identifying and then estimating the costs of the various aspects of burnout. Carroll and White list the major potential impacts, and applying cost-accounting principles to this long list will be a formidable task. Second, the cost data must be supplemented by individualized models that tie costs to causal factors that could be modified to reduce those costs. Unfortunately, these factors are interdependent **(Shinn)**.

Next, a rapidly developing area of law involves claims for damage due to work-related stress. At a minimum, stress-related damage can be used for workmen's compensation claims in many states. The organizational liability may be far greater, however, if the BOP leads to such consequences as a disabling illness, a successful suicide, or a defective project or decision that causes widespread damage. Finally, techniques for cost-benefit analysis should aid decision makers in assessing the various intervention techniques and strategies being touted as "cures" for the BOSS.

Part of the burnout problem can be traced directly to deficiencies in the ways professionals are trained. For example, some new professionals, to quote Golembiewski, "flame out" immediately on their first job and may permanently leave the field within a matter of months. A recent book by Cherniss (1980a) is the first longitudinal study to document the process during the first three years of employment. Little is known about longer-term patterns, including whether or not an individual can burn out repeatedly over the course of an entire career or if the process has discrete stages **(Carroll & White, Edelwich & Brodsky)**.

An area of considerable concern is the possible role of professional training in increasing students' vulnerability to burnout on their first job. **Wilder and Plutchik** present an analysis of this area. They were the first to survey faculty in different types of professional schools on this issue, and their chapter raises some fundamental curricular questions. Some of these issues also apply to on-the-job training. It is clear that both academics and professionals need to work together to ease the transition into and out of higher education. For example, Virshup (1982) recently published an interesting volume to aid medical students in dealing with stress.

Wilder and Plutchik also provide some thoughtful insights into how professional education can be modified to prevent subsequent burnout. They are fully aware of the problems encountered with curriculum reform in higher education and have attempted to stress practical solutions involving one general model.

These contextual issues will have continuing impact on our understanding of the BOSS. Developing such an understanding is the first step in planning interventions to prevent or reverse the process.

What Can Be Done?

As Carroll and White point out, the BOSS is best conceptualized within an ecological framework. Both causes and effects occur at all levels, from the biological through the societal. To be most effective, attempts to alleviate the problem must occur at multiple levels and should be linked within a general strategy that grows out of some attempt to model the BOP in a given work environment.

A wide variety of specific techniques and strategies have been proposed to deal with burnout, and it is difficult to relate them within a coherent framework. However, almost all can be grouped by primary goal and site of intervention. The major goals are:

(1) identification: techniques for the analysis of the incidence, prevalence, and characteristics of burnout in individuals, work groups, subunits, or organizations (**Shinn, Maslach**);
(2) prevention: attempts to prevent the BOP before it begins (**Wilder & Plutchik**);
(3) mediation: procedures for slowing, halting, or reversing the BOP (**Tubesing & Tubesing, Shapiro, Edelwich & Brodsky**); and
(4) remediation: techniques for individuals who are already burned out or are rapidly approaching the end stages of this process (**Freudenberger**).

Please note that many techniques can be used to facilitate the attainment of more than one goal. For example, the creative supervisory procedures analyzed by Constance Shapiro have a role in all four goals, and the Tubesings discuss stress management techniques that could be used for prevention, mediation, and remediation.

Interventions can also be targeted at specific sites or levels. The four most important sites are:

(1) individual: interventions designed to strengthen an individual's ability to deal with job-related stress **(Wilder & Plutchik, Tubesing & Tubesing, Edelwich & Brodsky)**;
(2) interpersonal: attempts to strengthen interpersonal relations or work group dynamics either to decrease stress or to support an individual's abilities to deal with stress **(Shapiro, Shinn, Golembiewski)**;
(3) workplace: modifications in the immediate work environment intended to reduce stress or ameliorate it in some way **(Pines)**; and
(4) organizational: changes in policies, procedures, or structure intended to deal with organizational factors related to burnout **(Golembiewski)**.

Again, it is clear that these levels are not completely distinct, since some interpersonal interventions have individual effects and organizational changes will often impact directly on the workplace.

These two sets of categories provide a basis for a useful table, which groups interventions used to change individuals and organizations (Table 1.1). To date, most work has been done on mediation efforts designed to strengthen individuals, and the other areas have received less attention. This may change as decision makers realize that some consideration should be given to all sixteen areas in Table 1.1 in order to develop comprehensive programs (Paine, 1982).

TABLE 1.1   Illustrative Burnout Interventions

Site Intervention	Identification	Goal of Intervention		
		Prevention	Mediation	Remediation
Personal	Self-evaluation	⬌ Professional training/ orientation	⬌ Stress management	⬌ Individual counseling
Interpersonal	Peer feedback	⬌ Support groups	⬌ Creative supervision	⬌ Group counseling
Workplace	Formal surveys	⬌ Professional development	⬌ Job redesign	⬌ Job/Career changes
Organizational	Performance monitoring	⬌ Organizational development	⬌ Quality assurance	⬌ Employee assistance

Strengthening Individuals

Any consideration of attempts to deal with the problem of burnout must start with a consideration of the individual. The three chapters in Part III suggest that individual professionals must take responsibility in at least four areas:

(1) to learn about burnout and job stress in general and how they may affect themselves and others;
(2) to develop techniques for monitoring personal levels of stress and burnout;
(3) to develop effective coping mechanisms to deal with job-related stress; and
(4) to work with others within the organization to deal with the problem.

In many job situations, particularly in human services, high levels of stress are an integral and largely unavoidable component of the work. Examples include air traffic control centers, burn units in hospitals, and social service agencies serving sexually abused children. Similarly, the ability to cope with complexity, ambiguity, conflict, and competing demands is assumed to exist when individuals assume higher-level administrative positions.

However, this is not to say that individuals have the only, or even the primary, responsibility to prevent, mediate, or remediate the BOSS. Indeed, Shinn suggests that individual coping skills may have relatively little impact on burnout. Industrial organizations have begun to recognize their responsibility to provide a safe and healthy workplace. As Minnehan and Paine note, the same logic applies in the area of stress. Organizations are often unnecessarily stressful and should be changed to reduce their negative impact on individuals' physical and mental health. They can also support techniques that strengthen individuals by supporting workshops on stress management techniques and other resources for training and intervention.

This volume focuses on three major strategies for strengthening individuals: workshops **(Edelwich & Brodsky),** the development of individual stress management skills **(Tubesing & Tubesing),** and focused, short-term counseling **(Freudenberger).** The chapters devoted to these strategies should be read together to provide a comprehensive view of the problems and opportunities involved in intervening at the level of burning-out or burned-out individuals.

Because this is a new area, there is a real need for introductory workshops that clearly communicate available information on the problem. These, in turn, would be supplemented by more specialized training efforts on specific topics such as time management or relaxation techniques. **Edelwich and Brodsky** draw on their wide experience in conducting workshops to present specific guidelines for the selection and presentation of training programs in general and workshops in particular. Since the quality of available training is quite variable, such guidelines are needed to aid in selection decisions.

At another level, the **Edelwich and Brodsky** effort is valuable because it provides trainers with many valuable suggestions on how to design, merchandise, and implement such workshops. A potentially large pool of adult educators, private consultants, and others could provide high-quality training once they develop the necessary skills. Some of this expertise should also trickle back into academia to influence the professional training programs discussed by Wilder and Plutchik.

The single largest area of intervention involves techniques intended to help individuals manage personal stress. As Nancy and Donald **Tubesing** point out, everything from aerobic dancing to zen has a potentially useful role in stress management. The Tubesings attempt to bring some order out of this chaotic area by stressing first of all that the complexity of the BOSS requires a holistic perspective on prevention and treatment. As do the other intervention authorities in this volume, they contend that there is no "magic bullet" that can be aimed at the problem. Instead, they recommend individualized prescription based on an understanding of an individual's needs and strengths.

This chapter is particularly useful because it catalogues different general strategies of stress management, including the common relaxation techniques. Additionally, the Tubesings present a stress skills model linking four overall strategies (personal management, relationship, outlook, and stamina) to twenty relatively specific skills that can be learned. Because additional references are given in each skill area, this chapter is an important guide for trainers in the area. (See also Tubesing, 1979, 1981; Tubesing, Sippel, & Tubesing, 1981.) This strategic approach should become even more valuable as we learn more about how best to diagnose individual needs in order to prescribe focused techniques for those needs. Wilder and Plutchik also discuss some basic stress management skills.

Burnout also raises a variety of fundamental ethical issues. These are particularly troublesome when discussing the legitimate role of an organization in dealing with burned-out employees. **Freudenberger** stresses the need for an appropriately structured referral process and the workers' right to confidentiality when involved with employee assistance programs. Shapiro summarizes some of the issues arising from supervisors attempting semiclinical roles, and the Tubesings clearly recommend that the focus be on individual, not corporate, responsibility and decision-making.

Unfortunately, malingering individuals are misusing burnout to excuse inadequacies in work performance. A wide variety of professionals are also seizing this opportunity to make money as consultants and trainers, despite their lack of expertise **(Edelwich & Brodsky, Tubesing & Tubesing).** Clinicians, particularly if they see the problem as synonymous with depression, foresee lucrative opportunities for long-term treatment **(Freudenberger).** Drug companies see a market for antidepressive medications or minor tranquilizers, despite the general potential for misuse. The extent of these abuses is likely to increase as the size of the need becomes clear.

Herbert Freudenberger also deals with the difficult question of what to do with the burned-out professional. It is likely that the trends discussed by Cherniss will result in increasing numbers of staff reaching the end points of the burnout process. Freudenberger's analysis indicates that many of these individuals can be salvaged and can continue to contribute productively within organizations. They are not mentally ill and do not seem to require intensive counseling and psychotherapy. The more productive emphasis is on short-term counseling oriented toward the types of reality issues and personal perceptions discussed in this book. This is an important alternative to the traditional and expensive solution of terminating burned-out employees.

Changing Organizations

Individual change unaccompanied by organizational change is often ineffective over the long term and may even be counterproductive. Training may generate expectations about the willingness of an organization to change; if these expectations are not met, the resultant frustration may accelerate the burnout process **(Edelwich & Brodsky).** Knowledgeable individuals may also become more likely to leave or to challenge the system and increase the stress on others.

There is an increasing consensus that one of the best barriers to burnout is interpersonal **(Pines).** Professionals able to relate closely to other professionals in their work and support groups are less likely to burn out on the job. A separate key is supervision. This organizational function can either reduce job stress or exacerbate the deleterious effects of stressors.

Constance **Shapiro** analyzes the role of such supervisory functions as orientation and evaluation, and presents some potentially useful procedures for creative supervision. A danger here is that requiring effective supervision may contribute to stress on supervisors and increase their burnout. Shapiro also discusses some of the major interpersonal issues involved in intervention, briefly summarizing assertiveness training, buddy systems, orientation programs, time management, the supervisor as role model, and peer support groups. By focusing on the supervisory role, she provides an interesting and useful overview of many related intervention options.

The work environment itself is an important focus for intervention **(Pines).** The literature on occupational stress (Cooper & Payne, 1980; Mac-Neill, 1981) has enumerated many different classes of job-related stressors and related them to such issues as job satisfaction and worker productivity. In her recent book (Pines & Aronson with Kafry, 1981), Pines has summarized research linking specific components of the work environment with self-reported burnout. Her work is an important supplement to the occupational stress literature because it documents in nonbusiness settings phenomena that have previously been studied mainly in industrial organizations. It also provides the beginnings of an empirical justification of intervention at this level.

Pines's effort is largely correlational in nature and will require additional empirical studies to document causal links among job stressors, burnout, and productivity. But it is an important start and suggests specific work-related features that could be modified to reduce the problem of the BOSS. Pines also sensitizes readers to some less publicized stressors: boredom, environmental factors in white-collar jobs, the sense of being confined by a job, inadequate career development practices, and the lack of positive work done in this area. Robert **Golembiewski,** a pioneer in the area of organizations to do this sort of analysis; but it is increasingly recognized as crucial to the prevention and mediation of burnout.

At the most macro level, policies, procedures, and organizational structure must be modified to reduce job stress. Little systematic work has been done in this area. Robert Golembiewski, a pioneer in the area of organizational development, makes the important point that change itself is often stressful over the short term, even if the longer-term effects are beneficial. He provides a stimulating and thought-provoking analysis of the relevance of organizational development and change strategies to the problem. His article lists potentially useful techniques and also discusses a number of important strategies.

Golembiewski's chapter also illuminates the utility of an organizational perspective in order to integrate other perspectives on the BOSS. Many of the interventions he discusses have important implications for individuals, for supervisors, and for those attempting to administer complex organizations in difficult times. Just as individuals must seek forms of assistance congruent with the rest of their lives, organizations must seek intervention congruent with their needs and philosophies, and both must work together to maximize effectiveness.

Ideally, changes would occur at all levels. Realistically, a more limited set of changes must be made. The three chapters just discussed provide the best available information on tools for reducing stress and its effects. All six chapters in Parts III and IV are relevant to the planning of comprehensive integrated institutional programs to deal with burnout.

This introductory chapter has focused on the burnout stress syndrome within the context of the present and the recent past. The closing chapter, by **Pfifferling and Eckel,** focuses on the present and the future in discussing some obstacles and prospects for work on the BOSS. It is, in one sense, an antidote to Cherniss's rather pessimistic analysis of trends, as it illuminates some of the concerns that will guide this rapidly developing area in the next ten years.

During the 1980s, burnout will probably cease to be a separate research area and will be incorporated into the larger area of stress. It will have served its purpose in focusing attention and resources on a phenomenon that incurs significant human and organizational costs. As the awareness of these costs grows, pressure to seek individual and organizational solutions will increase. Many of these solutions are summarized in this volume.

In the next decade, we should also move away from the present tendencies to utilize piecemeal interventions, apply techniques that have general rather than focused impacts, and rely on the implicit assumption that "if it works for stress it works for burnout." The ultimate goal is valid and reliable diagnostic procedures for individuals and organizations, leading to standardized, specialized, cost-effective techniques for dealing with specific aspects of work-related stress and burnout at different levels. These, in turn, will be combined into intervention programs that focus on identification, prevention, and human resource management rather than on mediation and remediation alone.

PART I

Models and Methodologies

2

Understanding Burnout
Definitional Issues in Analyzing
a Complex Phenomenon

CHRISTINA MASLACH

The current fascination with burnout is fairly recent. Ten years ago, very little was being said (at least publicly) about the phenomenon. The first articles appeared in the mid-1970s, and although they were few in number and scattered among lesser known publications, they generated an enthusiastic response. Interest in this topic mushroomed, and with all the writing, teaching, and consulting on burnout, it has become something of a small growth industry. All of this activity can be interpreted as a sign of how important an issue burnout is. Once neglected or swept under the rug, the problem is now getting the attention it deserves, and serious attempts are being made to deal with it. It has been called the crisis of the '80s and even the disease of modern life.

Although burnout is a byword to many people, it is viewed as a buzzword by others. According to these critics, burnout is simply old wine in a new bottle—a trendy name for a problem that has been around for a long time. "They used to call it depression, but now it's known as 'burnout,'" trumpets one newspaper headline; others suggest that it is alienation, apathy, boredom, blue-collar blues, mid-life crisis, or job stress that "burnout" now stands for. A more serious charge is that burnout is a copout; it is an excuse that gets people off the hook when they get into trouble and allows them to avoid facing up to their responsibilities.

Furthermore, some critics have argued that burnout is nothing more than a catchy term that essentially *creates* a condition or problem that then needs to be addressed. These critics often draw an analogy between burnout and the "identity crisis," noting the sudden influx of people into therapists' offices when the latter concept became popular. Burnout has also been dismissed as the junk-food term of the 1980s, and as an example of pop psychology at its worst—all surface flash but no substance. An explosion of written materials, with all their emphatic pronouncements, quickie tests, exercises, and how-to-beat-it hints, has led many people to proclaim that they are burned out on burnout.

Problems

These conflicting (and often impassioned) perspectives on burnout are not simply petty bickering, but reflect some serious problems in the development and usage of this concept. In searching for the truth about burnout—whether it is real or fake, important or trivial, and so on—we need to recognize and address these problems, and to avoid repeating past mistakes. My own feeling is that there is some truth to both the negative and the positive perspectives on burnout: I believe that burnout is a bona fide phenomenon and a very significant one, but I also believe that much of what has been said and done in the name of burnout has provoked some well-deserved criticism. What I deal with here are only the definitional problems; the various research problems are discussed in **Shinn's** chapter.

To understand burnout, we need to know first what it is. Herein lies the major source of confusion and controversy about the concept. There is no single definition of burnout that is accepted as standard. There is no clear consensus among consultants, clinicians, or researchers, nor is there much agreement among staff, managers, or administrators. Reports in the mass media have contributed their own definitions of the phenomenon. Most individuals have their own personal definitions of burnout as well.

Definitions of burnout include the following:

- A syndrome of emotional exhaustion, depersonalization, and reduced personal accomplishment that can occur among individuals who do "people work" of some kind.
- A progressive loss of idealism, energy, and purpose experienced by people in the helping professions as a result of the conditions of their work.
- A state of physical, emotional, and mental exhaustion marked by physical depletion and chronic fatigue, feelings of helplessness and hopelessness, and the development of a negative self-concept and negative attitudes toward work, life, and other people.
- A syndrome of inappropriate attitudes toward clients and self, often associated with uncomfortable physical and emotional symptoms.

- A state of exhaustion, irritability, and fatigue that markedly decreases the worker's effectiveness and capability.
- To deplete oneself. To exhaust one's physical and mental resources. To wear oneself out by excessively striving to reach some unrealistic expectations imposed by oneself or by the values of society.
- To wear oneself out doing what one has to do. An inability to cope adequately with the stresses of work or personal life.
- A malaise of the spirit. A loss of will. An inability to mobilize interests and capabilities.
- To become debilitated, weakened, because of extreme demands on one's physical and/or mental energy.
- An accumulation of intense negative feelings that is so debilitating that a person withdraws from the situation in which those feelings are generated.
- A pervasive mood of anxiety giving way to depression and despair.
- A process in which a professional's attitudes and behavior change in negative ways in response to job strain.
- An inadequate coping mechanism used consistently by an individual to reduce stress.
- A condition produced by working too hard for too long in a high-pressure environment.
- A debilitating psychological condition resulting from work-related frustrations, which results in lower employee productivity and morale.

Not only do these definitions vary from each other to greater or lesser degrees but different terms are sometimes used for similar concepts. Some definitions are limited, while others are more wide-ranging. Some are precise, while others are global. Some refer to a purely psychological condition, while others include actual behaviors. Some describe a state or syndrome, while others talk about a process. Some make reference to causes, others to effects. Most of these definitions have been proposed independently, without regard for the others (and possibly without knowledge of them). It is rare that later definitions follow up on earlier ones, either positively (by incorporating or improving them) or negatively (by explicitly rejecting them and showing why they are inadequate).

The Common Core

However, all is not total chaos. Despite the differences, there are also similarities among definitions of burnout. An analysis of these common threads may reveal a working definition of burnout that is shared by most people.

First of all, there is general agreement that burnout occurs at an individual level.[1] Second, there is general agreement that burnout is an internal psychological experience involving feelings, attitudes, motives, and expectations. Third, there is general agreement that burnout is a negative experience for the individual, in that it concerns problems, distress, discomfort, dysfunction, and/or negative consequences.[2]

Beyond these basic points, the consensus begins to break down. Nevertheless, there are some key dimensions of burnout for which there is majority agreement. The emphases placed on particular dimensions and the terminology used to describe them may differ from one definition to the next, but a definite pattern is discernible.

The dimension on which there is the most agreement is exhaustion. It is also described as wearing out, loss of energy, depletion, debilitation, and fatigue. Although sometimes this exhaustion is a physical one, more often a psychological or emotional exhaustion is described as central to burnout: a loss of feeling and concern, a loss of trust, a loss of interest, a loss of spirit.

A second dimension of these definitions is a negative shift in responses to others: depersonalization, negative or inappropriate attitudes toward clients, loss of idealism, and irritability. Most discussions of this dimension emphasize its movement (in a negative direction) over time—a movement that may also be called a shift, change, development, or accumulation.

A third dimension found in these definitions is a negative response toward oneself and one's personal accomplishments, also described as depression, low morale, withdrawal, reduced productivity or capability, and an inability to cope. Some definitions are limited to feelings of failure or sense of low self-esteem; changes in actual behavior are considered to be an outcome of this psychological state. In other cases, these behaviors are considered to be part of the basic definition of burnout.

Causes and Effects

Just as there are different definitions of burnout, so there are different theories or ideas about what produces it and what results from it. Since most of these theories have not undergone rigorous empirical tests, it is impossible to say what are the "true" causes and effects of burnout. However, just as with the definitions, it is possible to discern some major themes.

Most discussions of burnout emphasize contact with people and the factors that make contact particularly difficult or emotionally stressful. The bulk of the burnout literature to date deals with the helping professions (human services, health care, education), probably because these are people-work situations par excellence. In addition to considering the dynamics of interpersonal relationships, causal analyses have focused on job stress and the characteristics of the organizational setting in which work takes place. There have also been discussions of individual causes of burnout (such as personal expectations, motivations, and various personality traits). However, the emphasis so far has been on situational and social causes more than on personal ones. Numerous outcomes, or effects, of burnout have also been proposed (see **Carroll & White** for a summary list of personal outcomes).

Expansion of the Concept

As use of the term "burnout" has increased, so has the number of phenomena to which it refers. With each new or modified definition, the boundaries of burnout have been stretched to accommodate even more within this framework.

One way the concept has broadened is through the use of hypothesized outcomes or correlates of burnout as a direct index of it. For example, self-tests will use physical symptoms as a measure of burnout, while others ask for reports of behavior. If these responses are considered symptoms of burnout, then the implicit assumption is either (1) by definition, these responses *are* burnout, or (2) these responses are outcomes, but because they have such a strong and exclusive link to burnout they can be used as a direct index of it.

The concept of burnout has also expanded as a result of more knowledge about it. Earlier definitions have been changed or modified to reflect the theoretical insights gained from new information. In almost all cases, these modifications have been in the direction of including more, rather than less. What has probably been the most significant change over the past few years has been the shift from simple to complex models of burnout. Current theorists are arguing that it is an ongoing process, that it is multidimensional, and that there is a developmental sequence of phases or stages.

At first, burnout was considered a problem that was found primarily (or even exclusively) within the helping professions, and the major reason for this was the intense involvement with people that characterized these jobs. Burnout has now expanded beyond these original borders and is now considered applicable to many other sorts of occupations, and not just a problem exclusive to service providers. Although a few analyses specify what types of work should be linked to burnout, more often the argument is that burnout can occur in *all* occupations, for anyone at any level. According to this view, burnout *is* job stress, not just a particular subcategory of it.

The term "burnout" has been extended to include not only all forms of work stress but also to nonwork spheres of life. The emotional strain of contact with people has been discussed in terms of people in one's personal life (spouse, child, friend, neighbor) and not just those people one works with on the job. Moreover, burnout has been applied to nonpeople aspects of the nonwork life, such as household chores and leisure activities ("I burned out on jogging").

Finally, burnout is being used as a metaphor for some fundamental problems facing our society. The overwhelming stresses of life and the difficulties in coping with them, the failure to achieve one's goals, the dissatisfaction and malaise of the worker, the search for personal fulfillment and meaning in life—these are the sorts of global issues that have been included in the ever-broadening concept of burnout.

Consequences of an Expanded Concept

What are some of the implications of this broader notion of burnout? On the positive side, it has been argued that the original concept was far too narrow and limited and that expanded definitions have overcome this weakness. Extending burnout to more job and home situations allows us to compare a variety of settings and discover the core characteristics of burnout. Expansion has also brought burnout from the backstage into the spotlight, changing it from a little problem to a big one. Rather than an issue of concern to only a few professional helpers, burnout is now everybody's business. Because it has become such a "hot" topic, the likelihood is greater that both remedial and preventive actions will be taken.

However, there are several negative consequences of expanding the concept of burnout. They are serious enough, in my opinion, to outweigh the possible gains. They not only impair our investigation and understanding of burnout, but also are the major reason some people are so cynical about the concept and reject it altogether.

To begin with, as the range of a concept expands, its usefulness as a concept shrinks; bigger is not always better. If burnout means everything, then it means nothing at all. As more and more phenomena are pulled in under the umbrella term, it becomes increasingly difficult to say not only what burnout is, but what it is *not*. If we cannot clearly distinguish burnout from other problems, then the concept serves no functional purpose. A parallel situation exists with the related concept of stress. There are so many different definitions of stress, and so many phenomena considered to be examples of it, that today's theorists not only consider it meaningless, but also see it as detrimental to future progress in the field. Unfortunately, burnout seems to be heading toward a similar fate.

When burnout means so much, clear communication and meaningful discussion are almost impossible. The same term is masking many underlying differences. The failure to recognize these differences and to seek a resolution of them in a common, shared definition means that in any subsequent discussion of burnout, people will be talking past each other.

Another drawback of an expanded definition is that it begins to tap into problems other than burnout. This is especially true if the expanded concept includes various outcomes as indicators of burnout. Although these outcomes may indeed be associated with burnout, the associations are neither particularly strong nor exclusive to burnout. Thus, the problem in using a certain outcome as an indicator of burnout is that it may, in fact, be an indicator of something else (as an example, see **Shinn's** analysis of the link between burnout and turnover).

The point is that if you cast a wider net, you are going to pull in a lot more fish—but they may not be the particular fish that you are after. While it is a serious mistake to assume that various physical symptoms, job behaviors, and coping strategies are always clear signals of burnout, it is a mistake that is easy to make. With a greater number of indicators, there will be a greater number of people categorized as "burned out." The phenomenon will therefore appear to be more pervasive and important, and this "evidence" will then be used as support for the broader definition.

This is not to say that a concept should never be expanded or made more complex, only that there should be a good theoretical reason and some empirical evidence for doing so. I am willing to accept a broad definition of burnout, but I need to be convinced by more than words. It is not enough simply to note some similarities between two phenomena and then assume they are two examples of a more global concept. Focusing on the similarities may blind us to the differences, and what is different about two phenomena may be more important than what they have in common.

Another difficulty arising from the variety of burnout definitions is that different people measure it in different ways. Consequently, many assessments of burnout cannot be compared with each other (the proverbial apples and oranges problem); nor can they be combined into a meaningful, overall statistic. This prevents people from using the results of other studies and building upon them; instead, it forces people to duplicate the efforts of others. Moreover, different modes of assessment make it impossible to answer some of the most basic questions about burnout, such as how prevalent it is in various occupations or how the burnout rate in one job setting compares with the rate in another.

Finally, a broad concept of burnout implies more causes and suggests more solutions. On the one hand, this is a positive consequence; an expanded concept stimulates more creative thought about an issue. On the other hand, it has the potential drawback of leading people to propose solutions that do not directly address the problem (or at least do not address what someone else thinks is the problem).

Disagreements about the viability of various solutions may also stem from the erroneous assumption that solutions for burnout must be at the level of the presumed causes. For example, if the belief is that the work environment causes burnout, then (according to this reasoning) the only solution is to change the work environment—individual solutions are not possible and, by implication, the individual is not responsible for taking action. In fact, this assumption is incorrect. Potential solutions or changes can occur at many levels, regardless of what the presumed causes are. Furthermore, the causes themselves can be modified in some instances, despite the common assumption that causes of burnout (particularly at the institutional level) are too big and too fixed ever to be influenced.

Sources of Definitional Problems

Burnout is not the first concept to be plagued with definitional confusion. To some extent, this is to be expected in the development of any new concept. Yet the problems with burnout seem to go beyond this. It seems to me that the term itself and the imagery involved are at the heart of these definitional difficulties.

In contrast to many other psychological concepts that use dull, technical jargon and seem divorced from experience, "burnout" is a catchy term and evokes strong images to which everyone can relate. As a result, it is easy for people to "know" what is meant by burnout (even when they have not been given a formal definition) and to respond to it in terms of their personal experiences.

Ironically, the same qualities that make "burnout" such a popular term are the ones that make it so problematic: The word can be *too* evocative. The image it conjures up can be easily applied to all sorts of different experiences, and therefore it lends itself to definitional confusion. One can imagine firewood in ashes or a candle that has melted away—something that was present but is now gone. Thus, burnout can be used equally well to describe emotional feelings that once existed but are now gone, good health that is now gone, creative thinking that is now gone, personal interests that are now gone, idealism that is now gone—experiences that are all rather different from each other.

Another drawback of the term's vivid imagery is that people get too caught up in it. They rely on the image to define the phenomenon and to provide the ultimate truth about it, failing to recognize that the image is amenable to many different interpretations. One of the popular "truths" that has been derived from the imagery is that "you have to be on fire in order to burn out." The implication is that a person who is highly energetic, enthusiastic, and idealistic is the only person who is prone to burn out.[3] In this particular image, there is an internal "fire" that consumes the person, much like a candle is consumed by its own flame. However, in other images of burnout, the fire is external to the individual—it is the outside situation that is "too hot to handle," and the person is like a pot that is being heated up. These different images suggest not only different causes of burnout (personal passions versus situational stressors), but also different types of solutions: building the fire up (replenishing resources) in the internal case, and putting the fire out (eliminating stressors) in the external case.

Given all the reasons why "burnout" confuses rather than clarifies, one is tempted to banish the word entirely and replace it with a more precise term (or set of terms) for the phenomena it has come to denote. I doubt that this will ever happen voluntarily, since the term is still too popular and alluring, but it may eventually die out through continued overuse and growing skepticism about its meaningfulness. However, if "burnout" is ever discarded, we must be careful not to toss out all of its underlying phenomena as well, for they represent some serious problems that should not be ignored.

Progress

While there have been, and continue to be, many problems facing us as we seek to understand burnout, progress has still been made. First of all, that burnout is now recognized as a legitimate issue is a major step forward. It was not so long ago that the topic was somewhat taboo and for the most part went unacknowledged. Since so little was being said about burnout, people often attributed their experience of it to personal inadequacy: "I must be the only person who feels like this; something must be wrong with me." Now that the problem is receiving attention and there is open discussion about it, people are realizing that "it's not only me" and that there must be more to burnout than their own personal flaws.

With the realization that burnout may be more common and widespread than previously thought, the focus has shifted to situational factors that may be involved. One effect of this shift has been the development of clearer conceptual links between burnout and both job stress and job satisfaction. As a result, there is now a more substantial research literature on which to draw, as well as a new group of researchers who see burnout as relevant, even central, to their other interests. The development of a multidisciplinary approach to burnout has enriched burnout research both by stimulating new ideas and by introducing improved measures and methods.

Although the burnout research literature is only a few years old, it has grown in both quantity and quality. Instead of general descriptions, there is now greater precision in defining terms and specifying critical variables. More carefully developed sets of hypotheses and working models are replacing intuitive hunches and informed guesses. Standardized measures with good psychometric properties have been developed. Studies with larger and more representative samples are supplementing those using case studies and self-selected groups. Self-report measures still predominate, but other kinds of data (observer ratings, work behaviors, physical health) are beginning to be collected. Recent findings are confirming some original ideas, modifying or challenging others, and suggesting directions for future research.

The changes in my own work over the years illustrate many of these trends. Having stumbled across the burnout phenomenon while studying something else, I did not begin with a clearly developed conceptual model or research methodology. Instead, my initial approach was an exploratory one in which I asked lots of open-ended interview questions, made many on-site observations, and generally went where my data led me. The research participants were few in number but studied in more depth. The working conceptualization of burnout that evolved from this exploratory approach was an attempt to pull all the bits and pieces together into a meaningful pattern (Maslach, 1973, 1976, 1978a, 1978b, 1979, 1981a). There was more speculation and description than systematic data, and the definition of burnout was somewhat narrow but fuzzy. Some of these general ideas began to be pinned down and studied more carefully in a series of survey studies. The first two were done in collaboration with Ayala Pines (Maslach & Pines, 1977a; Pines & Maslach, 1978a, 1980), and subsequent ones were undertaken with Susan E. Jackson (Maslach & Jackson, 1978, 1979, 1982; Maslach, Jackson, & Barad, 1982; Jackson & Maslach, 1982a, 1982b). Specific variables were targeted for investigation, and comprehensive questionnaires were developed. The samples were larger in number and were more broadly representative groups (although studied in less depth). In addition to self-report measures, ratings were often collected from colleagues or spouses.

With each subsequent study, the conceptualization of burnout was modified and made more precise. A standardized scale measure, the Maslach Burnout Inventory (MBI) was then developed (Maslach & Jackson, 1981a, 1981b). The use of the MBI by many researchers has facilitated the comparison and integration of various research findings, is generating a data bank for standardized norms, and is stimulating new ideas about patterns or phases of burnout. (The work of **Golembiewski** and his associates is especially noteworthy.) More integrative studies, in which both personality and situational factors are assessed, have been completed by two of my doctoral students (Gann, 1979; Heckman, 1980). A more fully developed conceptualization of burnout has emerged from all of this research (Maslach, 1982). Furthermore, it has stimulated some new ideas about empathy, and these will be investigated with a different research paradigm (laboratory experiments).

All of this current research, by both myself and others, is uncovering important correlates of burnout. For example, it has a connection with turnover, it is tied to the impairment of family relationships, and it appears to be linked to various types of health problems (see **Pines's** chapter for a summary list of work environment correlates). These findings undercut the argument that burnout is a trivial and unimportant issue ("just the usual staff griping") by showing that it has major ramifications and can be costly for both the individuals and for institutions. Burnout is not just a fad of the 1980s; it is a serious problem that deserves serious attention and action.

Promise

What progress is to come? Basically, it will be the development of new strategies for dealing with burnout and the implementation of solid research programs to evaluate their effectiveness. I am hopeful that, as our understanding of burnout progresses, we will be able to propose new and creative approaches to the problem, rather than trotting out the same old recommendations for coping with job stress. The concept of burnout can suggest new connecting links between various experiences and may make sense of seemingly disparate responses (for example, work with clients and hassles with one's children). Standard measures of burnout can be developed into diagnostic tools that permit the early identification (and possible treatment) of people who are headed for problems. Such an analysis could lead to innovative interventions that are more effective than traditional ones. For example, as **Golembiewski** points out, if there are distinct patterns or phases of burnout, then the most effective intervention might involve tailoring the remediation to the phase (e.g., lateral job transfer if the person is in one phase; personal counseling if he or she is in another).

In addition to generating better ideas for intervention, the burnout concept may stimulate a greater commitment to implementation *and* long-term evaluation. Currently, follow-up assessments of intervention programs for any type of job stress are almost nonexistent. Perhaps the great interest and concern about burnout are sufficiently motivating that, at last, these crucial evaluations will get done.

Most conceptualizations of burnout have hypothesized a direct link between experienced burnout and a deterioration in the quality of service or care provided to clients. Presumably, the person who is burned out and has negative feelings and attitudes about clients will not be inspired to try harder for them, and will provide a minimal level of care at best (and possibly even poor care). This is a very serious consequence of burnout and is probably the bottom line for most agencies and institutions. Staff complaints and absenteeism are one thing, but bad treatment of clients is quite another.

In spite of its importance, the quality of staff members' work with clients is almost never assessed. This is largely because of the difficulty in determining just what "good quality" and " poor quality" are in this context: the eventual outcome of treatment? certain characteristics of the treatment process? how the client felt about it? how the supervisor evaluated it? Often, the measure of quality that is used is a measure of quantity (e.g., how many clients were seen per month), and, quite understandably, objections have been raised about the validity of this approach.

The problems involved in assessing the quality of job performance are ones that people have struggled with for years. However, it may be that a real breakthrough will come about because of burnout. The quality of client contact is so central to burnout that it is imperative that it be clearly defined and well measured. The extensive thought that has already been given to the dynamics of the staff-client relationship in burnout could be the source of an innovative approach to the quality issue.

The promise inherent in understanding burnout is the possibility of doing something about it. We need to go beyond all the speculation and fancy jargon to discover what is actually going on and what will actually be effective coping strategies. If we can overcome the many definitional and research problems that confront us, and continue to build upon the progress we have made so far, then the ultimate promise of preventing burnout may indeed become a reality.

NOTES

1. Although there are a few instances in which organizations have been said to burn out, it has not been clear whether this means that all the individual workers are experiencing burnout or that some unique occurrence takes place at the organizational level.

2. Although the experience is negative, some have argued that it may still serve a positive function, as when it leads to personal growth or acts as a screening device to "weed out" incompetent employees.

3. Interestingly, some people have reversed this sequence and used their burnout as proof that they were once wonderful and caring individuals—much as a battle scar is shown off with a certain pride.

3

Theory Building
Integrating Individual and Environmental Factors Within an Ecological Framework

JEROME F. X. CARROLL and WILLIAM L. WHITE

Burnout is a construct used to explain observable decrements in the typical quality and quantity of work performed by a person on the job. Presumably the people who are burning out are experiencing psychobiosocial distress or dis-ease as a consequence of their exposure to stressors and frustrations that exceed their tolerance and resources for successfully coping with stress and frustration.

Since burnout is a work-related concept, the work environment generally receives considerable attention; however, other environments or ecosystems can and do play an important role in determining whether or not, to what degree, and in what fashion a person will experience burnout.

To appreciate the multiple and complex roots of burnout, we have chosen an ecological frame of reference. According to this perspective, burnout is viewed as a form of *ecological dysfunction* (Carroll, 1980).

The Ecological Perspective

Ecology concerns the interrelationships of organisms and their environments or ecosystems. Therefore, to apply this perspective to the phenomenon of burnout means that a *person,* his or her *ecosystems,* and the *reciprocal impact* each has on the other must be understood. Unfortunately, most writers on the subject of burnout tend to overemphasize either personal variables (the need to excel or overachieve, having unrealistic expectations, and so on) or environmental variables (such as noise levels, crowding, and

41

environmental obstacles), while either ignoring or giving only cursory attention to the other.

Typically burnout occurs whenever a person with inadequate stress management and need-gratifying skills must work in a stressful and need-frustrating work environment. The dynamic interaction of personal variables (such as poor physical health and unresolved emotional conflicts) and environmental variables (such as poor supervision and excessive paperwork), which also includes the influence of other ecosystems (for instance, the family), generates burnout. This interaction can be expressed by the formula:

$$BO = f(P \leftrightarrow E)$$

Several writers (e.g., Pines, 1981) have taken the position that the term "burnout" should only be used to describe those decrements in worker performance that occur as a result of "prolonged, emotional involvement" between a service provider and those whom he or she serves. We disagree with this attempt to restrict the meaning and use of the term. We fear it may unintentionally lead to the development of an Orwellian hierarchy of concern for the quality of worklife, one that implies that some workers' psycho-biosocial distress is more deserving of our attention than others'.

In one sense, burnout is not new. Job-related distress, with its concomitant decrement in the quantity and quality of work output, is as old as work itself. "Back then," burned-out workers either quit their jobs, got fired, or were laid off until they recovered from whatever it was that was "troubling them."

Today, we are a bit more sophisticated in our understanding of the many causes of burnout and therefore exercise more caution in order to avoid "blaming the victim" (Ryan, 1971). In addition, the socio-politico-economic reality of the latter half of the twentieth century dictates that certain minimal standards for the quality of worklife must be upheld. In other words, unions and equivalent organizations for professionals and management personnel can do much to prevent arbitrary and insensitive terminations of burned-out workers through legal recourse.

Signs of Burnout

Signs of burnout may appear anywhere within the ecological system or life space, including the person and the various parts of the individual's environment, namely, the microsystem, mesosystem, exosystem, and macrosystem (see Figure 3.1). Whenever and wherever signs occur, they indicate an *ecological dysfunction*.

Personal signs of burnout (see Table 3.1) should not lead one to conclude that something is wrong *only* with the person and/or that "fixing" whatever is wrong with him or her will be sufficient to correct that person's problem. Signs of burnout, rather, should trigger an *ecological system analysis*, which should, in turn, lead to the development of a *systemic intervention* that addresses the key components of the ecological system, namely, the person, the salient elements of the various ecosystems, and their interactions.

Signs of Burnout Within the Work Environment

Some typical signs of burnout within the work environment (microsystem and mesosystem) include, first and foremost, a significant decrement in the quality of services provided to clients or customers, even though the organization's statistical reports may continue to "look good" or even to "improve"; subsystems (e.g., divisions, departments, offices) increasingly interrelate in a distrusting, competitive, and hostile manner; bureaucratic "turf" becomes increasingly sharply defined and jealously guarded; authority conflicts emerge more frequently and with greater rancor; important organizational decisions are more frequently decided by an increasingly isolated, elitist group which, less and less, seeks meaningful input from lower-level staff; communications within the system are poor; and humanistic, friendly, and informal staff encounters are increasingly replaced by stereotyped, fixed-role, formal, but "quite proper," staff interactions.

Other signs of staff burnout within the work environment include poor staff morale, as evidenced by workers and management expressing increased feelings of mutual disrespect and distrust that may lead to both sides insisting that their respective rights, responsibilities, and relationships be legally codified; staff members arriving late or failing to show up for important meetings and appointments; and management spending more and more time away from the organization and otherwise reducing the amount of time spent in direct contact with line staff.

Other signs include increased absenteeism, especially sick leave; higher staff turnover and a decrease in average length of stay on the job; fewer staff leaving the organization amicably due to an increase in firings and/or forced resignations; increased accidents on the job; increased employee theft; increased drug and/or alcohol use on the job or during breaks; and worsening

TABLE 3.1 Personal Indicators of Staff Burnout

Health Indicators	Excessive Behavior Indicators	Emotional Adjustment Indicators	Relationship Indicators	Attitude Indicators
Fatigue and chronic exhaustion	Increased consumption of caffeine, tobacco, alcohol, over-the-counter medications, psychoactive prescription drugs, illicit drugs	Emotional distancing	Isolation from or overbonding with other staff	Grandiosity
Frequent and prolonged colds		Paranoia		Boredom
Headaches		Depression: loss of meaning, loss of hope	Responding to clients in mechanical manner	Cynicism
Sleep disturbances: insomnia, nightmares, excessive sleeping	High-risk-taking behavior: auto/cycle accidents, falls, "high-risk" hobbies, general proneness to accidents and injuries, gambling, extreme mood and behavioral changes	Decreased emotional control	Increased isolation from clients	Sick humor—aimed particularly at clients
Ulcers		Martyrdom	Increased expressions of anger and/or mistrust	Distrust of management, supervisors, peers
Gastrointestinal disorders		Fear of "going crazy"		Air of righteousness
Sudden losses or gains in weight		Increased amount of time daydreaming/fantasizing	Increased interpersonal conflicts with other staff	Hypercritical attitude toward institution and/or peers
Flare-ups of preexisting medical disorders: diabetes, high blood pressure, asthma, etc.	Increased propensity for violent and aggressive behavior	Constant feelings of being "trapped"	Increased problems in marital and other interpersonal relationships away from work, including relationships with one's children	Expressions of hopelessness, powerlessness, meaninglessness
		Nervous ticks		
Injuries from high-risk behavior	Over- and undereating	Undefined fears		
	Hyperactivity	Inability to concentrate	Social isolation: overinvolvement with clients, using clients to meet personal and social needs	
Muscular pain, particularly in lower back and neck		Intellectualization		Value Indicators
Increased premenstrual tension		Increased anger		Sudden and often dramatic changes in values and beliefs
Missed menstrual cycles		Increased tension		

relationships between the organization and other agencies/companies, funding sources, regulatory agencies, legislative bodies, boards, and surrounding communities.

Some Assumptions

Our assumptions about burnout are derived primarily from our personal experiences with burnout, those of our co-workers, and studies we have made of burnout in other organizations. The writings of other experts on this topic have also contributed to these assumptions.

(1) Since burnout is caused by prolonged exposure to stress and frustration, all of the various personal and environmental factors that generate stress and frustration for humans must be considered as potential causes of burnout.

(2) Burnout is a holistic or psychobiosocial concept. To construe it solely or even principally as a psychophysiological stress management issue is to oversimplify it. How an individual fulfills or fails to fulfill his or her needs, especially those needs that are dependent on interpersonal relationships for their fulfillment, deserves co-equal status with the concept of stress management.

(3) Since environmental settings other than the work environment can generate stress and frustrate important needs, they must be considered as potential contributors to the experience of burnout on the job. Efforts to ameliorate and/or prevent burnout, therefore, must take these ecosystems into account.

(4) The quality of interpersonal relationships that distinguish the work environment and other ecosystems of the worker is especially important to consider.

(5) Signs of burnout will occur in the individual and his or her ecosystems. Which of these signs will be most easily recognized will depend as much on the sign's origin, severity, and duration as it does on the observer's theoretical orientation to burnout, his or her experience and sensitivity to burnout, and the honesty of the observer.

(6) To the outside observer, the behavioral manifestations and negative consequences associated with burnout may sometimes appear to emerge suddenly, dramatically, with little or no warning. More typically, however, the signs of burnout occur slowly, over time, with ever-increasing severity.

(7) Burnout is a process, not an event. Whether or not it occurs in distinct stages is a matter under study.

(8) Burnout may occur in varying degrees; for the individual, it varies from relatively mild distractions and energy loss through serious and debilitating illnesses that may result in death.

(9) Since the duration of burnout may vary considerably, the signs of burnout will also vary in duration. Moreover, the signs of burnout may vary with respect to their consistency and intensity.

(10) Burnout may be experienced more than once by the same individual. How and to what degree the first experience of burnout affects subsequent experiences of burnout is a matter to be determined by research.

(11) A worker's awareness of his or her burnout status and concomitant decrement in the quantity and quality of work performed may vary from complete denial to nearly full consciousness of the experience.

(12) Burnout can be infectious, in the sense that one person's burnout constitutes an additional source of stress and frustration for his or her co-workers and others with whom he or she interacts in other ecosystems.

(13) Burnout is especially common and severe among professionals who deliver direct care and assistance to emotionally distressed, indigent clients in public institutions or agencies.

(14) When the aggregate level of stress and frustration among workers within the work environment prevents the completion of tasks essential to the primary mission/purpose of the organization, the organization itself may be described as burned out.

(15) Although certain characteristics are shared by all burned-out workers and organizations, there will always be aspects of the burnout process that are unique to particular persons, work sites, and organizations. Restorative interventions and prevention efforts, therefore, will always have to be individualized.

(16) There is no known personality trait or personality configuration that, in and of itself, will cause someone to burn out. It is possible, however, that certain personality characteristics may predispose and/or make someone more vulnerable to burnout in certain ecosystems. Research is desperately needed in this area.

(17) Burnout is not a disease; the medical model, in other words, is *not* an appropriate analytical model for understanding and coping with burnout, even though physical disorders may arise as a consequence of burnout.

(18) Burnout should *not* be confused with malingering; we believe burnout is more likely to be experienced among highly motivated than among less motivated workers.

(19) Burnout may lead to subsequent personal and professional growth and development, as well as greater despair and trauma. Which outcome will follow the experience of burnout will depend on changes made in the individual, the various ecosystems, and their interactions.

Employing an Ecological Model for Analysis of Burnout

Using the seminal work of Lewin (1935, 1936) and the more recent contributions of community-oriented, preventive mental health experts such as Bronfenbrenner (1977), Cowen (1977), Moos (1979), Holahan and Spear-ly (1980), and Belsky (1980) as a guide, we can depict the individual's work environment and larger life space as containing the following key components: (1) the *person,* and (2) environmental components: the *microsystem,* the *mesosystem,* the *exosystem,* and the *macrosystem* (see Figure 3.1).

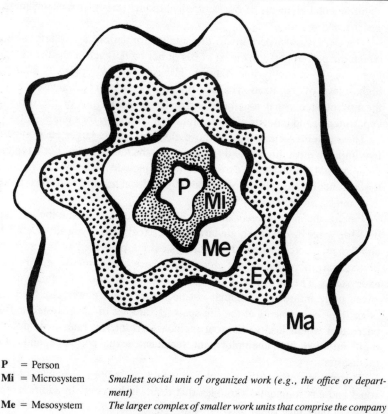

P   = Person
Mi = Microsystem   *Smallest social unit of organized work (e.g., the office or depart-ment)*
Me = Mesosystem   *The larger complex of smaller work units that comprise the company or institution/agency*
Ex = Exosystem   *Non-work eco-systems that directly impact on the worker and his/her company's or institution/agency's operations (e.g., surrounding community, legislators, accountability systems, his/her family)*
Ma = Macrosystem   *The larger cultural and world-wide complex*

Note: Each element is complex, dynamic, and unique. All elements interact to varying degrees. The consequences of all these interactions are experienced throughout the entire system and are reciprocal in nature.

FIGURE 3.1   An Ecological Model for the Analysis of Burnout

Most readers will be familiar and comfortable with the person (worker) element of our ecological model. Anything and everything that can influence a person's work performance must be considered and evaluated: for example, physical and mental health status; the amount of education and training completed; and the person's coping skills, frustration tolerance, goals, needs, interests, and values. People may be less familiar with the environmental elements of our ecological model (the microsystem, mesosystem, and so on).

The *microsystem* pertains to the smallest organized ecosystem within which the person performs most of his or her work (such as the office, the home, or the assembly-line station). The *mesosystem* represents the next highest level of organization of the work environment. It encompasses all of the microsystems that together form a larger whole (all of the offices, departments, and bureaus of an institution or company, for example).

The *exosystem* encompasses those elements of the larger environment that impinge most directly and frequently on the mesosystem. For a typical company or institution, the exosystem would include the board of directors, the surrounding neighborhood or community, local legislative bodies, funding sources, and regulatory agencies.

Finally, the *macrosystem* includes all other elements within the individual's life space beyond the boundaries of the exosystem. Typically, elements and dynamic forces within the macrosystem are perceived as larger, more impersonal, more distant and global than those of the micro-, meso-, and exosystems. The influence of the macrosystem, moreover, is often experienced more indirectly, although not necessarily less powerfully than the other three components of the life space. Examples of macrosystem influences that would lead to burnout include high interest rates and "double digit" inflation, high unemployment, racial and sexual prejudice, and natural disasters.

This model reflects the complex, interactive, reciprocal impact of personal and environmental variables that result in burnout. In addition, the model should also make it abundantly clear that no two individuals can possibly experience burnout in quite the same way.

The model also illustrates why a multidisciplinary effort is needed to study and cope with the phenomenon of burnout. The personal element, for example, calls for inputs from disciplines such as biology, chemistry, neurology, psychology, and psychiatry. The environmental element invites contributions from such diverse disciplines as economics, sociology, group dynamics, organizational development, political science, labor relations, and architecture.

Obviously an eclectic approach is needed, since theoretical constructs from many disciplines need to be integrated. On the positive side, many valuable, relevant constructs from diverse disciplines are already available to us; on the negative side, it is a difficult challenge to integrate many diverse concepts across disciplines.

Specific Personal Factors
Contributing to the Experience of Burnout

A proper consideration of *personal factors* contributing to burnout will include such broad categories as genetic endowment and congenital factors; temperament; growth and development; physical health status; education and skills training; motivation and interests; behavior patterns, especially those relating to interpersonal relationships; personality dynamics; mental health status; work history; and general life experiences.

When addressing the ecological sources of stress and frustration—the root cause of burnout—it is most important to consider the individual's perceptions and interpretations of their meaning and significance (Lazarus, 1966; Lazarus et al., 1965; Lazarus & Launier, 1978; Baum et al., 1981). Previous experiences and attitudes, as well as existing coping styles and behavior patterns, will also influence how an individual perceives and responds to any given stressor and/or frustration (Meichenbaum, 1977b).

One frequently encountered specific, personal cause of burnout is inadequate training and/or education needed to do the job. Individuals with educational and/or training deficits must continually confront challenges and problems with which they are ill equipped to cope. Their resultant experiences of personal and professional failure on the job invite burnout (Larson et al., 1978; Warnath, 1979; Edelwich & Brodsky, 1981; Shapiro, 1981b; Wilder & Plutchik, 1981).

A related cause of burnout concerns individuals with highly developed, specific job skills (such as a recovered alcoholic working as a therapist), but who also have serious deficits in more general job skills, such as writing, speaking, and group problem-solving. Such persons often feel "trapped in their jobs," since their present skills and knowledge do not qualify them for advancement to higher administrative positions and/or permit them readily to transfer to other career fields.

Limited insight into significant, unresolved, unconscious conflicts are another source of distress for workers, especially in the human services fields. Persons with such conflicts are likely to mismanage the dual problems of transference and countertransference commonly encountered by all direct care service providers. This usually results in therapeutic failure for their clients and a sense of defeat for the service providers.

Perhaps the most damaging of all the dynamics associated with a negative self-concept is the inability or refusal of the insecure human service provider to seek assistance from others. As the demands of the job increase and stress mounts, this worker, fearing that his or her hidden inadequacies will soon surface for everyone to see and ridicule, has only one option: to redouble his or her already overextended efforts to get the job done. More often than not, this last-gasp effort will fail, leaving the worker with but one thing to do, namely, burn out.

Paradoxically and tragically, this inability to admit to personal limitations and seek assistance from others will not usually be seen as an irrational act. More often than not, it will be viewed by some supervisors and co-workers as a sign of "true dedication" to one's job. Rather than getting help, the worker will usually be given the equivalent of "tea and sympathy"—a palliative treatment at best.

Specific Ecosystems Factors

As the individual moves across boundaries from one component of his or her life space to another (for instance, from the mesosystem to the exosystem), he or she encounters new norms, power hierarchies, communications patterns, decision-making processes, levels of intimacy, demands, challenges, roles, stresses, needs, and feelings. How well the person performs in one area of the life space, moreover, will affect his or her effectiveness in other areas—sometimes dramatically, sometimes subtly. Therefore, to appreciate burnout we must examine *more* than what transpires in the work environment (that is, the microsystem and the mesosystem), since we are dealing with an *interactive, holistic system.*

In applying an ecological dysfunction perspective to burnout, it is essential to consider how an individual adapts to a particular environment, as well as how and to what extent a given environment is changed by the inclusion of a particular person within its boundaries. The degree of harmony or disharmony in this person-environment matchup will determine to a great extent the quality of life to be experienced within this ecosystem.

We would also suggest that in each environmental component, special attention be directed toward the nature and quality of interpersonal relationships transpiring therein. In this regard, we recognize the invaluable contributions of Sullivan, especially his principle of communal experience (Sullivan, 1965; Mullahy, 1970). Since interpersonal relationships may be a rich source of both need gratification and dispiriting frustration, they can significantly influence whether or not one will experience burnout, the extent and intensity of the experience, and one's recovery from it.

Systems Factors That Contribute to Burnout

Boundary Issues

Boundaries serve to delineate "territories" (such as departments, companies) and "tribes" (such as social workers, upper management) to control who and what enters or leaves and to regulate the communications and transactions with other components of the life space. At certain points, boundaries may be impenetrable, while at other sites quite open, depending on who and/or what is attempting to come in or go out. Obviously the nature of the boundaries separating various ecosystems and the dynamics that regulate their boundary functions have a tremendous influence on the experience of burnout.

The recruitment, selection, and training practices of companies and agencies (and their numerous and sundry components) constitute important dynamics for regulating the ebb and flow of traffic and commerce across their respective boundaries. If, for example, a company or agency for fiscal reasons elects to recruit and hire only people with relatively limited work experience, they may well be creating conditions within their ecosystem that will add to the level of burnout within that system.

Moreover, the nature of a company's or agency's boundaries (that is, its policies and procedures for determining access to or exclusion from its territory) will also be instrumental in determining the level of heterogeneity or homogeneity among its workforce and managerial staff. White (1978a, 1978b, 1978c, 1980, 1981a, 1981b) has warned of the dangers of "organizational incest," which we agree constitutes a major cause of burnout.

Task/Role-Person Match/Mismatch

It is axiomatic that no two individuals are equally well endowed to undertake a particular task or role, yet the quality of the task/role-person match/mismatch is often a major determinant of the experience of burnout. Elsewhere, we have described twelve role conditions that contribute to burnout (White, 1981b; Carroll & White, 1981). Two examples are:

- *role-person mismatch:* the incongruity between (1) an individual's knowledge and skill level and the skills required to perform tasks of a given role, (2) an individual's level of stress tolerance and the level of stress endemic to a particular role, and (3) an individual's style of stress management and the methods of stress management officially and informally sanctioned within an organization.
- *insufficient role feedback:* the nonavailability of regular information on (1) the adequacy of role performance, (2) the methods of improving performance, and (3) the adequacy of adjustment to the work milieu.

Governance

Internal norms and standards (both formal and informal), the style of leadership, the exercise of power and decision-making processes, and the mode of evoking sanctions and conferring recognition, reward, and status are all vital elements to consider when seeking to analyze burnout within any ecosystem. It is equally important to consider how the governance of one ecosystem interfaces with that of another ecosystem (for example, how an executive director's powers articulate with those of his or her board of directors).

Goals and Objectives

The clarity, feasibility, and overall support for an ecosystem's goals and objectives will also determine the degree and extent of burnout. Where goals are ambiguous, impractical, and dictated from "above" without building an adequate base of support, we would predict higher rates of burnout. Similarly, the absence of clear, realistic, and consensually agreed upon objectives and criteria for evaluating one's work also contribute to burnout.

Obstacles and Resources

Each element of the individual's life space (the microsystem, mesosystem, and so on) contains numerous obstacles and/or resources that will, *on balance*, facilitate or impede the worker's efforts to accomplish goals and objectives. Obstacles and resources may be physical, psychological, or social in nature.

In examining the relationship between obstacles/resources and burnout, one must consider not only their absolute number but also their relative significance to the individual. The greater the relative weight of obstacles to resources, the more likely it is that the individual will experience burnout.

Interface Issues

Since life is dynamic, people are always moving from one element of their life space to another (for example, microsystem to mesosystem). What transpires at the interface between two ecosystems, therefore, can be as critical as what happens within any one of them. The compatibility of ecosystems thus becomes very important, as do the "boundary spanning" skills of the individuals who must operate in different ecosystems. Where elements of one ecosystem are incompatible with those of another, where individuals are inflexible and unable to adapt to changing systems' demands, one may expect burnout to be high.

Inappropriate Strategies for Amelioration and Prevention

The ecological approach to burnout requires that interventions be multi-faceted and attend to *both* individual and environmental issues in a *balanced* fashion. Unfortunately, this balance is often neglected, as is illustrated by the following approaches. These examples can only effect transient "success" at best, since they address only *part* of the ecological dysfunction. Typically they will worsen the situation, because the failure to effect meaningful changes in the ecosystem will only add to the existing level of bitterness, cynicism, and hopelessness already in the system.

The Authoritarian-Moral Approach

The authoritarian-moral approach to burnout is reflective of what McGregor (1960) has called the "theory X" view of management. Theory X is based on the assumption that most people dislike work, lack ambition, are essentially passive, avoid responsibility, resist change, and are self-centered and unconcerned with the needs of the organization. The role of the manager is thus to direct, motivate, manipulate, persuade, control, reward, and punish the worker to respond effectively to the needs of the organization.

Within an organization managed via the propositions of theory X, even the existence of professional burnout is adamantly denied through such flippant statements as, "There's no such thing as burnout—only staff who don't want to work." Behavioral signs of burnout are viewed as emerging from an indolent and evil character.

The individual experiencing burnout may also be impugned with malicious motives toward the organization and organizational leadership. Professional burnout is, in essence, seen as a "cop-out" to avoid one's responsibilities or is seen as an act of sabotage against the organization and its leaders.

The authoritarian-moral approach is also immune to corrective feedback due to its self-justifying moral rigidity and the tendency of the organizational ideology to become self-prophetic. As staff become increasingly burned out from high-stress conditions, they do indeed avoid responsibility, develop malicious attitudes toward the organization, and commit acts of sabotage (decrease production, damage equipment, and the like) against the organizational leadership.

Clinical Approach

The clinical approach to victims of professional burnout defines burnout as emerging from *individual* "psychopathology." This approach to burnout is remarkably similar to the response of a family system to an acting-out adolescent.

As a particular staff person experiences a stress-related deterioration in performance, the organization identifies the inappropriate behavior and attitudes of the worker (acknowledgement of deviancy). The problem is seen as emerging from the personality of the worker (diagnosis of psychopathology).

The worker, who is perceived as "sick" (identified patient) is then typically advised by the supervisor to seek therapy for his or her problems. What was once an employee-supervisor relationship now becomes a patient-therapist relationship. If the worker's behavior does not change, he or she is fired or manipulated out of the organization (the equivalent of institutionalizing the adolescent).

By focusing the worker's attention on his or her own intrapsychic processes, the clinical approach decreases the worker's ability to mobilize external resources of support at the exact time he or she is in most desperate need of such supports. The definition of the problem as psychopathology also increases the workers' feelings of isolation, paranoia, and loss of control; in short, it escalates the symptoms of burnout.

The clinical approach also stigmatizes the worker through the diagnostic process. Having been officially diagnosed as "sick," workers often fail to connect their distress with events transpiring in their work environment. They tend to assume they are responsible for the distress they are experiencing. In addition, they often fear that they are "going crazy." The clinical approach to burnout inadvertently confirms the worst fears of these victims.

Training Approach

The training approach to victims of professional burnout defines burnout as a reflection of skill deficiency, especially in the area of stress management. It assumes that work-related stress is inevitable and that workers vary in their ability to cope well with stress.

Remediation measures typically include the provision of stress management training to increase the worker's level of stress tolerance and the worker's repertoire of stress management techniques. The training approach also assumes that a significant amount of job-related stress and frustration occurs as a result of the individual's not having the skills needed to perform the job effectively.

Whereas the training approach should be an integral part of any organizational strategy to address professional burnout, there are some limitations to this approach. Training approaches that focus *only* on deficiencies in stress management skills may actually be used to immunize workers against stress generated from intolerable conditions within the work environment. Such training may inadvertently distract the organization from eliminating sources of stress and frustration and/or increasing supports within the work environment.

Training approaches that focus exclusively on skill development to remediate burnout may contribute to a misdiagnosis of the very conditions that are responsible for inadequate job performance and high levels of stress and frustration by the worker. For example, the problem may be due to unclear or outmoded organizational policies, a lack of role clarity, and excessive and contradictory demands upon a worker's time, rather than a deficiency in the worker's skills.

The Work Environment Approach

The work environment approach to professional burnout views burnout as a breakdown due to inadequate structures, policies, and functions within the work environment that engender stress and frustration. This perspective is especially sensitive to the extent to which an organization is "open" or "closed" to external inputs and specific role conditions that may subject workers to conflict, stress, and frustration (White, 1978a, 1978b, 1978c, 1980, 1981a, 1981b). According to this view, burnout is considered to be due to the progressive loss of support and sources of replenishment from sources outside the organization. This loss increases the worker's vulnerability to burnout.

Organizational strategies designed to address burnout that are based *solely* on a concern with the work environment would seek:

(1) to maintain the openness of the organizational system to assure members access to outside sources of personal, professional, social, and sexual replenishment;
(2) to reduce role stressors within the work milieu;
(3) to increase role supports within the work milieu; and
(4) to enhance each member's stress management skills.

Due to this approach's heavy focus on broad organizational processes and role conditions, inadequate emphasis is typically afforded to the personal sources of stress and frustration. In addition, stressors originating from ecosystem components outside the work environment (the exosystem and the macrosystem) are often ignored and/or not addressed.

An Ecological Approach to Assessment and Intervention

Having described what not to do, we shall now describe what to do according to our ecological approach to burnout. In this regard, it is essential *both* to evaluate person and environmental variables and their interactions, *and* to develop and implement intervention strategies that address, *simultaneously,* both the person and the environment.

For convenience in reading, we have separated individual interventions from environmental interventions. In actually dealing with burnout, they cannot be so separated if an effective program is intended. The lack of *multiple interventions* addressing *both* personal and environmental issues, is what was criticized in the four imbalanced approaches we have described (the authoritarian, clinical, training, and work environment approaches).

Interventions Designed for the Individual

Perhaps the most immediate need for the staff member suffering from staff burnout is relief from stresses on the job. This can be done in many ways: for example, giving the person time off away from the institution, assignment to a different and less stressful job within the organization, or allowing other staff to pick up some of the person's workload. It is most important that supervisory staff ensure that the person being granted time off not view this action as a response to weakness or failure; the same is true for the person's co-workers. If other staff are asked to pick up some of the burned-out staff member's workload, they must be helped to do this in a cooperative, positive manner.

Having made this recommendation, however, let us quickly add that limits should be mutually agreed upon regarding the length of time such workers may be granted time off or carry a lighter workload. In addition, specific, concrete plans should be mutually agreed upon and carried out by the worker during this period. To do otherwise encourages the burned-out worker to delay unnecessarily returning to normal duties, to the detriment of the burned-out worker, his or her co-workers, and the ecosystem.

The importance of good physical and mental health should not be overlooked in treating staff burnout. It is advisable, therefore, to recommend or provide a thorough physical examination, as well as some personal counseling. The latter ideally should focus on assisting the burned-out staff member carefully and objectively to identify both personal and environmental sources of stress and sources of potential support or need gratification. More effective stress management techniques and need gratification skills (relaxation therapy, desensitization, biofeedback, assertiveness training, and so on) could also be provided through the medium of personal counseling. Very stressful therapeutic modalities (such as marathon or encounter groups) should be avoided, at least as an initial intervention.

Additional education and training may also be beneficial, especially in conjunction with removal of the person from his or her immediate job situation. In pursuing this, a careful inventory of the staff member's training needs is vital and should address such areas as expectations, values, and standards the staff member is using to judge performance of duties (for example, they may be unrealistically high); interpersonal skills, especially communication and listening skills; committee work skills; and maintaining a healthy and constructive distance in working with clients.

Interventions for the
Work Environment

The treatment of staff burnout also entails making changes in the structure, policies, and operating procedures of the organization in order to mitigate or eliminate stresses and frustrations emanating from the work environment.

We have identified a number of interventions, including improving hiring procedures and on-the-job training; offering high-quality, relevant, realistic, practical orientation programs for new employees; providing adequate nurturing of staff through such means as granting guilt-free time-out periods, job changes, and recognition of personal effort; providing carefully graduated levels of responsibility for new staff; obtaining training outside the agency or from nonagency staff; encouraging and assisting staff to identify and achieve career goals and objectives; preventing the same individuals from always working overtime; ensuring that staff are adequately compensated for their work and, if their workload is increased, salaries are increased and/or other aspects of the workload decreased; and, for paraprofessionals who have been patients, formally marking their change in status from patient to staff (White, 1978a, 1978b, 1978c, 1980, 1981a; Carroll, 1980).

It is Freudenberger (1975), however, who suggested the ultimate intervention. When and if the organization as a whole shows signs of being burned out, he recommends closing down the facility for a period of time. Although at first glance this recommendation seems rather extreme, there are many ways it can be implemented while continuing to satisfy mandated minimal requirements for services. For example, a treatment facility could host an activities day or an organizational self-examination study day for both staff and clients. The change in pace that accompanies such activities would, in effect, constitute an organizational shutdown, at least in terms of business as usual.

Interventions for the
Nonwork Ecosystems

Interventions directed toward nonwork ecosystems are much more difficult and risky to implement, but nonetheless important to attempt. If, for example, a major source of stress is the individual's homelife, the work agency could refer the worker and his or her family to an appropriate treatment facility, preferably with some financial assistance to defer costs.

Although no agency can single-handedly overcome societal "isms," each organization can do its best to confront racism, sexism, ageism, and the like as each of these social dynamics operates within its own boundaries. Cleaning up one's own work environment strengthens the resolve of people to cope with "isms" in other ecosystems.

Conferences can also serve to enhance the quality of life, both on the job and in the nonwork ecosystems. Through our sharing of theoretical constructs, information, suggestions and guidelines for future research, and strategies for coping with and preventing burnout, as well as our full and rigorous discussions of these matters, we cannot help but raise the overall level of consciousness and understanding of this phenomenon throughout the entire "macrosystem." Our work here also will encourage others to add to what we have accomplished at the First National Conference on Burnout.

Suggestions for Assessment

Since our ecological emphasis stresses a *balanced* attention to *both* person and environmental variables and their interactions, it follows that assessment, too, should reflect this balance.

Unfortunately, most efforts to assess burnout (such as those of Maslach & Jackson, 1981a; Freudenberger & Richelson, 1980; Golembiewski, Munzenrider, & Phelen, 1981) have tended to overfocus on the person and the relative intensity with which he or she may be experiencing burnout. These instruments, to the extent they are reliable and valid, have some merit in that they will enable an agency to identify workers who need assistance in coping with burnout.

The failure to address environmental dimensions of the burnout phenomenon, however, limits the utility of such instruments. If, for example, someone wishes not only to measure the extent of burnout in an organization but also to identify and understand the various factors that contribute to the problem, focusing on the individual's experience of burnout will be of limited help.

What we would like to see developed are ecologically oriented assessment procedures. These instruments would enable the user to not only assess the level of burnout a particular person is experiencing, but also to identify various predisposing, precipitating, and sustaining factors—within both the person and the environment—that are associated with the experience of burnout. Such approaches, while more complex and time-consuming, will, in the long run, provide more valuable data for the purpose of alleviating the ecological dysfunction.

To illustrate our contention, let us consider the following two illustrations involving two individuals manifesting severe signs of burnout. In one instance, the stressors are directly related to the work environment (the microsystem and mesosystem); in the other, the exosystem.

Steve works in a department that has inadequate staff to service many needy, indigent clients. The budget is to be cut so severely that even cost-of-living adjustments are in jeopardy. Competition among Steve's peers for one middle-management opening is intense. The quality of supervision and training Steve receives is horrendous. Furthermore, other departments within the agency show little respect for the work done by Steve's department; interdepartment cooperation is the exception rather than the rule.

In the second instance, Ken's wife, whom he loves, just informed him she is leaving him for another man. His son was recently arrested for possession and use of marijuana. Ken's daughter is dating someone he dislikes intensely—actually, he suspects they are sleeping together. The neighbor next door is fighting with Ken over who owns a hedge separating their homes. On the other hand, at the work site everything is relatively pleasant. The pay, workload, interpersonal relationships, supervision and training, and career advancement opportunities are rather good.

Ascertaining that both men are experiencing burnout to the same degree does little to identify the causes of the distress and resultant diminution in the quantity and quality of work each man performs on the job.

Conclusions

Attempting to summarize one's conclusions on burnout is a bit disconcerting for several reasons: (1) Little "hard" evidence as a result of vigorous research is in hand; (2) the issue, especially from the ecological frame of reference, is most complex; and (3) our thoughts on the subject are still being formed.

With these qualifications made, our conclusions are as follows. Staff burnout must be viewed as stemming from the interaction of debilitating individual *and* environmental factors that together detract from a person's ability to do his or her work. Treatment and prevention must be approached from many directions and at various levels, involving many different disciplines and professions, in a coordinated and well-integrated fashion. Staff burnout, simply stated, is not an individual disease. Nor is it due only to negative, environmental conditions. It is an ecological dysfunction and must be dealt with as such.

4

Methodological Issues
Evaluating and Using Information

MARYBETH SHINN

The increasing concern with burnout in the human services these days is evidenced in books, scholarly journals, popular magazines, and on television. Advertisements for conferences and workshops flood the mails, and newspapers reprint scales allowing readers to assess whether they, too, are "burned out." This chapter is directed to consumers of information on burnout, whether administrators, practitioners, or researchers, to help them sort out what from this plethora of materials is valid, important, and relevant to their situations. In evaluating findings about burnout, three questions are crucial: (1) What is being described? (2) Who is being discussed? (3) How is the information obtained?

What Is Being Described:
Burnout and Related Concepts

As **Maslach** notes, and researchers and theorists usually define burnout in terms of the psychological experience of the individual. Administrators, on the other hand, are concerned with possible behavioral consequences of burnout for their agencies, namely, employee absenteeism, turnover, and poor job performance. And organizational and social psychologists and sociologists have studied related concepts, such as job satisfaction, alienation, and psychological and physiological manifestations of job strain, for years.

AUTHOR'S NOTE: Preparation of the chapter was supported, in part, by a grant from the National Science Foundation, #BNS-8011824. The views expressed herein are those of the author and do not necessarily reflect National Science Foundation policies.

All of these concepts are interrelated, to a greater or lesser extent, and all are legitimate topics for study and targets for change. But not all of them operate in the same way, and an intervention designed to affect one variable may have no effect, or even the opposite effect, on another. For example, introducing a generous pension system may reduce turnover by making it difficult for workers to leave their jobs, without reducing their emotional exhaustion. Cynicism may even increase as older burned-out workers stay on the job and inculcate their values among their younger and initially more enthusiastic peers. Some would argue that this process is different from burnout (Cherniss, 1980b), but the end result of alienation, detachment, and low job satisfaction may be the same. Let us follow the example of turnover a bit further before turning to a broader discussion of selecting and measuring variables in research on burnout.

The Example of Turnover

Several researchers have suggested that burnout may lead to turnover among human service workers (Freudenberger, 1975; Maslach, 1976, 1978b; Pines, Aronson, & Kafry, 1981), and a few studies have reported empirical relationships between various measures of burnout and intentions to leave one's job (Jones, 1980a; Kafry, 1981; Maslach & Jackson, 1979). Certainly turnover is a greater problem for the human services than for other professions. Professionals in social work and rehabilitation services leave their jobs at about twice the rate per year (25-30 percent) of professionals in nonservice fields (8-15 percent; see Katzell, Korman, & Levine, 1971). Rates in one high-stress human service setting, residential treatment programs for youths, may run as high as 200 percent per year (Connis, Braukmann, Kifer, Fixsen, Phillips, & Wolf, 1979; Shinn, 1979). But the relationship between burnout and turnover is more complicated than may be supposed.

Many factors residing in the job, the person, or the external environment may contribute to job turnover. The relationship between job dissatisfaction and turnover has been replicated consistently in the literature with prospective as well as retrospective designs (see reviews by Mobley, Griffeth, Hand, & Meglino, 1979; Muchinsky & Tuttle, 1979; Porter & Steers, 1973), although the relationship rarely accounts for more than 15 percent of the variance in turnover (Mobley et al., 1979).

The type of satisfaction studied can make a difference. For example, a causal model of satisfaction and anticipated turnover in a sample of child-care workers showed a strong relationship between overall satisfaction and turnover. Satisfaction with growth needs (such as the need to develop skills and abilities) was the strongest predictor of overall satisfaction, but satisfaction with existence needs (such as pay and benefits) made an independent contribution to the prediction of turnover (Shinn, 1981). That is, even satisfied workers were more likely to leave their jobs if they could not make ends meet.

Job design factors, such as role clarity and autonomy, are consistently related to turnover (Porter & Steers, 1973). Other predictors include personal background factors, especially prior tenure in the organization (Mobley et al., 1979), and physical and emotional indicators of strain (Katzell et al., 1971), but personality factors are not related in any consistent way (Muchinsky & Tuttle, 1979). External conditions, such as the state of the economy and the availability of alternative jobs, also play a role (Mobley et al., 1979).

So far I have discussed turnover as though it were a single, uniformly defined concept. But turnover can be voluntary or involuntary, anticipated or actual, and the way that it is measured can affect the results. For example, Mobley, Horner, and Hollingsworth (1978) found a relationship between two psychological variables, the expectancy of finding another job and the intention to quit, among hospital employees, but no relationship between the expectancy and actual turnover. Turnover also has a very different meaning for the human service professions and for our understanding of burnout if workers who leave their jobs go on to similar positions in other human service agencies as opposed to leaving the field entirely. Thus, it may be important to assess not only when workers leave but also where they go and why.

There are several lessons to be learned from this extended discussion of turnover. First, it is important to distinguish carefully among concepts like burnout, turnover, and satisfaction, and even among different sorts of turnover and satisfaction. (We shall see that there are different sorts of burnout as well.) What is true of one variable may not hold true for another.

Second, statements such as "burnout is related to turnover" are too simple. They may be true, but they do not tell the whole story. More careful attention to all, or at least to a greater proportion, of the relevant variables will increase our understanding and give better guidance to change efforts.

Third, the way one measures a variable may affect what one finds. In evaluating quantitative research or clinical observations, one should demand precise definitions of what is being observed.

Fourth, there has already been a vast amount of relevant research on turnover and other variables, some of it on human service workers. However, most of this information has not yet been incorporated into the literature on burnout. To the extent that one evaluates each new research report or intuition against what is already known, one is less likely to be led astray. These lessons apply to other variables in the study of burnout. Next I shall discuss outcomes, such as burnout, and give a brief overview of stressors that are assumed to cause burnout and coping strategies that may reduce it. I attempt to distinguish among some different concepts that go by the same name and to show relationships among concepts with different labels. Throughout, a major theme will be the importance of specifying what one is studying.

Although I focus on research tools, the need to specify topics of concern is even greater when informal observations, clinical wisdom, introspection, and intuition are the sources of information. Research instruments have the value of pinning down vague concepts with specific questions, so that one can judge the fit between them and theory. Common parlance is much more slippery. In fact, a major criticism of thinking about burnout is that it seems to refer to everyone and everything (**Maslach**). In order to advance theory or to choose promising points for interventon, one must distinguish carefully between concepts with potentially different antecedents and consequences.

Burnout and Other Outcomes

Measures of Burnout

The various definitions of burnout that **Maslach** lists are reflected in the variety of measures of the concept. There are at least five published burnout scales in the literature. The most widely used is the Maslach Burnout Inventory (MBI; Maslach & Jackson, 1981b), with items that measure Emotional Exhaustion (e.g., "I feel emotionally drained from my work"), Personal Accomplishment (e.g., "I deal very effectively with the problems of my recipients"), and Depersonalization (e.g., "I've become more callous toward people since I took this job"). An optional fourth factor assesses Involvement in recipients' problems.

Each statement is rated for both frequency and intensity, yielding similar factor structures and patterns of correlations with other constructs. The different subscales of the MBI are not highly intercorrelated, and they have somewhat different patterns of correlations with other criteria, suggesting once again the importance of specifying what is being discussed in burnout research.

Pines and Kafry (Kafry, 1981) have developed a Tedium measure that expands the first factor and part of the second in the MBI into a measure of physical, emotional, and mental exhaustion (being physically exhausted, feeling energetic, being emotionally exhausted, feeling burned out, feeling disillusioned and resentful about people, and so on). Unlike the MBI, the Tedium measure contains no reference to work. Pines et al. (1981) define burnout as identical to Tedium in its symptoms and measurement, but use the term "burnout" to refer only to tedium resulting from work with people. The Tedium measure is also more highly associated with work satisfaction and life satisfaction than is the MBI.

The median correlation between Tedium and Work Satisfaction is .44 across 24 studies reported by Kafry (1981), and .54 between Tedium and Life Satisfaction across 22 studies. Maslach and Jackson (1981a) report correlations between MBI subscales and Job Satisfaction ranging from .17 to .23.

The Staff Burnout Scale (SBS; Jones, 1980b) is also based on Maslach's conceptual framework, but includes reported behavioral and physiological items as well as cognitive and emotional ones. A Job Dissatisfaction factor is explicitly included, and assesses feelings about the workplace (e.g., "I find my work environment depressing") and attitudes related to turnover (e.g., "I often think about finding a new job"). A Psychological and Interpersonal Tension factor measures tension, as does Pines and Kafry's Emotional Exhaustion scale, and interpersonal problems with supervisors, co-workers, and clients. The Physical Illness and Distress factor (e.g., "I experience headaches while on the job") assesses fatigue and physical complaints often found in measures of somatic symptoms (Caplan, Cobb, French, Harrison, & Pineau, 1975; Langner, 1962). The final factor, Unprofessional Patient Relationships, covers some of the same ground as Maslach's Depersonalization factor (e.g., "I have lost interest in my patients and I have a tendency to treat these people in a detached, almost mechanical fashion"). The instrument is thus quite broad, and it is not yet clear whether the different factors have the same causes and consequences.

The SBS also contains an index of Social Desirability, or the tendency of respondents to give answers that are skewed in the direction of socially desirable responses. This tendency may be a problem for the MBI. Maslach and Jackson (1981a) report a nonsignificant correlation between the MBI and Social Desirability in a small sample, but Golembiewski, Munzenrider, & Phelen (1981) report a significant correlation in a larger sample. Neither paper reports the magnitude of the effect.

A fourth measure of burnout is provided by the Berkeley Planning Associates (1977), who define burnout as job alienation. Their scale assesses alienation from clients (e.g., "I feel optimistic about our clients"), the project (e.g., "This organization has problems which a person cannot do anything about"), co-workers (e.g., "My co-workers and I work closely together"), the job (e.g., "My job is meaningless"), and opportunities in the job (e.g., "I have the opportunity to really help other people"). The scale is highly related to job satisfaction ($r = .59$).

A final scale, intended as a self-assessment tool, is presented by Freudenberger and Richelson (1980). It measures exhaustion, sadness, and withdrawal from routine activities (e.g., "Do you tire more easily?" "Is joy elusive?" "Are you seeing close friends and family members less frequently?"). Freudenberger's scale, like the Tedium measure, is unrelated to work settings.

The first four of these scales have adequate psychometric properties and relationships with various validity criteria. (The fifth is not intended as a research tool.) However, all five scales measure different content areas, and one would not expect them to affect or be affected by other variables in the same way. In fact, I would be surprised if these five measures of burnout were correlated as highly as some of them correlate with satisfaction, a supposedly different concept. This is not a criticism of any of the scales so much as a caution to the consumer of research information to take note of what is measured and how, and how well it conforms to theoretical concepts of interest.

Related Measures

Even these scales do not exhaust the possible ways of assessing burnout. For example, some theorists conceptualize burnout as a process rather than an end state (Cherniss, 1980a, 1980b; Edelwich with Brodsky, 1980). Although a few of the scales contain a few items designed to assess change—for example, "I've become more callous toward people since I took this job" (Maslach & Jackson, 1981b) and "I no longer believe this project can accomplish any good" (Berkeley Planning Associates, 1977)—most define static states. Golembiewski, Munzenrider, and Phelen (1981) suggest that the subscales of the MBI may indicate progressive phases of burnout but have not yet provided evidence for this temporal sequence.

Cherniss (1980a) dealt with the problem by interviewing workers, novices in a variety of helping professions, across several points in time and rating their attitudes toward the job and their clients at the initial and follow-up interviews. He then defined those workers who showed the most negative changes in attitudes as the most burned out.

Yet another approach, which I have adopted in my own research, is to choose a fairly narrow measure of burnout (such as the Berkeley Planning Associates' alienation measure) and then to examine related measures, such as job satisfaction and psychological and somatic indicators of job strain. This allows comparison of findings with the existing literature on these topics. Psychological strain asks respondents how often they feel depressed, anxious, angry, and so on (see Caplan et al., 1975, and Pearlin & Schooler, 1978, although the latter authors call their measure "stress"). Somatic strain asks respondents how often they experience a variety of physical symptoms, such as headaches, loss of appetite, and trouble sleeping at night (see Caplan et al., 1975, and Langner, 1962, among others).

We have already seen that measures of job satisfaction include overall satisfaction and satisfaction with the extent to which the job meets various individual needs. A third measure of satisfaction, which is perhaps more common, is the assessment of satisfaction with different job facets, such as the work itself, pay, promotion opportunities, the supervisor, and co-workers (Smith, Kendall, & Blood, 1969).

Again, these measures differ from one another in subtle and not so subtle ways. Somatic strain is often less responsive to job conditions than other measures, probably because physical symptoms may result from illnesses unrelated to work. If burnout follows uniform stages, as some authors have suggested (Edelwich with Brodsky, 1980; Golembiewski, Munzenrider, & Phelen, 1981), we might expect different forms of strain to manifest themselves at different times. Certain indicators (say, anxiety) might then serve as "early warning signals" for burnout. And different outcomes may be differentially affected by interventions. For example, LaRocco, House, and French (1980) show that social support has a direct effect in improving job-related outcomes, such as satisfaction, but a moderating effect on health outcomes, like psycholgoical and somatic strain. That is, social support has little effect on these strains when stress is low, but prevents high levels of stress from leading to increased strain.

Using Multiple Measures

Most of the measures I have discussed so far are measures of attitudes, and the best way to assess attitudes is by asking people. However, often we are interested not in attitudes but in behavior—in absenteeism, turnover, job performance, and health problems like high blood pressure. Again, one can ask workers how often they are absent from their jobs or how well they perform at them. But program attendance records, ratings from co-workers and supervisors, actual observations of behavior, or medical examinations may be better sources of data.

Each type of data has its own problems. For self-report information, researchers are concerned with social desirability and with internal consistency reliability, or the extent to which questions measuring the same construct are correlated with one another. (Other forms of reliability, such as stability over time, may also be important.) For observer ratings, we want to know whether two independent observers looking at the same situation will give the same report. Often they will not.

Program records can be sloppy or inaccurate, and sometimes systems of recording data change over time. Some physical measures, such as blood pressure, vary considerably during the course of a day. But effort can be made to make each sort of measure as reliable as possible (for example by training raters to use common criteria, keeping careful and accurate records or averaging several measures).

Even greater advantages accrue from using multiple measures that share theoretically meaningful components but differ in the types of errors to which they are prone. This triangulation of measurement processes leads to more persuasive evidence than any individual measure (Webb, Campbell, Schwartz, & Sechrest, 1966). Research on burnout now relies heavily on the self-report and would do well to diversify its portfolio of assessment tools.

Of course, simply assessing burnout and related outcomes is, by itself, of little interest. Most theorists and practitioners are more concerned with the causes of burnout and what to do with it. The next subsections deal briefly with the stressors that lead to burnout and with coping strategies to reduce it. Again, my major concern is with what is being studied, but the problems here are not primarily problems of definition.

Stressors

The term "stress" refers to events "in which environmental or internal demands (or both) tax or exceed the adaptive resources of an individual" (Lazarus & Launier, 1978). French (1973) argues that job stress occurs when the job either poses demands that the worker cannot meet or fails to provide sufficient supplies that the worker needs.

For years, researchers have demonstrated that job stress leads to dissatisfaction and psychological and somatic strain among workers in a variety of occupations (see Caplan et al., 1975; French & Caplan, 1972; Kahn, Wolfe, Quinn, Snoek, & Rosenthal, 1964). Beehr and Newman's (1978: 682) review of the literature concludes that "the finding that perceptions of stressful situations are related to employee health and well-being has been replicated consistently." **Pines** catalogues many of the stressors that have been implicated in burnout.

The problem is not with the specification of these stressors, most of which are well defined, but with the fact that they are interdependent, making patterns of causality difficult to determine. For example, Cherniss (1980a) found eight workplace factors, all of which distinguished between the most and least burned-out workers in his sample. Kafry (1981) reports statistically reliable relationships between tedium and thirty-seven different work features in one or another of the studies she conducted with Pines. **Golembiewski** found similar links to twenty-two of twenty-four work-site descriptors. These results undoubtedly reflect reality: Many aspects of the work environment can contribute to burnout. But they provide little guidance to administrators who want to change their agencies so as to reduce burnout, and less comfort to theorists seeking parsimonious explanations of the phenomenon.

One step toward simplifying this picture is to test for the relative importance of different causal variables in a multivariate model (see Berkeley Planning Associates, 1977). But even statistical modeling is ambiguous when the predictor variables are highly intercorrelated, as Robinson (1980) found in a re-analysis of data on workers in residential child-care programs. Conceptually distinct variables, such as worker-rated quality of supervision and role overload, were highly related. Again, this makes some theoretical sense. **Shapiro** describes ways that good supervisors can reduce job pressures for workers. Alternatively, supervisors may become scapegoats when workers are unhappy about job pressures; or perhaps organizational characteristics, such as client load and bureaucratic demands, create role overload for the supervisors too, thus affecting quality of supervision at the same time that they affect employee overload. As always, the correlation tells us nothing about the direction of causality.

Ultimately, we must rely on more sophisticated research designs to untangle these relationships. I shall return to this point in the last section of this chapter. In the meantime, consumers of information on burnout should be aware that any particular stressor identified as a cause of burnout is likely to be one of a constellation of interdependent factors, and that one-shot efforts to "cure" burnout, say, by adding variety to a dull job, are unlikely, by themselves, to be successful.

Thus far, I have considered organizational stressors as causes of burnout but have given no attention to individual personality variables. Muchinsky and Tuttle's (1979) review suggests that personality traits are not consistently related to turnover. In fact, personality theorists argue that traditionally conceived personality traits like conscientiousness or honesty are not consistently related to much of anything, because behavior depends not so much on individual predispositions as on transactions between people and their environments (Mischel, 1968). Individual variables that do make a difference often have to do with expectations and styles of appraising or interpreting the environment (Mischel, 1973). Personal background factors, such as training, may also be important. The next section discusses individual differences in coping styles and resources such as social support.

Coping Strategies
to Reduce Burnout

A final set of variables that are important in understanding burnout are coping strategies that reduce stress and its consequences. Again, it is important to ask what is being studied; as in the case of burnout, definitional problems abound. But I believe a more crucial problem is that much discussion of coping with burnout centers on individual coping when other levels of coping, namely strategies undertaken by groups of workers and by agencies, may be more effective.

Research on coping has a long history, but surprisingly little of it assesses the effects of coping on outcomes outside the laboratory. An important exception is Pearlin and Schooler's (1978) study of coping in four domains: marriage, parenting, household economics, and jobs. They found that coping, in the sense of reducing strain, works in the first three realms but has little impact on strain associated with jobs. Other studies have shown that individual coping explains relatively little variance in burnout (Shinn & Mørch, 1982; Shinn et al., 1981) or tedium, and that inactive or emotion-focused strategies, like drinking, may actually be harmful (Pines et al., 1981: see Table A.15 by Kafry).

Mechanic (1974) argues that many of the problems with which people must cope are too large and complex to yield to individual efforts, but that these problems may be amenable to organized, cooperative efforts. This may be true of burnout (**Cherniss** shows political, economic, historical roots of the phenomenon) and of work-related problems generally.

The picture is much rosier for the group-level strategy of social support. Several reviews have shown the benefits of social support for psychological and physical health in the face of general life stressors (Cobb, 1976; Dean & Lin, 1977; Kaplan, Cassel, & Gore, 1977) and for occupational stress in particular (LaRocco et al., 1980). Several writers on human service agencies stress the importance of social support (see Cherniss, 1980b; Lenrow, 1978a, 1978b; Pines et al., 1981), and some have reported empirical data on its negative relationship with burnout (Pines et al., 1981; Shinn et al., 1981; Shinn & Mørch, 1982).

Agency-level coping is a potentially important variable that has received too little attention. Newman and Beehr (1979) outline a number of adaptive responses that organizations can use to reduce job stress and resulting strain, and Cherniss (1980b) provides a similar catalogue focused on human service agencies, but few of these strategies have been systematically investigated. **Golembiewski** summarizes the sparse evidence that organizational development ment interventions can reduce stress. My students and I found that agency coping was associated with low levels of strain in one sample of human service workers (Shinn & Mørch, 1982) but was used too rarely to receive a fair test in another (Shinn et al., 1981).

This is not an area where I would discourage administrators from acting before all the research results are in. Change efforts should be monitored— they may easily backfire—but if changes seem to be improving morale or reducing burnout, they should be encouraged. From a practitioner's perspective, specification of the precise causal sequence of events and demonstrations of the generalizability of results to other settings can wait.

In sum, to evaluate information on burnout, one must pay careful attention to what is being discussed. Burnout itself has been variously defined and measured, and related outcomes, on which there is much research, have been slighted. Stressors are better defined but tend to be interdependent, so that it is difficult to untangle their effects. Discussion of coping is too often confined to the individual level, where its effectiveness in dealing with burnout is questionable, and the demonstrated and potential effects of social support and agency coping are too often ignored. Throughout, there is a tendency to rely too heavily on self-report measures. The next section deals with the equally important questions of who is being discussed when one talks about burnout.

Who Is Being Discussed?
Professions and Work Settings

Most research on burnout has concerned professionals in a variety of human service settings. However, Golembiewski, Munzenrider, and Phelen (1981) have found the MBI useful in a commercial setting, and much of the research I have advocated consulting on satisfaction, strain, turnover, job stress, and coping has been conducted in business and industry. Several authors have described the special stresses of human service work (Berkeley Planning Associates, 1977; Cherniss, 1980a, 1980b; Maslach, 1978a). But other workers, like air traffic controllers and bomb squad members, also experience high levels of stress. Ultimately, the extent to which conclusions about job stress and burnout hold across different occupations and work settings is an empirical question.

There are two ways to answer this question. The first is to examine the consistency of findings from numerous studies, each of a different occupation. To the extent that findings hold up across studies in spite of differences in the samples and methods employed, they are robust and are likely to apply to new population groups and new methods that do not differ drastically from the old ones.

The second method for assessing the generality of findings is to include several different occupations or work settings in the same study, so that each is assessed with the same techniques. This allows greater precision in describing differences among the groups but provides less information about the overall generality of the findings, which may be limited to the samples or the measures chosen.

A major study of the second type is Caplan et al.'s (1975) research on job demands and worker health. The researchers studied how patterns of job stress and strain differed among 2,010 workers from twenty-three occupations. For example, physicians and administrative professors reported the highest workloads, the greatest responsibility for other people, and, along with policemen and administrators, the highest levels of job complexity. Forklift drivers, machine tenders, and assembly-line workers reported the most underutilization of abilities and ambiguity about their job futures. The authors show both that there are significant effects of stress on strain that hold across occupations, and that some of these relationships vary from one occupation to another and for people of different ages and educational levels. They thus caution that intervention programs that work well in one occupation may have little effect in others.

In a much more modest effort, my students and I surveyed members of a statewide professional organization of human workers (Shinn et al., 1981). Some of the most interesting comparisons were between therapists (primarily psychologists, social workers, and psychiatrists) in private practice and their colleagues who worked in mental health centers or university counseling centers. Private practitioners experienced fewer psychological symptoms, lower alienation, and greater satisfaction than did therapists in mental health and counseling centers. The private therapists, not surprisingly, reported almost no stress associated with agency membership (primarily inadequate, incompetent, or nonsupportive administrators) but relatively high amounts of stress associated with clients (emotional demands or failure to improve) and with the professional helping role (feeling inadequate relative to one's own expectations or feeling pressure to cure clients). These results suggest that patterns of stress and strain may differ markedly among different types of human service workers and workers in different settings, just as they do for occupations more generally.

Although there is systematic variance in stress and strain from profession to profession and from one type of work setting to another, there can also be tremendous variability among workplaces of a given type. Cherniss (1980a) describes high-stress and low-stress schools and poverty law agencies and Pines and Maslach (1980) report how a day-care center transformed itself from a high-stress to a low-stress environment.

Even within a given organization, people in different roles are subject to different kinds of stress. For example, persons at high levels in organizational hierarchies tend to view all aspects of their work more favorably than do persons at lower levels (Tannenbaum, Kavčič, Rosner, Vianello, & Wieser, 1974). Novices and experienced workers in any setting will have different sorts of problems (Cherniss, 1980a), as will members of different professional groups, such as doctors, nurses, orderlies, technicians, and social workers at a hospital. The particular types of stress that are most potent for different occupations remain to be spelled out.

As research accumulates, we shall discover and empirically verify some of the dimensions that explain variance in patterns of stress. For example, Pines et al. (1981) have suggested that stressors differ in their mutability, intermittance versus continuousness, and in their predictability. Relationships between stress, burnout, and coping might be expected to differ in systematic ways in work settings where stress is intermittent and unpredictable (as in many hospital emergency rooms) from those where stress is persistant and predictable (as in many institutions for the profoundly retarded). Generalization will be safer between jobs that are similar on most relevant dimensions than between jobs that differ on several of them. For now, we must be wary of overgeneralizing from one occupation, workplace, or role to another.

Another sort of generalization is even more dangerous. This is generalization from unusual or extreme groups of people to the human service professions at large. Psychotherapy clients, members of self-appointed grievance committees, and people who attend burnout conferences may all offer important insights into phenomena such as burnout, but they are likely to differ in systematic ways from their peers who do not get involved in the same activities. Researchers should also be wary of comparing samples of people who are unrepresentative of their populations. Biased sampling is always a potent threat to validity.

The last section of this chapter deals with other threats to validity and with research designs that may minimize them. How information is obtained is a final concern in evaluating findings about burnout.

How Information Is Obtained: Validity Issues

Information comes in many forms, from armchair speculation to carefully controlled experimental studies. Different sorts of information are subject to different threats to validity (Campbell & Stanley, 1966) and permit different degrees of inference about causal relationships.

There is a tendency, as fields mature, to progress from speculation to systematic qualitative observations, to quantitative studies of relationships among variables, to experimental manipulation of events and empirical tests of theory-based models. That is not to say that quantification necessarily makes research more valid or sophisticated. We have all seen thoughtful, informative qualitative studies and silly uses of statistics. Premature efforts at quantification may lead to study of unimportant variables, simply because they can be measured easily. And different levels of precision may be required for different purposes.

In this section I describe the advantages and disadvantages of several methods of data collection on burnout, from informal observations to designs that permit causal inferences. This is not intended as a research primer, of which there are many available (for example, Babbie, 1973; Campbell & Stanley, 1966; Selltiz, Wrightsman, & Cook, 1976), but as a brief discussion of what we can learn and what we should be wary of in using different types of information.

Informal Observations

Informal observations are attempts to understand a problem where the methods of collecting information are unsystematic or not clearly specified. They include the observations of administrators, clinicians, and grievance committees, and "studies" whose methodology is not spelled out. Such observations are as good as the observer, and if the observer is thoughtful and well placed for collecting information, they can be very good indeed.

Some of the earliest descriptions of burnout took this form (Freudenberger, 1974, 1975; Maslach, 1976). These descriptions played the valuable role of defining the problem and outlining potential antecedents and coping strategies.

The problem with informal observations is that they are very difficult to evaluate. One can judge whether their logic is internally consistent and whether they fit with common sense and one's own experience. But beyond these minimal criteria, one must take or leave their conclusions on faith, because of the lack of specificity in what is being described, who is being described, and how the information is obtained. The conclusions have the status of hypotheses awaiting verification or falsification; and, by now, the study of burnout should move beyond reliance on them.

Systematic Description

Substantial advantages accrue from systematizing observations, as in questionnaire or interview studies or management information systems where the what, who, and how of data collection are specified. Systematization may come from the way open-ended interview material or entries in program log books are organized, coded, and analyzed, as well as from asking respondents to quantify their answers, say, on seven-point scales.

Unstructured or semistructured interviews allow respondents to specify the domains of concern. The researcher then attempts to bring order to the material, showing commonalities and differences in the experiences of different individuals. Such a process is time-consuming, so usually only a small sample of people are interviewed, often in considerable depth. The data gathered are typically very rich, but different researchers interpret the material in different ways. Although small sample sizes and lack of comparability of answers across respondents make systematic tests of hypotheses difficult, unstructured and semistructured interviews are invaluable for gaining a phenomenological understanding of the problem.

More structured interviews may involve specific, open-ended questions. Unfortunately, interviewees often use different frames of reference in their answers. One never knows whether respondents neglected a particular dimension because it seemed unimportant, because another dimension came to mind first, or because they assumed the interviewer was concerned with something else. One can remove some of the ambiguity by designing a series of increasingly specific probes to follow open-ended questions, but some uncertainty always remains.

In the later stages of research in a field, when researchers have a better idea of the range of possible responses and dimensions of concern, they can develop questions with predetermined response options. Such questions allow greater precision in describing relationships among variables. One can be sure of covering the domains of interest with each respondent. Moreover, the quality of the measures themselves can be judged in part on the basis of their psychometric properties.

On the other hand, premature specification of response options can be harmful if it eliminates consideration of important domains of variables. For example, a researcher who studied job stress in human service agencies by borrowing one of the standard questionnaire instruments developed in industrial and commercial settings would have good, psychometrically adequate measures of concepts like role conflict, but might miss entirely such other problems as the emotional demands of working with clients.

The degree to which data are quantified is only one dimension along which descriptive studies differ. A second important dimension is the degree to which analyses are multivariate. Most studies of burnout assess many variables but, unfortunately, analyze them only one or two at a time. Thus, we learn that burnout is correlated with a long string of stressors or a series of other outcomes like satisfaction without ever learning of the relationships among stressors, their relative potency, or the extent to which they interact in predicting various outcomes. Some of the difficulties of interpreting these analyses were described in the discussion of job stress.

Descriptive studies can be improved by careful attention to the what, who, and how of data collection and by using multiple sources of information (for example, program records as well as workers' reports) and multivariate analyses. If researchers present enough information about their methods, we can at least recognize the problems in their studies and judge how seriously they may distort the results. Most current research on burnout is based on either informal observation or systematic description, and the latter is far superior to the former. But research would be improved still further if it relied more heavily on designs that permit causal inferences.

Designs That Permit
Causal Inferences

Foremost among these designs is the true experiment, which assesses the effects of one or a small number of key variables (the experimental treatment) while keeping all other variables as constant as possible. The series of experiments summarized by Wanous (1977), showing that realistic job previews reduce employee turnover, are good examples.

In the true experiment, subjects are assigned randomly to treatments. In the Wanous studies, some new employees received a realistic preview of the job they were about to undertake, emphasizing the difficulties they might encounter; others saw a recruiting film or received the usual orientation. Randomization assured that the groups were equivalent at the start. This, and equivalent treatment of the groups after the job previews, eliminated several potential threats to internal validity, that is, threats that something other than the special treatment caused differences between the groups (Campbell & Stanley, 1966).

External validity, or the extent to which a finding can be generalized beyond the immediate test situation, can sometimes be a problem in experimental studies, especially if efforts to ensure internal validity lead to the creation of unusual test conditions. However, if the experiments take place in the settings and under the conditions to which one wants to generalize, external validity is not a problem. This was the case in the studies of the realistic job preview. The external validity of the research was further enhanced by several replications of the effect with different populations and different stimulus materials (Wanous, 1977).

Experiments have the advantage of allowing clear inferences about causality and of enabling us to untangle relationships among variables that are ordinarily confounded. However, they can be criticized on two grounds.

One criticism is that random assignment and maintenance of experimental controls are almost impossible outside the lab. I believe these difficulties have been overstated. By making research participants into collaborators rather than guinea pigs, it is possible to gain their cooperation to do experiments in naturalistic settings. However, there is some validity to a milder form of the criticism. Experiments are difficult to conduct and tie up time and resources, especially when one replicates the results in a variety of settings. Other methods of garnering knowledge may be more efficient, if less sure.

A second criticism of experiments is that they are designed to deal with the effects of a small number of statistically independent variables at a time. For problems such as burnout, where large numbers of variables probably play a causal role, experiments provide only a partial picture of the underlying relationships. Experimentally untangling the effects of naturally correlated variables may be valuable for theory but may not provide an accurate picture of what typically occurs under natural conditions. This is not an argument against experimentation, which at least can provide an unambiguous picture of the independent effects of a few variables. But it does suggest that we need other weapons in our research arsenal.

A second class of designs that permit varying degrees of causal inference has been labeled "quasi-experimental" by Campbell and Stanley (1966). Many of these designs take advantage of the types of information typically available in human service agencies. For example, to study the effects of a new policy permitting flexible time off or unauthorized absenteeism, one might examine program records of absenteeism before and after the policy is implemented in a time-series design. If the new policy does make a difference, one would expect to see a reduction in absenteeism at the time the policy is introduced, with this reduction superimposed on seasonal or other existing trends.

Another common design uses nonequivalent comparison groups in place of randomly assigned control groups, as when an intervention is attempted for staff of one agency while staff in a second agency serve as a comparison group. The degree to which one can sustain causal inferences for these and other quasi-experimental designs depends on the plausibility of rival hypotheses or threats to validity. Any extraneous differences between the agencies studied could lead to an alternative explanation for treatment effects.

Quasi-experimental designs may be strengthened by adding tests to rule our specific rival hypotheses and by replication under different circumstances where new rival hypotheses would have to be invoked to explain treatment effects. Often these designs serve as a reasonable compromise between demands for experimental rigor and the practical exigencies of research in natural settings.

A third class of designs that permit causal inferences is multivariate longitudinal or panel designs, in which the same subjects give information at several points in time. One can then use the patterns of relationships over time to infer causality. A simple version of this design is known as the cross-lagged panel correlation (Campbell, 1963; Kenny, 1975; Pelz & Andrews, 1964; see also criticisms by Rogosa, 1980), but other models of causal relationships over time may be constructed and their parameters estimated.

Longitudinal designs, like experiments and quasi-experiments, extend one's conceptual reach in thinking about burnout because they permit study of causal relationships among variables. No single technique will solve all research problems, but greater use of these and other, more sophisticated methodologies will increase understanding of the causes of burnout and how to reduce it.

Of course, powerful methodologies are tools, not ends in themselves; sophisticated tools applied to trivial problems will yield trivial, if well-crafted, results. Research on burnout needs more sophisticated theories as well as better methods.

Research and Theory

In my own research on burnout, I have adopted a theoretical model in which job stress leads to strain (alienation, dissatisfaction, and psychological and somatic symptoms). Strain may lead to poor job performance and turnover, but it also motivates coping responses. And coping, at the individual level, the group level (social support), and the organizational level, can reduce both stress and strain. Group and organizational coping are hypothesized to be more effective than individual coping with job demands (Shinn, 1980; Shinn & Mørch, 1982; Shinn et al., 1981).

This model is not especially original; it borrows from theories developed by organizational, social, and clinical psychologists, sociologists, and medical researchers. In fact, one advantage of a theoretical model is that it suggests analogies with phenomena that others have observed in related fields and allows one to employ existing evidence to support or refute it. It guides further empirical investigation, which shows its successes and limitations. The model also suggests ways to reduce burnout by reducing job stress and enhancing coping responses. Thus, theory can aid interventions and careful research on the results of interventions can improve theory.

I have briefly sketched only one possible model for investigating burnout, and although we have some supportive evidence (Shinn & Mørch, 1982; Shinn et al., 1981), it may not be correct. But even incorrect models are valuable for guiding research and intervention, and if an incorrect model is carefully specified and not couched in vague generalities, the research it generates will eventually disconfirm it.

In sum, our understanding of burnout has benefited in the past from systematic descriptive research, but future progress is more likely to come from empirical tests of theory-based models using research designs that permit causal inferences. Careful specification of what is under investigation and to whom research applies is essential. Much can be learned from investigations of related phenomena in related fields. More rigorous research promises benefits not only for theory but also for preventing and coping with burnout.

PART II

Background Issues

5

Cultural Trends
Political, Economic, and Historical Roots of the Problem

CARY CHERNISS

There has been a significant bias in thinking about burnout. Most research and action has focused on the worker and/or work setting. However, both burned-out workers and their settings are strongly influenced by social, political, and economic forces in society. While these are difficult to "see" or change, our understanding is greatly limited if we fail to study this larger social context, a point also made by **Carroll and White.**

The following analysis will focus on one particular occupational area, the human services, because that is where interest in the topic of burnout first emerged. Obviously, job stress and burnout occur in many other occupations. However, recent concern about burnout in these other groups was sparked to a great extent by the popular attention that first emerged in the human services, and other areas are affected by similar trends.

Other writing on burnout has strongly suggested that a major cause is the bureaucratic arrangements, frustrations, and indignities experienced by human service providers (see **Pines**). What are the economic, political, and social roots of stresses such as red tape, an emphasis on quantity rather than quality, and role ambiguity? Part of the answer, as Dressel (1980) has pointed out, lies in the nature of our political system and the policymaking process. For example, inadequate funds result from legislation that is largely symbolic and meant only to serve the political needs of legislators. Fragmented and uncoordinated service systems, to take another example, result from the politician's efforts to satisfy the demands of competing interest groups. The politician's need to demonstrate visible results leads to goal displacement (such as emphasis on the number of clients served rather than on the quality of the service).

In addition to the political system, there are other factors that contribute to job stress in the human services and to the current popularity of burnout as a topic. These factors are historical in nature. They are related to important changes and events that have occurred in our society during the last century. One of the most important is our changing view of how society functions.

The Rejection of Progressivism

A significant amount of bureaucratic frustration is encountered in the human services because numerous interest groups have demanded that government agencies play a more active and scrutinizing role in the provision of services. This consumer disenchantment and activism has become especially marked during the last fifteen years, in part because of a profound change in our beliefs about society. According to Rothman (1978), public policy in this country during the first half of this century was guided by the Progressive Ideology, which assumed that the various interests in society ultimately coincided. The Progressives believed that a consensus could be achieved in any social conflict and that existing conflicts were neither necessary nor permanent. In the 1960s, the Progressive vision was replaced by a new perspective that saw conflict of interests as inevitable in any social system, including the system for human services.

Rothman, in trying to trace the historical roots of this fundamental change in ideology, concluded that the civil rights movement was the bridge between the old perspective and the new. About 1966, civil rights activists began to emphasize conflict, power, and separateness. Empowerment, rather than integration, became the central objective. Gradually, this emphasis on empowerment spread to other groups and created an ethos that eventually led to the consumer movement in the human services.

Like Blacks, consumers came to be seen as disadvantaged and unfairly treated. Promises of reform from professionals and administrators no longer appeased consumer activists, who began to agitate for more control over programs. The quest for empowerment led to demands for "accountability," vigorous lobbying for legislation such as mandatory special education, and the creation of community control boards. Through class-action lawsuits, the courts also were spurred to assume a more active and directive role.

The service providers themselves were influenced by the new ethos. They became more willing to unionize, and their unions were increasingly militant and open about getting as much as they could for their members (Oppenheimer, 1975).

Administrators were unprepared to deal with the many conflicts and demands generated by this emphasis on empowerment. Caught in the middle, unable to please everyone who needed to be pleased, they "coped" by formulating vague, ambiguous, even conflicting program goals. Because their actual control over staff behavior ultimately was limited (Prottas, 1979; Hasenfeld & English, 1974), they often relied on classical bureaucratic mechanisms resulting in more paperwork, more red tape, and less personal control for direct-care staff. As staff became angrier and more resistant, pressure on administrators intensified. Many burned out (Vash, 1980), and when they did, the burdens on staff further increased **(Shapiro).**

The new emphasis on empowerment also affected staff-client interaction. The "consumers" of service became less pliant, more resistant, and less appreciative. They increasingly saw providers as adversaries. Providers, already frustrated by bureaucratic machinations, had less patience for these clients and often responded in ways that confirmed the clients' worst fears and most cynical expectations.

Impatience with the rate of change in civil rights was an important factor leading to the decline of Progressivism and the new emphasis on empowerment, but it was not the only one. Several other events occurring at about the same time contributed to a widespread loss of faith in social institutions and the willingness to challenge their authority. The war in Vietnam, assasinations of popular, visionary leaders, and Watergate caused many to lose faith in the system.

Economic factors also contributed to the decline of the Progressive vision. As Rothman (1978: 91) noted, the slowdown in economic growth after the mid-1960s "shook people's faith in the idea that an expanding economy would ultimately solve all of America's social problems." When it became apparent that the economic pie would not expand indefinitely and that a larger piece for one group would mean a smaller piece for another, conflict and confrontation increased.

Thus, the decline of the Progressive image of society led to pressures for increased government intrusion in the management of the human services. This change led to structural changes in work settings that have contributed to staff burnout and made it such a popular topic today. But we also must take into account another factor. A critical examination of the helping professions suggests that they contributed to their own misfortunes.

Shortcomings of the Professional Model

When social unrest erupted during the 1960s, the helping professions initially were seen as part of the solution. However, they soon came to be seen by many as part of the problem. Some of this reaction can be traced to the public's high expectations. However, the professions themselves helped to create and perpetuate these expectations. Scholars who have studied the historical development of the professions suggest that in attempting to secure legitimacy, an emerging professional group strives to show that lay practitioners using common sense and tradition are worse than useless and that a formally trained and certified professional is superior in integrity and competence (Lasch, 1979; Bledstein, 1976). Increasingly, the public came to accept this argument. Unfortunately, professionals cannot always meet these expectations **(Wilder & Plutchik).** When they fail, the public's sense of betrayal leads to new calls for government supervision and control.

However, unrealistic expectations are only part of the problem. During the 1960s, several real abuses and shortcomings of the professions also came to light, and this added to the clamor for more external control of professionals and their workplaces. First, there were the gross inequities in the provision of services and in the outcomes of service (Hollingshead & Redlich, 1958; Sue, 1977). The cost of professional services also was attacked. Many observers noted that the professions maintained a monopoly on service, preventing competent persons from practicing and driving up the prices (Gross & Osterman, 1972). This monopoly limited the numbers of professionals and made it inevitable that there would never be enough to serve all who needed help (Lynn, 1965; Albee, 1959).

Critics also pointed out that the professionalization of care undermined self-reliance in clients (Lasch, 1979; Bledstein, 1976). Furthermore, the professional approach to the client's problem focused on causes within the client and ignored causes that might require social reforms (Gross & Osterman, 1972; Schein, 1972).

The professional's methods could be detrimental to the public in other ways as well. Even the medical profession, which seemed to have the best technological arsenal, could fail. Freidson (1970) and Bucher and Stelling (1977) have shown that the physician's expert knowledge often is inadequate and much medical practice is based more on prejudice than on firm scientific evidence. Public confidence was not enhanced when techniques that had been promoted as benign, such as X-rays, diethylstilbestrol (DES), and thalidomide, proved to be otherwise.

One other charge against the helping professions concerned their response to criticism itself. They often revealed themselves to be particularly arrogant and resistant to change. As Lynn (1965: xii) put it: "The American professions are enormously conservative when it comes to changing the club rules."

As these faults of the professions became more visible during the 1960s, there was more public pressure for external review and government intervention. Third-party payers also were prodded to exert more control. The result: further limitation in the provider's autonomy, more red tape, and more paperwork. Also, there was increasing pressure on human service programs to provide certain types of services to certain types of clients, such as aftercare services for deinstitutionalized mental patients or education for severely retarded children now kept in the community. Often these were the clients who were less rewarding to work with, and providers had not been trained to do so. Their methods were inappropriate. Thus, their opportunity to feel competent, as well as their sense of autonomy, were reduced.

As the credibility of the professions weakened, practitioners themselves joined in the assault. Many new professionals emerged from university training programs with a commitment to challenging the status quo in their fields **(Wilder & Plutchik)**. They believed that many of the traditional methods and concepts were obsolete and pernicious. Unfortunately, they had not learned alternative methodologies. New professionals could not easily develop a sense of competence, a major source of burnout (Cherniss, 1980a). Therefore, the professions themselves contributed to the erosion in public confidence, and one consequence was increased strain on the individual provider.

The Effects of Increasing Professionalization

Despite growing criticism of the professions, there has been a dramatic growth in the number of professions and the number of people practicing them. This growth also contributed to structural changes in the human service workplace that ultimately increased stress and burnout.

In seven decades, the proportion of professionals in the population increased over threefold. In 1890, 4 percent of the working population were professionals; in 1960, it had increased to 13 percent (Veysey, 1975). So many areas of life have become professionalized that one sociologist only half jokingly suggested that very soon, virtually everyone will be a professional (Wilensky, 1964).

This growth has been a mixed blessing. As the numbers of professional and allied groups in a field increased, each group sought more autonomy, status, and power vis-à-vis the others; and the problem of coordination became substantial. Organizationally, human service programs have become more complex, conflict and fragmentation have increased, and administrators have attempted to impose more control to secure order out of chaos. Staff have become frustrated because there is so much suspicion, so much paranoia, and so little cooperation among groups. They also resent the seemingly arbitrary and cumbersome bureaucratic control mechanisms that administrators have used to improve coordination.

Specialization has been another consequence of increasing professionalization. As each professional develops a body of knowledge, there is pressure to develop subspecialties. In some cases, however, increasing specialization is motivated by a desire for increased status, political support, or financial reward. But whatever the cause, increasing specialization has become the norm.

Specialization further hampers staff and administrative efforts to coordinate program functions, and it also can make professional work less stimulating. A study of new professionals suggested that it was difficult for most of them to feel professionally competent without specializing (Cherniss, 1980a). But as they became more specialized, many came to feel limited and stifled, because there was little variety in their work. Thus, growth and specialization within the professions have contributed to fragmentation, conflict, and boredom in a workplace which itself was changing.

Fallout from the 1960s

At first, the human services actually benefited from society's concern with the disadvantaged and growing support for government action in the 1960s. The public regarded them as the vehicle for the social reform that needed to occur. Elected officials authorized hundreds of new programs and allocated billions in new dollars. Unfortunately, the "golden age" was relatively short-lived, and its demise contributed to more frustration, disillusionment, and burnout.

In 1981 it is clear that our expectations for those new programs were unrealistic. Not only were the primary goals (to eradicate poverty, for instance) impractical, but the assumptions we had about the nature of the problems, the clients, and the political system were naive. This became obvious within a few years (Moynihan, 1969; Snow & Newton, 1976). However, while the original goals were too idealistic, they did inspire a certain amont of commitment. The more "realistic" goals that have replaced them cannot generate much excitement or zeal. As the optimism of the 1960s waned, the *Zeitgeist* became ripe for burnout.

Coming to terms with the failure of the new programs was particularly hard for the many young people from elite backgrounds who chose social work, education, or a related field rather than a higher-status occupation. The zeal that existed in the 1960s made the human services an especially attractive career option. Not since the Progressive era, when graduates of Vassar chose to do social work in the slums, had the human services become so appealing to the children of the privileged. Those who gave up high-paying careers in business and corporate law to become elementary school teachers and poverty lawyers were especially bitter when their occupations lost their glamour and sense of mission.

Even if public support for the human services had not declined after the 1960s, some disillusionment and burnout probably would have occurred as the new programs matured. Organizational settings tend to deteriorate over time as the enthusiasm, cooperation, and commitment of the honeymoon period give way to growing self-interest, conflict, and boredom (Sarason, 1972). Perhaps it was inevitable that many of the exciting, innovative programs created in the 1960s became marked by routine, trivialization, and petty bickering by the mid-1970s.

Not all human service providers worked in one of the innovative settings during the 1960s; and for those in traditional settings, whom history had left behind, burnout had other sources. In state hospitals, institutions for mentally retarded persons, or public welfare departments, new trends such as deinstitutionalization made one's work especially frustrating and meaningless. There now is little about these programs that can inspire a sense of purpose or accomplishment. The result is ever-increasing burnout among the staff.

As the 1960s gave way to the 1970s, affluence was replaced by inflation and recession. The public agenda shifted, and the human services no longer occupied center stage. Fifteen years ago, the important social problems were in education, mental health, drug abuse, and poverty. Today, the primary concerns focus on international conflict, energy, and the economy. College undergraduates no longer flock to psychology or education majors; now they go into business, law, and engineering. Many working in the human services must feel abandoned by the rest of society. The sense of specialness that they had in the 1960s has been lost; their efforts no longer are regarded as heroic. Burnout is the result.

Of course, as the human services have slipped in the public agenda, the loss has not been merely symbolic. Thousands of jobs are disappearing amidst massive budget cuts. College training programs, insensitive to changes in the job market, have continued to produce a surplus of new practitioners. The result has been fewer jobs and fewer options for those who are dissatisfied with their present work situation. When escape through job mobility becomes blocked, then psychological withdrawal (burnout) often appears to be the only option.

Prospects for the Future

This chapter briefly summarizes some of the historical forces that have made burnout in the human services such a pressing problem in recent years. This analysis is by no means complete; there are other factors operating in the larger society that have played a role, and some of these are discussed in a recent book (Cherniss, 1980b). Others are noted elsewhere in this volume (see **Carroll & White**).

The primary goal of this effort has been to show that there is a larger social context and that political and economic factors in society profoundly affect individual organizations, workers, and the prevalence of burnout. Thus, any analysis that leaves out these factors is misleading. Those who merely pay lip service to the existence of a larger social context ultimately will fail to understand, predict, and meaningfully alleviate the problem. Ignoring the larger context may be comforting, but it leads to ineffective interventions.

Will concern about burnout continue? Will the problem become worse in the future? History helps us to learn from the past and understand the present, but it is not an infallible guide for predicting the future. Nevertheless, this analysis highlights some of the factors that will influence the nature of burnout in the next few years.

One factor to be considered is that we have entered an age of "diminishing expectations." Increasingly, people expect the future to be worse. If burnout is exacerbated by unrealistically high expectations, this would suggest that the problem will diminish in the coming years.

However, even if burnout does diminish, the end result may be no different. New workers increasingly will *begin* their careers "burned out." They will not burn out on the job, simply because they will never be on fire! Young people will be alienated and preoccupied with personal survival before they assume their first job, and this attitude will make commitment, fulfillment, and idealism even more rare in the future than they are now. Thus, workers and programs in the human services will perform at lower levels, and there will be less concern about the problem. People at all levels of the system will simply accept things as they are and will not expend the effort or take the risks necessary to effect change. This will create even more frustration and stress for others. State psychiatric hospitals, public welfare departments, and the Penn Central will be the prototypes of the future.

Another factor to consider is the possibility of a radical change in public policy. For the first time since the 1930s, there is an administration in Washington committed to reducing the role of government in people's lives. A clear implication is reduced support and funding for the human services. Consequently, there will be larger caseloads, less clerical assistance, fewer ancillary services, and so on. Also, the status and prestige associated with work in this field will deteriorate further.

Another factor that will increase caseloads is growing unemployment. Brenner's (1973) research has suggested that all indices of social disorganization are linked to the unemployment rate, with a lag of about two years. Thus, even if unemployment becomes no worse than it is today (8.9 percent), social agencies will see a steady growth in their caseloads during the next year. With fewer resources to meet this demand, the burden inevitably will fall on the shoulders of service providers. And the long-term picture is not good: The current administration has made inflation its priority and seems to be less concerned about unemployment. Even if one accepts the validity of supply-side economics, the hoped-for benefits of greater productivity and less unemployment will not occur for several years.

Long-term demographic shifts also will produce more strain on the human services. One of these is the accelerating flight from snowbelt to sunbelt. The growing numbers of people moving to the South will be faced with the difficult task of creating new support systems in situations of economic uncertainty. Their incidence of psychological and social disorder will be relatively high, and the burden will be felt by sunbelt social agencies. At the same time, the North will suffer from a continual erosion and constriction in its resources, caused by a loss of population. Also, the people who remain in the North, the "residual population," may well be needier and more dependent than those hearty souls who set out to start new lives in more promising environments. Thus, the burdens will increase in northern social agencies as well.

A second important demographic trend is the increasing age of our population. As the "baby boom" population grows up and enters its later years, the social problems associated with growing old in America also will increase. Human service agencies will deal with new, complex issues. Many of their staff will be poorly prepared to do so, and this too will add to strain and burnout.

One other factor that will shape the future is the "stable fat" phenomenon.

In the 1960s, many human service programs were young, and a large percentage of the workforce consisted of new people. However, few new programs have been created in recent years, and there are fewer new recruits. Increasingly, therefore, programs will be run by a large cadre of workers who have worked in the same place for many years with no other place to go. This is the stable fat. As it grows, idealistic workers will find themselves in stifling, unstimulating environments, and they will burn out quickly.

The picture may be different in business, industry, and the military. As we all know, the federal government is committed to increasing support for the armed services and improving the general climate for American business. Even before the new administration was elected careers in business were popular, and enrollments in business schools were growing quickly. Thus, in business and the military, we are in a period of rising expectations. If these expectations become unrealistically high, burnout may increase, especially among younger executives and managers. Also, continuing demands for greater productivity will generate more stress and burnout. Because burnout is an obstacle to improved productivity, the business community may become more interested in doing something about it.

Postscript:
Coming to Terms with History

When I originally presented these ideas at the First National Conference on Burnout in Philadelphia, the audience response was both troubling and instructive. Most of the people I talked to reacted emotionally rather than intellectually. They did not like the presentation because it seemed to be too pessimistic and negative. It was perceived as negative because it did not offer any quick, easy techniques for alleviating burnout in individuals or settings. In fact, I argued strongly that any such efforts ultimately would have little success. Virtually no one attempted to disprove my thesis on the basis of facts or rational argument. Instead, people rejected it simply because it made them feel hopeless. In fact, a few audience members seemed to assume that to present such a bleak picture, I must be depressed and burned out myself. One individual even invited me to come to her workshop on yoga; with concern and sympathy, she said, "I think you're in a place now where you could really use something like this for yourself."

These responses were disturbing because my ideas were dismissed for the wrong reasons. However, the reactions also were illuminating. I began to realize that our tendency to define social problems such as burnout in terms of individuals or organizations, rather than history or culture, is based not on rational analysis or even political ideology, but rather on a strong desire to avoid emotional pain. It clearly is painful for many of us to accept the fact that our actions are influenced and constrained by a larger social context over which we have little control. Furthermore, to save ourselves from that pain, we tend simply to ignore any information that suggests such a state of affairs.

Admittedly, part of the pessimism felt by the audience was a reaction to my concluding remarks. I stated that we seem to be faced with a dilemma for which I have no solution. The dilemma is that we all want to do something to alleviate burnout, yet my analysis of the problem suggests that its roots are to be found in history, politics, and culture. What does one do to bring about change if the source of the problem is out of one's reach? Although I did not say that I thought this dilemma was insoluble or that burnout was inevitable and could never be reduced, apparently many in the audience made this extrapolation. (What I meant to say was only that the usual remedies, such as social support groups or jogging, would fall short, not that all remedies would do so.)

Since the conference, I have thought about what positive action might be valid, given the analysis presented here. By presenting some suggestions, I hope to show that addressing the larger social context does not inevitably lead to paralysis of action. There are no quick and simple "technologies" of social change comparable to behavior modification or relaxation training, but it is possible to implement a clear and coherent program that does take into account the societal sources of burnout.

The first step in any program of action must be to continue and extend the analysis that I have begun here. We must critically examine every important social policy initiative and political action in terms of its ultimate impact on burnout. We must carefully document how changes in funding patterns, accountability mechanisms, and program structures influence burnout rates. For instance, the city of Chicago currently is agonizing over the future of its public transportation system. Some kind of fundamental change in service routes and fare structures is inevitable, and various interest groups are lobbying for their particular choices. Professionals concerned about burnout should attempt to examine how the various options will affect job stress. A change in public transportation patterns may not substantially affect job stress, but this possibility should be explored before it is dismissed out of hand.

A second suggestion is that we return to the social action emphasis characteristic of the 1960s. We should do this not with the naive expectation that the world will suddenly change, but with the conviction that a more limited individual or organizational focus ultimately will be of little help in the long run. Some of us avoid engagement in social action efforts because of the risks involved, but even more avoid such activity simply because they feel that they, personally, can have little immediate impact. Such a reaction is a manifestation of the narcissism that is so characteristic of our age. We are not content with making a relatively modest and anonymous contribution to a larger social movement. We want to make a big splash on our own, and we want to see results quickly. Once we recognize the psychological roots of our disdain for political activity, we may be able to overcome our reluctance and become involved, content in the knowledge that we are making an important, necessary contribution, small though it may be.

One final suggestion concerns strategy. Almost any intervention activity can be used to "raise consciousness" and contribute to cultural change if that is a conscious goal. Even interventions that focus on individuals can do so. A good example is the consciousness-raising group developed by the women's movement. The prototypical group began with the personal feelings and problems of its members. Initial sessions were devoted to catharsis, social support, and individual problem-solving. However, members were not simply taught techniques for managing their difficulties; they were helped to see how their situations could be interpreted in terms of a feminist perspective. As women in these groups came to see their individual problems as manifestations of social problems, many began to feel better about themselves and took positive action to improve their situations (Cherniss, 1972). Soon many groups would begin to discuss and participate in political activity. In this way, an intervention initially focusing on individual help also contributed to one of the most successful social change movements of this century.

There are many other suggestions for action that could be mentioned. But the important point is that a cultural, economic, and political analysis of burnout need not lead to paralysis or even pessimism, if we are willing to assume a longer time perspective. History shapes people, but it is equally true that people shape history. If we are serious about reducing burnout in the workplace, we must come to terms with the social forces that create it.

6

Bottom Lines
Assessing the Economic and Legal Consequences of Burnout

ROBERT F. MINNEHAN and WHITON STEWART PAINE

The legal and fiscal implications of the burnout stress syndrome (BOSS) are slowly being defined. As Christina **Maslach** indicates, burnout does seem to exist, but there is controversy about its definition, and this complicates attempts to assess potentially significant economic and other consequences. These consequences are probably widespread and are becoming more serious as a result of the social, political, and economic trends noted by **Cherniss.** Thus, they should be of significant and increasing interest to decision makers, particularly those concerned about such issues as decreasing staff productivity, quality of life, burgeoning medical and legal costs, declining quality of output, deteriorating labor relations, increasing personnel problems, risk management, and long-range planning.

Carroll and White's and **Freudenberger's** discussions of the effects of burnout provide a depressing picture of multiple, potentially negative impacts on individuals and organizations. This has led to the widespread presumption that the BOSS must also have significant economic impacts and legal implications. However, to date there has been no detailed analysis of either area. The following is a preliminary attempt to summarize a strategy and concepts that can be used to apply such analyses to given situations, including work sites, companies, industries, agencies, or professions. Ultimately, as **Paine** notes, work must be done at all of these levels in order to maximize the impacts of intervention.

Unfortunately, the present body of empirical knowledge discussed by **Shinn** could only support preliminary economic analyses of the BOSS, and the directly applicable legal precedents are sparse. However, both areas are developing rapidly as researchers, economists, and lawyers begin to apply techniques and principles found useful in parallel areas. The increasing links between researchers providing data on incidence, prevalence, and characteristics of the BOSS, economists assessing the short- and long-term economic impacts of validated outcomes, and lawyers using the results in specific cases will further complicate the decision-making process in organizations. To some extent this will become yet another stressor for professionals and administrators.

Thus, the following analysis is inherently speculative, but it draws directly upon expertise in related areas, including cost analysis, and legal precedents in workmen's compensation and other cases. The reader should be aware, however, that any such effort must rely on assumptions that can, and should, be challenged. The authors have selected assumptions that are reasonable in terms of the currently available, and often incomplete, literature on the BOSS. When using this general approach, individuals must select the specific assumptions that appear most valid within their own contexts and according to their needs.

Background

Several general bodies of literature are relevant. Economists and others have developed useful approaches for estimating costs associated with a wide range of outcomes. Calculating the direct and indirect costs of burnout is a crucial step in any economic analysis of the process. For example, the costs of turnover, job-related accidents, plus product and other liability questions are some of the issues involved here.

Such an economic analysis is incomplete unless it is extended to include the causal variables involved in the process itself. With these variables the costs of intervention and prevention can be considered. Having these two types of costs provide a more comprehensive model of costs and cost/savings for studying the burnout syndrome. From the perspectives of decision makers, these cost and cost/savings models do not have to be comprehensive, but they should be complete enough to guide decisions regarding how to change the process to minimize costs.

One immediate use of a BOSS economic model is its application to a legal analysis. Here, only certain variables would be chosen on the basis of legal and other precedents. For example, it is potentially possible to claim workmen's compensation benefits on the basis of burnout and related injuries as a result of exposure to job stress. This may come as an unwelcome surprise to many administrators. Essentially, the issue in this area is how to limit the organization's legal exposure and what strategies should be pursued in estimating potential damages.

In a second use, the BOSS economic model can also be combined with particular cost data to aid in the analysis of identification, prevention, intervention, and treatment strategies for an organization. This analysis would draw heavily upon the available procedures for estimating the costs and benefits of alternatives. For example, one question would be: Is it better to ignore burnout and simply force out staff exhibiting the symptoms, or should an organization implement selected changes in its present structure, benefits packages, or ways of operation, and retain staff?

Thus, four related issues will have to be considered in the 1980s:

(1) how to define the impacts of burnout in economic terms;
(2) how roughly to link the impacts into a limited model;
(3) redefining the analysis in terms of legal precedents;
(4) using economic models to assess prevention/intervention alternatives

Because of space limitation and the present state of knowledge in this area, the text will focus on issues 1 and 3, the economic and legal implications. Each brief discussion will involve an analysis of the importance of the issue, a specification of a potentially useful strategy, and a discussion of its limits and potential problems. Obviously, each topic is complex enough for its own chapter or even a separate book.

Any approach to the analysis of the BOSS must utilize different levels of information, be modifiable to meet different needs, and be based on the available literature concerning inputs, processes, and outcomes of the BOSS **(Carroll & White)**. Because it is the first time that these analytic tools have been formally applied to the BOSS, the reader should keep the following general limitations in mind:

(1) At present, there is no agreed-upon, empirically validated general model of the burnout process. Thus, decision makers must select the variables of importance to them from the wide range available.
(2) Research on the BOSS is just beginning, and there is a general lack of "hard" data.
(3) Little is known about the interaction of the BOSS process with factors that are specific to different work settings. Setting differences may have major impacts on the costs of different outcomes.
(4) Clear legal precedents are few, and this area of law is only beginning to develop. There are generally acceptable approaches for the estimation of damages, however.
(5) Professionals have not come to any agreement about the optimum mix of

intervention/prevention options. This would require considerable additional data on the impacts of various procedures and on their costs.

(6) In complex areas such as the BOSS, procedures for estimating costs and benefits are necessarily imprecise.

These limitations are quite common for many issues related to the work environment, but they should be kept in mind when reading the present analysis. It is intended to be preliminary, limited in scope, and general in nature, and it focuses on an overall strategy that can be adapted to differing situations. As the literature on burnout develops, it is assumed that this strategy will become increasingly useful. Even now it should be useful, since some information, carefully devised, is better than little or no information, which is currently the case.

Issue I: Defining the Impact of Burnout in Economic Terms

Ultimately, the widespread acceptance of burnout as a legitimate phenomenon of concern will require hard data on the costs of this process. Determining the "bottom line" is a necessary first step in understanding the extent and seriousness of the problem and in the comparative assessment of possible solutions.

Obviously, any analysis of costs would differ according to the key questions of interest. The interests of state and federal policymakers are different from those of individuals experiencing BOSS. The same general procedure should apply at all levels, however. It involves the following steps:

Step 1: Defining the Key Multiple Outcomes of Interest

Carroll and White list many possible impacts of the BOSS. To select the outcomes of most importance in a given situation, administrators should use a combination of the available literature, industry and local data, consultants, limited surveys, discussions with colleagues, and personal experience. The recent work of Jones (1981a, 1981b) is particularly important here, as he has linked the BOSS to such impacts as police brutality and employee theft, impacts of obvious interest to employers.

Initially, the full range of expected outcomes should be delineated and efforts made to determine (1) probability and frequency of occurrence, (2) severity and intensity, (3) probability of recovery with and without intervention, and (4) expected time path. In some cases, such as turnover, good data will be available. Other outcomes will not be well documented and will have to be estimated using the best available data and information. For example, **Golembiewski** presents data on the number of individuals in one organization at different levels of the BOSS as defined by the Maslach Burnout Inventory (MBI).

In general, ignore outcomes where (1) little or no data are available; (2) the linkages to the organization's mission are remote, (3) the probability of occurrence is small, (4) severity and intensity are low, and (5) the time path is very long, if normal turnover may solve the problem.

These five points are general guidelines and may have to be ignored in specific situations. For example, if an effect such as low morale is perceived to be important, it may be necessary to collect data on its incidence, prevalence, and characteristics. A given effect may be peripheral to the stated goals of the organization but very important to the individuals involved, and thus should be included. Unlikely effects with major financial loss implications may be quite important. Finally, extended time paths are appropriate for the analyses of burnout in long-term situations, such as professional careers.

Step 2: Defining Costs

The multiple outcomes of the BOSS were selected in Step 1. A "price tag" or cost can be estimated for many of these effects, but the accuracy and precision of the cost estimate will vary. This list of effects to be costed out should include ones that can be identified as (1) direct, (2) indirect, (3) hidden, and (4) potential costs. If the BOSS is already a problem in your organization, you are already paying many of these costs. A separate issue is the probable increase in costs associated with increased staff burnout in the next year or over a longer period. Some typical costs are presented in Table 6.1.

The list of *direct* costs of the BOSS can begin with the direct health care costs to the employee, employer, and insurer. These costs represent the "value" of resources used to provide (1) prevention, (2) diagnosis, (3) treatment, (4) continuing care, and (5) rehabilitation of the health impairment. From the perspective of an organization, these medical-type costs for all affected employees can be measured with some precision, since data are usually available and can be collected.

A second type of cost, a loss in *productivity,* is defined as an *indirect* cost in the methodology used for cost-of-illness studies (Hartunian, Smart, & Thompson, 1981).

There is also a possibility that the absence of one burned-out person increases stress on co-workers. This consequence may be especially delete-

TABLE 6.1   Examples of Costs of Interest

Type	Examples
Direct for employee	—Medical costs for illnesses, accidents —Loss of earnings, pension —Intervention costs: prevention, treatment
Indirect to employee, but direct effects on employer	—Reduced worker productivity, increased reject rates —Cost of replacement or substitute worker —Sick leave —Increased insurance premiums —Payments for early retirement —Recruitment and orientation costs —Identifiable "lost" clients or customers —Employee theft, sabotage
Hidden to employee, employer	—Decreased flow of clients and consumers —Impacts on families and support groups
Potential costs to employer	—Possible early retirement —Industrial and other accidents —Potential health disability —Increased legal costs —Product liability suits

rious when the co-workers are experiencing the explicit behavioral changes of the BOSS. This type of effect can be difficult to estimate in quantitative terms, but a study of changes for an organizational unit might provide some quantitative ideas about an effect. These effects on co-workers can include changes in both (1) productivity or outcomes and (2) medical-type costs.

There can also be increases in the costs of doing business, costs such as insurance premiums, payments for early retirement, orientation, and training costs for replacement employees. Some estimates can be made for each of the identified effects, but these estimates may not be completely accurate.

There may be *hidden* costs outside the organization; these are effects borne by (1) family and related persons and (2) clients or customers. Some value of these hidden costs can be estimated, if the effects can be identified and carefully described, but the accuracy of the estimates may be poor.

An example of a health disability situation is the typical workmen's compensation case for stress-related health problems. (These types of cases will be discussed in detail below.)

To summarize the discussion of this step of defining costs, the first task is to define the nature of the effects, preferably in an extensive list; then the cost-estimating procedures for the effects of interest can be selected. For some effects, the costs are accurately estimated, such as direct medical costs and perhaps the indirect costs of productivity losses. Other costs, such as hidden costs or potential costs, can be more speculative, and estimating procedures may not be as accurate.

In large firms, some thought might be given to analyzing a cohort of workers in high-stress jobs who manifest some of the major BOSS symptoms (decline in personal productivity, turnover, increased absenteeism, increased use of benefits, and theft, for example) and comparing their productivity and costs of employment in their last year and during an earlier time period. This type of analysis, while crude, could generate a surprising amount of information on the costs of the BOSS and can also assist in predicting future costs.

A pragmatic approach here could be the preparation of two sets of cost estimates, that is, high and low cost estimates for the range of effects. In addition, the *probability* that each type of identified cost will occur must be considered in developing accurate cost estimates. Low probability effects with inordinately high potential costs may be very important in an organization concerned with liability issues.

Limitations

There are two general types of limitations for the cost analysis described here. First the list of different direct, indirect, hidden, and potential costs is difficult to develop in complete detail, especially since some costs are hidden or potential. Second, the accuracy and precision of the economic magnitudes and probability of each identified economic consequence are also difficult to estimate for the indirect, hidden, and potential costs. Third, as **Paine** has pointed out, the BOSS has some benefits as well as costs, and these may have to be factored into some analyses.

The best quality estimates would typically be the direct health (prevention and intervention) costs; the reliability (and even validity) of the other cost estimates may be poor unless there has been some explicit study of the BOSS effects within the organization. As better data become available, the accuracy of these estimates improves. However, cost estimates can, and should, be made, and these cost estimates can help to evaluate alternative strategies for dealing with the BOSS. In this situation, a decision based on some data is clearly better than one based on few or no data (which is usually the case).

Issue II: Building a Comprehensive
Economic Model of the Burnout Process

The previous cost analysis is incomplete because, while cost data are useful, they provide relatively few guidelines for intervention. Presumably, a fuller understanding of the entire burnout process is necessary to provide the information needed for decisions designed to modify that process. Building such models as the ecological one developed by **Carroll and White** is largely an art form, but it is necessary for such an understanding. These models are built on an understanding of complex cause-effect relationships, with the following possible linkages between cause and effects.

Linear Relationship. A major simplifying assumption is that a set of causal variables involved in Process A results in Outcome B in a direct, additive way. This makes model building much simpler, since possible nonlinear impacts can be ignored.

Probabilistic. The relationship between a causal variable and an outcome is not absolute, particularly given the social and psychological factors mentioned above. How strong is the relationship and what is the probability of the effect, given the cause, are important questions. Hence, a probabilistic relationship between A and B is the basis of a model.

Such models should be conceptualized as a comprehensive approach for analysis and decision-making. Both systems theory and ecological theory **(Carroll and White)** would apply here. This approach can begin by drawing a *picture* of the major probable chain of causes and effects for an existing environment. This picture could resemble a skeletal tree (as a tree appears in the winter), the branches leading to the different sets of possible costs and affected groups, as seen in Table 6.1. The purpose of the strategy study is to find optimal ways to minimize the size of the costly branches, yet not overspend on the process of "pruning" or tree maintenance.

Many different pictures of trees can be drawn, assuming certain combinations of prevention and intervention actions. A substantial number of pictures may be needed to analyze comprehensively the many possible strategies or ways of minimizing the costs of the BOSS. These pictures provide a very graphic way to understand a complex phenomenon. At this point, knowledge about all the costs and groups affected (as seen in Table 6.1) is limited, so any specification of the linkage between prevention/intervention actions and types of cost reductions is highly speculative. The main purpose of the tree is to suggest areas where intervention appears to be most useful, least costly, or both.

Model Building

A model is needed to find a good organizational strategy for the BOSS. Yet the process of model building can easily become inordinately complex and overwhelming. The basic rule is KISS—keep it simple and short. Other precautions include:

Precaution 1: Focus on a few key outcomes (effects), rather than a large list.

Precaution 2: Select process variables (or causes) that are meaningful. What characteristics of the work environment (and possibly changeable factors), discussed by **Pines,** seem logically or empirically linked to BOSS outcomes and to each other **(Shinn)?** A real problem here is the lack of an empirical literature that links causes and effects, but this is developing rapidly **(Shinn).**

Precaution 3: Model building is a learning process. It is unlikely that a perfect description or model (of all the important variables affecting a BOSS strategy) can be built in a short period, simply because the theoretical knowledge and data base are not yet available. Therefore, a discovery, successive-refinement, muddle-through process of model improvement should be expected. This learning process can result in an elaborate "tree" containing many process variables and outcomes. This is an expanded version of the tree discussed earlier.

Despite the limitations cited above, model-building attempts must be made. The complexity of the BOSS and its probable responsiveness to work-site characteristics suggests that, ultimately, individualized models will be needed to maximize the effectiveness and efficiency of intervention efforts. This is discussed in more detail in Paine (1981a).

Issue III: Impact of Legal
Precedents on an Analysis

We are in an era of legal confrontation, and in this context it is not surprising that there are important legal ramifications of the BOSS.

The basic argument is that the employer must provide a workplace that is not dangerous to an employee's physical and mental health. High-stress work settings have the potential to impact negatively on both areas of health **(Carroll & White).**

In some industries, enough information is becoming available to support these types of analyses. One example would be air traffic controllers. In this instance there is a considerable body of Department of Transportation data that could be combined with the results of such studies as the Air Traffic Controller Health Change Study (Rose, Jenkins, & Hurst, 1978) to develop a model of stress, burnout, and costs. This analysis would have some obvious policy implications.

Burned-out employees may present a workmen's compensation claim or other claims and may also, through decreased, inadequate, or inappropriate performance, increase the liability of the organization. The ideas identified in the previous two sections can also be applied to assess (1) potential general liability (potential costs), and (2) liability in specific workmen's compensation claims and damage suits. Obviously, the following analysis must be general in nature, since specific situations must reflect local statutes and precedents. Most states currently allow claims for work stress-related problems, a rapidly developing area of law which should be closely monitored by decision makers.

Economists and others working with the legal profession have developed a number of generally accepted procedures for determining liability and damage in individual cases. Indeed, the logic behind these analyses is very similar to the logic involved in modeling the burnout process and estimating the economic costs of that process. Legal precedents and related considerations act to restrict the scope of economic costs to costs that can be determined beyond a reasonable doubt (that is, the evidence must be adequate). This restricted view of costs can be useful here, since these costs are realistic and assessable against an organization.

There are two means of compensating for an existing injury: remedies under workmen's compensation and common-law suits. These will be discussed separately, since they have very different fiscal and other implications.

Workmen's Compensation

The purpose of workmen's compensation laws is "to guarantee each employee a weekly income, based on his past earnings experience, as a substitute for what was lost by reason of an accidental injury or diseases causally related to his employment. It is the rule of causal relationship which makes the difference. On the other side of the coin, the employer is protected against exorbitant claims" (Blair, 1975). This remedy of workmen's compensation is available for most industries and employers; excluded groups are generally employees of charities and nonprofit institutions. Job stress has been implicated as a causal factor for incapacitating medical conditions (such as hypertension) and increased job-site injuries.

There are legal precedents for workmen's compensation claims for stress-related disabilities. One basis for a claim is that stress gradually accumulates on the job and eventually disables the worker. For example, the Pennsylvania Supreme Court recently ruled that a worker who died of a heart attack at home while writing a speech was eligible for death benefits, because the heart condition was deemed the result of accumulated job stress. According to a September 17, 1980, *Wall Street Journal* article, California receives

3,000 to 4,000 psychiatric injury claims each year, and about half these claims are awarded.

The awards can be for a temporary period or for a lifetime, depending on the extent of the disability. The employer pays for workmen's compensation insurance, and if more employees claim disability their insurance rates can increase, so an increase in numbers of compensation awards can result in the highest insurance rate. If the BOSS is increasing, the implication may be significant in this area.

The workmen's compensation mechanism would be the usual response to stress-related disability, whether the disability were temporary or permanent—at least in those cases where there were no extraordinary or unusual circumstances that would support a common-law suit.

Common-Law Cases

As an alternative to workmen's compensation, damages may be sought through a civil court case. These cases typically require several types of convincing evidence for a successful judgment. First, there must be a finding of liability on the part of the employer—some negligence, malice, creation of conditions that are hazardous or stressful, or the like. Second, there must be some medical testimony (and evidence) regarding the degree of present and probable future disabilities or impairment. Third, there must be some testimony or demonstration of vocational effects. In addition, pain and suffering, or loss of companionship, may also be considered. The fourth kind of evidence must demonstrate and project economic consequences. The amount of the economic damages is usually based on an economist's estimate of the loss of an individual's income in past and future periods. (There can be additional amounts awarded for pain and suffering, as well as exemplary damages.)

In the case of a surviving disabled worker and strong evidence of employer fault, the award may equal the projected value of lost earnings and can be considerably higher than that provided under the workmen's compensation law.

The types of factors that affect the earnings-loss evaluation, the estimated medical and vocational effects, and the economic projection methodology are often examined by experts for both the plaintiff and the defense. The result of employing separate sets of experts for each of the adversaries is usually a substantial disagreement of testimony about the magnitude and duration of effects. Quite often the experts for the defense are chosen because they will present evidence that adds to a minimal economic loss estimate. Hence, the estimated economic values for earnings loss can be extraordinarily different. These common-law cases can require several years to resolve (four years or more is not uncommon in Delaware), and the attorney fees and court costs must be added to any damages award.

The claim can total to hundreds of thousands of dollars easily, but claims of $2 and $6 million (for men 50 years old), as cited in a recent article (Rice, 1981) are unreasonable in some states' courts. A more common situation is presented in the following hypothetical case. The assumptions and procedures utilized to compute damages are those commonly employed in cases in Delaware and Pennsylvania. Cases in other states would differ somewhat in their computations, but the final figures would, in most cases, be of a similar magnitude.

Example of Economic Damages
Claim for Burnout

This is a simulated case based on data from some actual law cases. The employee's perspective on economic losses is taken here. Assume two executive employees at two different points in their careers: one is age 35 and earning $30,000 per year; the other is age 50 and earning $45,000 per year. The calculations shown here assume that the ultimate effect of burnout is a presumed injury leading to a downgrading in actual position and earnings level, with the individual attempting to recover his or her long-term losses. A downward transfer within the company or relocation to another company are possible actions leading to a claim.

The following economic losses and claims could be considered in this instance:

(1) *Decrease in Earnings Level:* The economic assumption is that the 35-year-old would progress to a $50,000 level by age 50 (ignoring inflation), while the 50-year-old is at or near the maximum level. The effect of burnout is (a) to reduce the 35-year-old to a $24,000 position without growth potential and (b) similarly to reduce the 50-year-old to a $30,000 level.

(2) *Loss of Earnings and Pension Value:* A further assumption used here is that one longer-term effect of burnout would be an early retirement (arguable but possible). The 35-year-old would retire at age 50, and the 50-year-old would retire at age 55. In each case there would be 25 years of service and qualification for early retirement. Early retirement means both fewer years of earning and a smaller pension value (due to actuarial reasons, retirement at age 50 means a 50 percent reduction in pension, and at age 55 means a 25 percent reduction of the pension based on the lower salary level). The calculations for the loss in earnings and pension are summarized in Table 6.2.

The magnitude of earnings and pension loss is (possibly) surprising for this example, as the loss for the 35-year-old who is downgraded totals to $1

TABLE 6.2   Estimation of Damages

Person	35-year-old	50-year-old
Part I: Normal Earnings		
a. Normal earnings to age 65	$1,237,500	$675,000
b. Minus expected reduced earnings	− 360,000	150,000
c. Predicted loss in earnings	$ 877,500	$525,000
Part II: Pension Earnings		
d. Normal 65 pension: earnings until death	$ 237,600	$226,800
e. Early retirement pension: until death	− 93,600	148,500
f. Loss in pension payments to end of life	$ 144,000	$ 78,300
Part III: Losses		
g. Sum of losses	$1,021,500	$603,300

million! This total occurs even though this person continues to work for fifteen years. Working longer will lower the damages, but half a million is still possible for a permanent "disability" claim. The loss of salary is always recognized, and the loss in pension value is allowed with supporting evidence. The realistic impact of the reduced earnings and pension values may be *understated* by these projections, since the affected person earns less, saves less, and receives a much smaller pension for a longer period of retirement. Such a person could be quite impoverished in the retirement years without the compensation demanded!

In this type of situation, the attorney for the company would argue that the damage was not permanent—that there would be a recovery of functioning and thus of earning potential and future employability and that early retirement was unlikely. These arguments would be weaker in the case of the 50-year-old. However, if the damage is apparent and the evidence reasonably strong that it was work stress-related, it is likely that the company would prefer to settle prior to a trial. The minimum expected settlements are still substantial and would probably be over $300,000 for the 35-year-old and over $200,000 for the older employee. This money would cover the cost of rehabilitation and the permanent loss of earnings due to diminished employability and similar factors not including pain and suffering.

(3) *Other Claims:* In addition to the earnings and pension losses, there can be (a) medical costs not covered by insurance, and (b) "pain and suffering" costs for the individual and his or her family. The medical costs for some inpatient care, long duration outpatient therapy, and medication could easily total $10,000, although this seems small in comparison to the earnings and pension losses. The claim for pain and suffering is typically related to earnings level and the duration of pain and suffering. In some cases, this claim can be large.

In a lawsuit, the "demand" for settlement could include separately item-ized claims for a loss of each type listed above, and more. The total demand can be quite large, even with the reasonable assumptions used above. How-ever, it is very possible that the total loss to the organization and society could be much larger than the individual losses identified above.

The legal basis for common-law cases is being expanded with new law-suits that will set precedents regarding how employer liability for the BOSS should be computed. Also, outside parties, including clients/consumers/patients, professional organizations/unions, and regulatory agencies, are increasingly becoming interested in this area of law and may generate their own estimates. In any case, the potential cost to organizations is substantial and probably growing. This vulnerability is likely to increase as the general literature on the BOSS strengthens.

Limitations

The basic logic behind the estimation procedure is accepted within the legal community. It has been tested in a wide variety of workmen's compen-sation and other situations. However, within each case and within each group of cases, there will be considerable disagreement about the severity and duration of injury and hence about the magnitude of economic valuation. This is normal in a legal adversarial situation.

A Note on Risk Prevention

Typically, the lost-earnings analysis is done in response to a threatened or actual claim or suit. Administrators should give some thought to obtaining a similar analysis to estimate their risk of liability prior to possible legal proceedings. In medical settings, for example, decreased and inappropriate professional performance has immediate risk management implications. In industry the equivalent risk involves product liability suits. Space does not permit any analysis of these questions, but they should be of concern to decision makers, particularly those involved in insurance, quality control and assurance, legal issues, and related areas.

Issue IV: Economic Models and Prevention/Intervention Decisions

Up to this point, this chapter has focused on estimating the impacts of burnout and understanding its process. The very limited and preliminary analyses discussed above suggest that the BOSS is indeed a problem with significant legal and economic implications. Future, more detailed and valid analyses are likely to reinforce and extend this basic conclusion. What, then, are administrators and others to do to limit the negative impacts of the BOSS? This is essentially a set of cost-benefit questions that can be answered using information drawn, in part, from the procedures discussed above.

Basically, we are suggesting that decision makers utilize such information to analyze the expected short- and long-term costs and benefits of alternative integrated strategies for dealing with the BOSS. The analytical device here is to create a chart (Table 6.3) listing costs and benefits. This approach suggests that intervention actions should attempt to maximize four main goals—detection, prevention, mediation, or remediation—at four levels of the organization: (1) personal/individual, (2) interpersonal, (3) work site, and (4) overall organizational. These categories are discussed briefly in the introduction to this volume and in a more detailed paper by Paine (1982b). Specific intervention techniques are presented in depth in this volume's six chapters on strengthening individuals and changing organizations. Some salient cost/outcome concerns are discussed below to alert decision makers to some of the questions that they should consider in this type of analysis.

Limitations and a Suggested Strategy

The following are some of the limitations to this type of analysis:

(1) The more sophisticated approaches to cost-benefit analyses require data that are unavailable.
(2) The monetary costs of the various alternatives can often be determined, but the estimation of benefits and the assignment of monetary values to benefits is far more difficult.
(3) Many intervention alternatives have the potential of generating paradoxical effects. A short-term benefit may also result in a high cost over the longer term and vice versa.
(4) One intervention may effect the impacts of another intervention.

Under these circumstances, a simple approach to cost-benefit or cost-outcome analysis seems most appropriate. For each possible intervention, one should calculate the expected short- and long-term costs and benefits. Where numbers or dollar values are available, they should be included.

Interventions can then be grouped into alternative integrated plans for dealing with burnout. One possible way of summarizing such an alternative

TABLE 6.3 Suggested Format for Studying Alternative Strategies

Alternative Strategy: _____ *Cost/Benefit Ratio:* _____
Total Projected Costs: _____

Level in Organization	Types of Possible Interventions	Short-Term (1 year) Projections of		Long-Term (3 years) Projections of		Confidence in Projections and other Comments
		Costs	Benefits	Costs	Benefits	
PER-SONAL	1. 2. 3.					
INTER-PER-SONAL	1. 2. 3.					
WORK-SITE	1. 2. 3.					
OVER-ALL ORGA-NIZA-TION	1. 2. 3.					

is to use the chart presented in Table 6.3. A chart or tabular listing such as this one is literally a picture worth a thousand (or more) words! A separate chart for each set of integrated actions is suggested. Such an approach should significantly contribute to planning and to the most effective internal utilization of the analysis of the economic and legal implications of efforts to deal with the problem of burnout. As better information and data become available, the sophistication and utility of cost-benefit approaches should increase. But even at present, primitive approaches are almost certainly superior to the piecemeal approach. They also represent one way of facilitating decisions when selecting from among the wide range of intervention options discussed in this volume.

For example, a recent article by Carrington and her associates (1980) presents an unusually clear example of a situation that would support simple cost-benefit analyses as an aid to decision-making. Carrington did a study of three alternative meditation training techniques which were evaluated with telephone company employees. The training costs were reasonably specific and the impacts relatively clear. All of the various strategies suggested in this chapter could have been applied to this industrial setting to aid managers in deciding whether or not to continue this type of training.

At another level, a recent article by Kaplan & Bush (1982) summarizes a decision strategy that links a unit of health status (a well year) with the costs of interventions. The authors' focus is on national health policy, but the techniques they describe could be used by large corporations to assess the potential utility of BOSS-related intervention programs.

Summary

This chapter is a very brief summary of the complexities inherent in any attempt to analyze the economic and legal implications of burnout. We know enough to feel that there are such implications and that they are important. An estimation of their ultimate importance will require a great deal of additional valid and reliable data on the burnout stress syndrome and on the burnout process. At present, it is possible to use available tools to assess roughly the economic costs of burnout in a given work situation, to build limited cause and effect models of the process, to support both workmen's compensation and common-law legal proceedings, and to begin to estimate the costs and benefits of different prevention, mediation, and remediation strategies for intervention. As better data become available, the precision of these types of analyses will increase, and so will their utility. We hope that in ten years a discussion such as this one will answer more questions than it raises.

7

Preparing the Professional
Building Prevention into Training

JACK F. WILDER and ROBERT PLUTCHIK

The negative changes in attitude and behavior that characterize the burnout syndrome in the professional is an individual phenomenon, and not all professionals experience burnout. It has been recognized that many factors in the job situation can make burnout more or less likely to occur **(Pines).** The issue raised in this chapter is whether there are factors in the *training* of professionals that influence the likelihood of burnout.

In an attempt to explore this issue, the authors have turned to the literature, to a survey of educators in professional schools, and to their own extensive experience in the mental health and health fields.

The Literature

Three areas of the literature were reviewed: first, the writings specifically on burnout; second, publications describing changes in the curriculum of professional schools in components that authors on burnout believe to be related to the phenomenon (such changes were instituted largely for reasons other than for preventing burnout); and third, writings describing training programs specifically aimed at preventing untoward reactions in stressful life situations that are not job-related. The reasons for the successes or failures of such programs may help us design effective interventions in training programs for the prevention of professional burnout.

Burnout

The writings on burnout (for example, Edelwich & Brodsky, 1980; Pines & Aronson with Kafrey, 1981; Cherniss, 1980a; Kramer, 1974; Kramer &

Schmalenberg, 1977) identify five "problems" associated with professional training programs: (1) They tend to create unrealistic expectations. (2) They are often not practical, thorough, or relevant enough. (3) They do not train professionals in interpersonal skills to a sufficient degree. (4) They do not provide adequate knowledge of the nature of bureaucratic organizations and of how to function effectively within those constraints. (5) They do not train professionals on how to cope with uncertainty, change, conflict, stress, and burnout. There is evidence, albeit not conclusive, that correcting these weaknesses will reduce burnout.

Changes in Professional Curriculum

The educational literature on professional training has been concerned with the five problems noted in the writings on burnout. It is the impression of the authors that there has been a major interest in bringing about changes in the areas of developing interpersonal skills, understanding the functioning of organizations, and coping with stress, in descending order of priority.

There are many writings on the teaching of communication skills and the enhancement of interpersonal skills in professionals. Recent research in medical education describes the characteristics of such successful educational programs and their lasting effects on physicians (for example, Grayson, Nugent, & Oken, 1977; Hartings & Counte, 1977; Kahn, Cohen, & Jason, 1979; Kauss, Robbins, Abrass, Bakaitis, & Anderson, 1980; Pacoe, Naar, Guyett, & Wells, 1976; and Robbins, Kauss, Heinrich, Abrass, Dreyer, & Clyman, 1979). Of course, such new programs are not unique to medical schools.

Related to improving interpersonal skills is the concern with training professionals who are more humanitarian. For example, suggestions are made to alter the selection criteria and broaden the curriculum in medical schools by Keniston (1967), Pellegrino (1974), Rose and Osterud (1980), Kutner (1978), Merton (1957), Coe, Pepper, and Mattis (1977), Becker, Geer, Hughes, and Strauss (1961), and Zola (1975). The Human Dimensions Institute in La Jolla, California, has conducted seminars with physicians—faculty and medical students—for several years and has actively consulted with a number of medical schools on how to train a more humane physician.

A cursory look at the course announcements in the catalogues of professional schools demonstrates the increased interest in understanding the functioning of organizations. The courses, required or elective, come under a variety of names, ranging from "organizational theory" and "organizational development" to "human behavior in organizations."

There is also an increasing interest in understanding the attitudinal changes that occur in professional trainees during their training and the techniques used for coping with stress during training. For example, again in medical education, the psychosocial processes whereby medical students acquire the professional role of physician have been studied by Becker et al. (1961), Bloom (1963, 1965), Coombs (1978), Eron (1955, 1958), and Lief and Fox (1963).

Changes in curriculum are taking place. But are the changes adequate? Are courses enough? Will the effect be in the direction we seek?

Models and Prevention

During the past ten to fifteen years, there have appeared many articles in the mental health field describing programs aimed at preventing emotional disturbances and promoting well-being. One approach to prevention is to expose individuals to a special training program prior to their entering a stressful situation. If the world of jobs is viewed as a stressful situation, then professional training programs might include a preventive intervention component. How successful have parallel prestress training programs been?

There are only two programmatic areas that have anything that approaches hard data: premarital counseling programs to reduce marital distress (see Gurman & Kniskern, 1977; Schumm & Denton, 1979), and educational programs for teenagers to prevent substance abuse during those difficult years (Goodstadt, 1978). The results of the research in these two areas may be interpreted in the following ways in terms of preventing job burnout through training.

First, it may not be possible to help an individual cope with stress on a job until he or she is actually on the job. As Mudd (1941) stated in commenting on the potential effectiveness of premarital counseling, "how far can one help to prepare another person for an experience he has not had?"

Second, the effectiveness of any prejob intervention is probably enhanced by continuing such a program when the individual is actually on the job.

Third, just giving knowledge to professional trainees about stress and the phenomenon of burnout during training will probably have few long-term effects.

Fourth, interventions aimed at preventing burnout might be counterproductive. For example, if a training program helps professionals become more humanitarian in their attitudes toward patients, they might burn out sooner on a job in which they find they cannot give the level of care that meets their standards.

Fifth, long-term effectiveness might be achieved by having trainees actively engage in stressful situations and learn, step by step, how to cope with them. These stressful learning situations can be in field experiences, in simulated job experiences, or in the actual experiences that a student faces in the stressful world of graduate education.

Survey of Educators in Professional Schools

A survey was conducted with fifteen schools in the Northeast that train professionals in graduate programs. Three schools were contacted in each of five professions: business, education, medicine, nursing, and social work. The names of one or two faculty members who were active in designing the school's curriculum and/or had an interest in the topic of professional burnout were obtained by the authors from personnel in the dean's office of each school. Extensive telephone interviews with these faculty members were conducted by one of the authors. Although the interviews were open-ended, all the respondents were asked the following two questions: "Do you consider job burnout an important issue in your profession?" "What are your training programs doing which might possibly contribute to or prevent burnout on the job?"

The sample in the survey—probably the first of its kind—is selective and limited. Conclusions drawn from the fifteen schools are at best tentative, and generalizations made about any one type of professional school are even more speculative. Anecdotal reports from informants are presented primarily to highlight issues common in varying degrees to all five types of professional training.

It must be kept in mind that the main purpose of the inquiry was to explore the relationship between professional training and burnout on the job. The survey was not intended to elicit opinions on whether a teacher's college produced a highly competent teacher, a business school an ethical executive, a social work school an empathic professional, a nursing school a caring nurse, or a medical school a physician who would practice in a geographic or patient area of great need.

"Do you consider job burnout an important issue in your profession?"

All respondents were familiar with the phenomenon of burnout and believed that it occurs in many of their professional graduates. Faculty in education, social work, and nursing were more concerned about burnout than those in business and medicine. The former group believed that burnout was more prevalent and generally occurred earlier in the professional careers of their students. They attributed these differences in vulnerability to the conditions their students encountered on the job. Teachers, nurses, and social workers usually have starting positions in public bureaucracies with low salaries, poor working conditions, heavy caseloads, difficult clients or students, repetitive tasks, and little opportunity for career advancement. In contrast, in business schools, "our graduates see themselves as entering a hierarchical career, not a flat career," noted a faculty member. "They perceive, perhaps unrealistically, a career line with unlimited opportunities for advancement. They may burn out later in their careers when they reach a plateau. This time often coincides with a mid-life crisis."

Physicians, likewise, have many options in starting positions. Although aspects of their work may be repetitive, the financial rewards, public acclaim, and opportunities for achievement and stimulation are considerable even early in their careers. "Those clinicians who work in areas with high emotional stress, such as in cancer therapy, or in bureaucratic institutions which provide care for chronic patients, such as state hospitals, may burn out earlier." Physicians who pursue a career in research are somewhat like graduates of business schools. "They may burn out later when they have no new ideas or when old ideas have been proven wrong—when they reach a dead end."

"What are your training programs doing that might possibly contribute to or prevent burnout on the job?"

The educators surveyed discussed four areas and their interrelationships: students, faculty, curriculum (both didactic and experiential), and "mission."

Students

In keeping with the literature on burnout, respondents expressed concern about the unrealistic expectations many students have about how they will be received, the day-to-day work that they will do, the results of their efforts, their career advancement, and the self-actualization they will experience on the job. A few respondents suggested that more attention might be given to unrealistic expectations in the selection of students for training. For example, a dean of a nursing school considers potential for burnout in her applicants. "I see nursing as a lifetime career. I like to see someone who is flexible. I get uncomfortable with an applicant who rigidly insists on being a full-time nurse and a full-time wife and mother at the same time. I don't have any hard and fast rules, but at times I might turn down such an applicant because I feel she will not last in a nursing career."

However, high expectations are not viewed as totally undesirable. Professional schools want students who start their careers with a reasonable amount of energy and enthusiasm. These high expectations are understandable. They spring from many sources: the historical mystique of professionalism, the portrayals of professionals in the mass media, the optimism of youth, and the highly personal and individual needs of the men and women who become executives, doctors, teachers, nurses, and social workers.

Almost all respondents, however, raised the question of whether the faculty in many professional schools promote unrealistic expectations in their students or at least do not try to modify unrealistic expectations to a realistic level. When pressed, most respondents in the survey believed they did.

Faculty

A number of faculty types emerge from the survey with respect to how adequately they prepare students for the real world of jobs. These types are briefly identified in Table 7.1. There are obviously no pure types, and each type described by the authors has both positive and negative effects on students. However, the "realist" and the "professional" were seen as the most desirable role models for preventing or delaying burnout in students.

Curriculum

The respondents discussed at length the possible relationship of their curriculum to later burnout. All five professions described the strengths and weaknesses of their classroom exercises, including lectures, seminars, conferences, and electives. The faculty members of the four professions that graduate trainees in the human services—teachers, social workers, nurses, and physicians—also described the strengths and weaknesses of the field experiences they provide their students, including student teaching, field placements, ward duty, clinic and agency assignments, and clerkships and clinical electives. These four groups of faculty members considered both the classroom exercises and the field experiences to be essential. The faculty members believed, however, that the field experiences were more important than the classroom exercises in preparing their graduates for the real world of jobs.

TABLE 7.1   Faculty Types Identified by the Survey

Type	Description
Elitist	A faculty member who is interested in a small, discrete area of knowledge in the field
Rip van Winkle	A faculty member who is 20 years behind the times, teaching in the 1980s what applied to the 1960s
Futurist	A faculty member who is 20 years—he believes—ahead of his time, teaching in the 1980s what may or may not apply to the year 2000
Faddist	A faculty member who is fascinated with what is new and in vogue—whether proven or not proven to be helpful or effective
Double-Binder	A faculty member who does not practice what he preaches, creating a conflict in the students about whether to comply with what they see or what they hear
The Exception	A faculty member who has achieved a meteoric success, unwittingly raising the expectations for success to an unrealistic level for many students
Cynic	A faculty member who believes that nothing was good in the past, is good now, or will be good in the future—he is burned out
Realist	A faculty member who sees the job for what it is and gives students hope that a professional can be competent and reasonably satisfied in a job characterized by high work stress
Professional	A faculty member, highly respected by both students and colleagues, who serves as a superb role model for preparing trainees for the world of their noble profession

Business schools do not provide formal field placements, although some students take summer jobs in businesses. Stated a faculty member in a business school, "What would our students do at their level of training and for a brief period of time? We probably provide a field experience in the way we conduct our educational program. In many ways students are forced to be managers while they are students. They are required to process a great deal of information, make decisions, and defend these decisions before their superiors and their peers. Like the business world they will face, they are in a very competitive setting."

There was consensus by the faculties in the human services that field experiences should approximate the real world but be couched in an academic environment. Three questions arise about this approach. First, "How close should the approximation be?" Second, "How much of a student's training should be spent in field experience?" Third, "Who should do the teaching in a field experience?"

A faculty member in a school of education commented: "They have a saying in the Marines, 'The more you sweat in peace, the less you bleed in war.' The Marines, however, have a captive group of trainees. If we put a teacher through a student-teacher experience that is too stressful, our trainee may never want to work in such a setting. On the other hand, if we place the trainee in a cushy setting, the trainee may get culture shock if she later takes a job in a tough school."

The faculties in social work and medical schools are generally pleased with the amount of time their students spend with clients and patients. Most social workers spend three days a week in field placements during their two years of training. They usually spend one year in one setting and the second year in another. Medical students spend two of their four years of training on the wards and in the clinics. They then train in clinical settings for an additional two to five or more years. The respondents in the schools of education would welcome more student-teaching experiences before they enter practice. There was no consensus among the nursing faculty on how much of the training time of nurses should be spent with patients and what percentage of that time should be spent in a hospital or in an outpatient setting.

The respondents of the four human service professions agree that the faculty member at the training site is critical to the learning experience. Most favored an apprentice model. "There is no substitute for having a teacher work in the same world as the student," said a nursing faculty member. Opponents of the apprentice model felt that faculty members who have the academic qualifications to teach should not be burdened with demanding service responsibilities.

As noted above, the burnout literature criticizes professional training programs for not giving enough emphasis in their formal curricula to preparing their students for the practical realities of governmental regulations and funding, organizational structure and functioning, on-the-job interpersonal stresses and strains, and work-home stresses and strains. The respondents in the survey did not always agree with this assessment. They stated that their training programs do have courses in these areas under a variety of titles. The question, however, is one of emphasis and focus. Many of the courses are not comprehensive, are given late in the training, and are electives. Some of the required courses are given by a "low-status" department, are poorly attended by students, or are derided by faculty members in other departments. Furthermore, the focus of such courses is often highly theoretical. To learn theories about organizational functioning and role conflicts is one thing; to appreciate how working in a hospital and in a team may affect "my" expectations, accomplishments, and well-being is something else.

There is more agreement by respondents that little is being done to teach students about the phenomenon of burnout and about ways of dealing with stress physiologically and psychosocially. As noted above, some respondents fear that lectures or courses on burnout could easily become counterproductive. They also see such courses as "dry" or "irrelevant" to the student experience. Most respondents, however, do describe opportunities they have instituted in their programs for students to meet with each other (and sometimes with spouses), with or without faculty, to share stressful experiences they are facing in their academic programs. Some groups are short-term and some continue throughout the entire training program. Respondents generally view these peer support groups as helpful. This sets an excellent example for the future, because one of the early symptoms of burnout on the job is withdrawal from the very support group that could help professionals deal with this syndrome.

There was full agreement among respondents that the curriculum should place more emphasis on teaching students how to cope physiologically and psychosocially with stress. "Maybe it could start as an elective," said a faculty member in a business school. "I'm sure it would be popular—with faculty, too."

"Mission"

A few respondents made references to an area the authors have labeled "mission." They referred to the overriding importance of the "purpose," "goals," or "commitment" of the particular school.

A faculty member in a school of social work described it this way: "If your goal is not to train social workers for the public sector—or it could be any other profession—but to survive, grow, increase the status of the institution, or to promote some special interest of the faculty, then no matter what course you offer, you will not be preparing students with realistic expectations and the skills needed to survive in the public sector. If you send the right messages to your students, they will enter a job with more momentum and more staying power. In the long run, however, it will be up to them and, hopefully, you have made it clear to them that it will be up to them."

In summary, respondents from fifteen professional schools in five types of training programs view burnout as follows: (1) They believe it occurs in many of their graduates. (2) They blame most of the problem on the stresses and strains of the job. (3) They probably do not address themselves sufficiently to the issue in their programs, yet they do not want to do anything that would turn students off to opportunities in the field. (4) They generally do not consider potential for burnout in student selection, and some question if they should gear their selections to the needs of the types of public agencies in which burnout is most likely to occur. (5) They believe students enter training with unrealistic expectations about the job world, and the programs probably unwittingly reinforce these unrealistic expectations. (6) They see no substitute for knowledgeable, practical, interested, professional, and great teachers. (7) They see the opportunity to experience stress and to learn how to cope with it in field experiences as more important than courses. (8) Many favor an apprentice model in the field experiences; that is, the teacher is doing what the student will be doing. (9) They favor less theoretical courses on what it is like to work in organizations and with people, and strongly endorse a formal curriculum in learning techniques of stress reduction. (10) They see no simple answer to a complex educational problem; many believe that the basic commitment of the professional school is overriding.

A Model for a Training Course on Preventing Burnout

The limitations of formal courses on preventing burnout have been noted above. There is general agreement that if they are given, they have to be supplemented with realistic experiences. The two complement each other. Respondents expressed some difficulty in presenting courses related to burnout that interest the students and have practical value. They also noted that the prevention of burnout is not simply an issue in training but a lifetime pursuit in which the professional plays a central role. We have developed a training approach that appears to deal effectively with these two issues, and present it here as a model.

The NAC training method for preventing burnout (Wilder and Plutchik, forthcoming) is a tripartite method for helping individuals understand and cope with problems of burnout. It has use both in the training of professionals and as a self-help technique for trainees once they are functioning on a job.

The acronym NAC stands for Needs Assessment and Coping Assessment. Let us consider each of these ideas in more detail.

Needs Assessment

Among the various solutions that have been proposed for burnout, one of the more important ones from the point of view of training is needs assessment. The idea behind this is simple: each person has a profile of needs that are relevant to his or her performance on the job. At the same time, each job, often by its very nature and sometimes because of the organizational structure, has a likelihood of satisfying certain needs and not others. We assume that when the job needs of the worker and the need-fulfilling properties of the job are closely matched, burnout is less likely to occur. When they are quite diverse, burnout is more likely to occur.

We have developed a somewhat simplified schema that we believe will be useful in preventing burnout. First, it sensitizes the individual to his or her own needs. Second, it helps an individual assess the need-fulfilling characteristics of a potential job. Third, it increases the probability of an appropriate match between an individual and a job. Fourth, since a perfect match is highly unlikely, it focuses an individual's attention on the areas that he or she should work on to provide maximum satisfaction on the job.

We have identified two sets of needs. The first recognizes needs that are more closely related to personality characteristics; the second recognizes needs that are more closely related to job characteristics. Needs Assessment I identifies eight needs in the former group: recognition, stimulation, family and social life, achievement, competence, autonomy, advancement, and collegiality. Needs Assessment II identifies eight needs in the latter: ambience and working conditions, variety and change, security, workload, emotional demands, participation in decisions, time pressures and deadlines, and interpersonal relations. Each need is defined explicitly. For example, autonomy is "the need to be able to make decisions about my work on my own"; interpersonal relations is "the need for trust, support, and cooperation between myself and my superiors, peers, and subordinates."

We ask each person to rate these needs for himself or herself on a scale of 0 to 100 percent and then plot the strength of the self-reported needs on a circular diagram as shown in Figure 7.1. "One hundred percent (100%) means that the need is absolutely essential for me to be satisfied in my work. Zero percent (0%) means that this need is totally unimportant for me to be satisfied in my work."

It is apparent from Figure 7.1 that trainees give the following priorities to their needs: competence is highest, then collegiality, stimulation and recognition next, then family and social life, then autonomy and achievement, and finally, advancement.

A person is then asked to rate the extent to which his or her individual needs can be met in a particular job. It is important to note that a need may *not* be met by either experiencing too little *or* too much in the need area. For example, the need for advancement (NA I) would not be met if the job

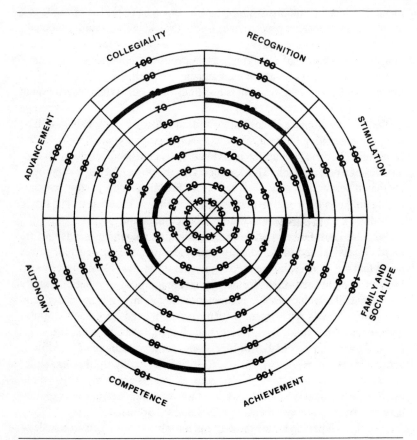

FIGURE 7.1   Needs Assessment I: Before Ratings

required less or more responsibility than the individual wanted to assume at that point in his or her career. Similarly, the need for workload (NA II) would not be met if a person had too little or too much to do on a job.

A faculty member and peers may help in this assessment. Especially informative are the opinions of peers who have taken their field placement in the facility under question, and written assessments of recent graduates from the school who are working in such settings. The shaded areas in Figure 7.2 depict the extent to which each of the individual's needs might be readily satisfied on the job. For example, the collegiality need would be very highly satisfied (about 4/5), but the autonomy need poorly satisfied (about 1/4). The blank areas between the two assessments in Figure 7.2 identify the

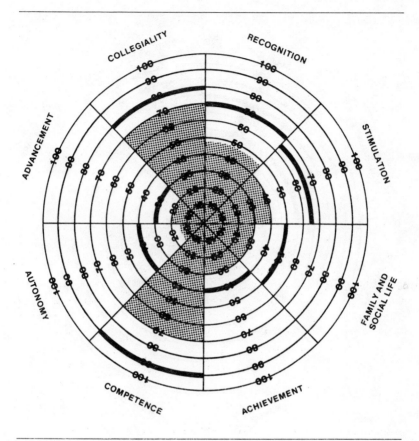

FIGURE 7.2   Needs Assessment I: After Ratings

extent of need dissatisfaction—potential stress—that the individual might experience in a particular need area.

In Figure 7.3 the trainee presents a circular profile for the eight needs that are more closely related to job characteristics. He or she anticipates that the greatest stress in the job under consideration will be in the areas of workload and variety and change.

The graphic representations of Figures 7.2 and 7.3 assist a person in applying for or accepting a job that is most likely to meet his or her individual needs. This self-help approach can also be used once the worker is on the job. In such a case, the shaded areas represent the degree to which the individual has actually experienced the satisfaction of his sixteen needs.

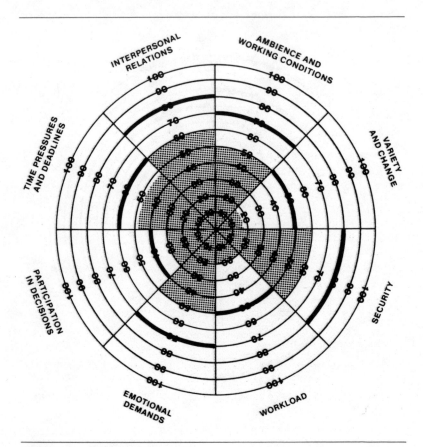

FIGURE 7.3   Needs Assessment II

Coping Assessment:
Ways of Dealing with Stressors

We can reasonably assume that few persons will find an exact match between their professed needs and the need-satisfying characteristics of the jobs they have or want. To some degree everyone has to learn to cope with stress and with discrepancies between what they want and what they get.

During the past several years we have developed a theoretical model for describing coping styles that may be useful in this context. The model of coping styles is based on the theory of emotion proposed by Plutchik (1962, 1980).

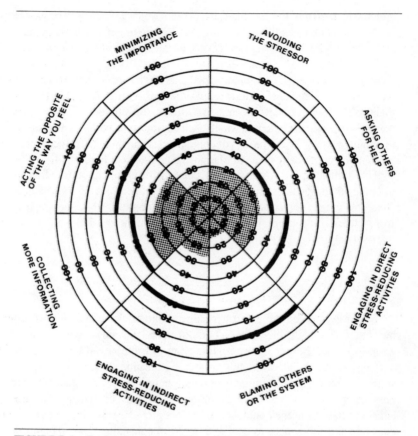

FIGURE 7.4   Coping Assessment: Ways of Dealing with Stressors

The schema assumes that there are eight basic coping styles that are used in attempts to reduce stress: avoiding the stressor, asking others for help, engaging in direct stress-reducing activities, blaming others or the system, engaging in indirect stress-reducing activities, collecting more information, acting the opposite of the way one feels, and minimizing the importance of the stressful event. The technical names for these coping styles are, respectively, suppression, help-seeking, replacement, blame, substitution, mapping, reversal, and minimization. More than one coping style may be used in any stressful situation. A case example of each coping style is given in the instructions for Coping Assessment provided in the NAC Manual.

None of these coping styles is inherently either good or bad. How well the styles work depends on the situation, how they are used, and the degree to which they are used. For example, if a person avoids a superior because of a disagreement between them, this might make him or her feel better temporarily, but might, in the long run, have a deleterious effect on his or her job.

Individuals in training rate their own typical styles of coping on a scale from 0 to 100 percent. "One hundred percent (100%) means that this is a very likely way in which I deal with stressful situations. Zero percent (0%) means that this is a way in which I never deal with stressful situations." A person is then asked to rate the extent to which each coping style works for him or her in reducing stress. These ratings of coping styles and their effectiveness can be depicted graphically on a circular profile as shown in Figure 7.4.

This figure reveals a person who copes with problems most often by blaming others and least often by asking others for help. As the shaded areas show, blaming is not particularly helpful in the long run, while seeking help from others—a coping style that the person might use more often—is relatively effective.

Summary

We have explored the role of training programs in relationship to job burnout, reviewed the literature on burnout and related areas, and conducted a survey of educators representing five types of professional schools: nursing, medicine, social work, business and education. There is a striking similarity between the comments in the literature and the comments of the respondents in the survey. Schools, to varying degrees, contribute to unrealistic expectations in their students and do not provide them with the knowledge and skills they need to deal with stress in demanding jobs in complex organizations. There is less agreement on what can be done about it. There is even some fear by educators that efforts at intervention may be counterproductive. Where does that leave us?

Preventing burnout is clearly in the interests of professional schools. After all, their educational aim is to train individuals who are likely to remain productive throughout their professional careers. We believe that if schools can make matters worse, there is a reasonable chance that they can make matters better.

It seems that professional schools could reduce or delay burnout in their graduates to some degree if they could do the following:

- be committed to training students to work in jobs that are demanding, frustrating, and stressful;
- select faculty who value such jobs;

- select students who are interested in taking such jobs;
- offer courses that provide students with the practical expertise and the realistic expectations they will need to carry out such jobs;
- offer courses and supervision that teach students to appreciate the interpersonal and organizational context in which their expertise must be applied;
- give students real-life or simulated experiences to apply that expertise;
- supervise students in these experiences with teachers who are themselves engaged in the same experiences;
- encourage students to be aware of the frustrations and stresses they are experiencing in their professional training programs and to learn ways of avoiding disillusionment and reducing stress;
- help students become aware of their own personal needs for professional satisfaction and help them identify ways of meeting these needs in their careers;
- make students aware that burnout is an individual phenomenon—that some professionals become disillusioned and worn down, while others, with the same training and in the same job, remain enthusiastic and energetic—and that stress on a job, rather than an intrusion, is as much a part of any job as it is of life in general.

Above all, we must encourage our professional schools to kindle a commitment and inspire a sense of responsibility that will enable students to endure as professionals.

PART III

Interventions with Individuals

8

Training Guidelines
Linking the Workshop Experience to
Needs On and Off the Job

JERRY EDELWICH and ARCHIE BRODSKY

Workshops, training programs, and consultative services for dealing with job burnout are proliferating at such a rate that harried professionals in both the private and the public sectors may soon find the resulting pile of brochures and proposals to be a cause of burnout rather than a remedy. Individual workers must decide which of these programs are worth the expenditure of time and, in some cases, money. Administrators must decide when to have in-house personnel run training programs within an agency, when to hire an outside consultant to run a program for the agency, and when to authorize or otherwise support employee participation in programs conducted outside the agency. These decisions require an evaluation of which programs and which trainers are likely to be most effective for a given purpose.

In this chapter we provide initial guidelines for answering these questions, guidelines derived from hundreds of workshops conducted in a variety of organizational settings, together with related experience in teaching, consulting, field supervision, problem-solving, team-building, and staff development. The recommendations given in the final section of the chapter focus on the following areas: (1) needs assessment, (2) purpose, (3) design, and (4) evaluation. Structural, procedural, and substantive features of an effective workshop are included in the consideration of workshop design.

To put these guidelines for the selection and presentation of training programs in perspective, we begin by relating the objectives of burnout training in the 1980s to the particular stages of disillusionment that constitute the burnout process (Edelwich with Brodsky, 1980). Although the focus of

133

this chapter is on acute intervention in the form of concentrated training experiences, we also address briefly the issues of ongoing management and organizational climate that are more systematically treated by **Pines, Shapiro,** and **Golembiewski.** Special training events, however soundly designed, must be supplemented by the sound day-to-day management and supervision they recommend, so that the benefits gained by attendance at an occasional daylong workshop will be sustained rather than dissipated.

The Context for Training and Other Interventions

The context in which burnout has become an issue, as analyzed by **Cherniss,** is one of limits. We find ourselves talking about burnout, job stress, and need fulfillment in an era of fixed or declining resources and dwindling opportunities. As employee turnover becomes less of an option, the individual worker asks, "This is my job; how can I make the best use of it?" The administrator asks, "These are my personnel; how can I make the best use of them?" Along with these questions there are the perennial ones: for the worker, "How can I take pressure off myself?" and for the administrator, "How can I take pressure off myself without putting it on someone else?"

Administrators who seek to answer these questions must reckon with the same limiting conditions that precipitate the individual worker's discouragement and frustration. The agency or firm operates in an environment whose responses (such as the behavior of human service clients, or the market demand for a product or service) are beyond the control of the entire organization, let alone anyone in it. Even within the organization, an administrator's power does not extend very far, whether upward, downward, or laterally. Competing priorities, budgetary constraints, bureaucratic conflicts, and the sheer size and complexity of the organization make the connection between actions and results a tenuous one.

Nonetheless, our experience indicates that the intelligent use of training opportunities, together with good day-to-day management, can have a desirable effect on how workers experience burnout. Although it is unrealistic to think that training alone can either prevent or cure what is a natural and virtually universal process of adaptation to experience, training plus enlightened management can help employees respond creatively to stressful events or situations and avoid the costly pitfall of apathy. Not all workers will benefit from such intervention, but those who do benefit will lessen the contagion of chronic disillusionment that impedes organizational effectiveness and productivity.

Intervention by Stages:
Frustration versus Apathy

Before considering how to achieve this objective, we need to clarify the nature of the phenomenon we are dealing with. This is not to attempt to duplicate the rigorous work of definition undertaken by **Maslach.** Rather it is simply to clear up some common misunderstandings about burnout by stating what we have observed it to be, with emphasis on the implications for educational and therapeutic intervention.

In the experience of the many individuals we have studied, burnout is an ongoing process that varies both in severity and in frequency of repetition. People go through a series of predictable stages in their relationship to their work. The first is *enthusiasm,* a period of high hopes, high energy, unrealistic expectations, and overidentification with the job. The second is *stagnation,* in which personal, financial, and career development needs begin to be felt. This is followed by *frustration,* in which one questions one's effectiveness and the value of one's efforts in the face of obstacles to meaningful accomplishment. Frustration is a crossroads that can lead either back to enthusiasm (via a constructive rechanneling of energy) or down to the fourth stage, *apathy,* an abyss of chronic indifference that defies most efforts at intervention. A more detailed discussion of these stages is found in Edelwich with Brodsky, 1980.

The term "burnout" sometimes is used to refer to this entire cyclic process of disillusionment. It is also used to refer to the end product, as in the expressions "burnout syndrome" or "burned-out" person. If the word is to be used at all appropriately in the latter sense, a crucial distinction must be kept in mind. *Frustration is not burnout. Burnout means apathy.* Frustration is the experience of learning to cope with limitations. It is a normal experience that everyone goes through. Indeed, it can be a source of creative energy leading to innovation and renewed enthusiasm. One may go through the cycle from enthusiasm to frustration many times in the course of a career, even in the course of one's tenure in a single job. This is not true of apathy. Apathy, although common, is not normal. Nor does it offer an encouraging prognosis for training interventions, although **Freudenberger** reports a better prognosis for limited counseling.

What we call burnout is more simply and clearly understood as apathy. Indeed, the fashionable status accorded the term "burnout" is cause for concern. Apathy is characterized by denial, which is abetted by the availability of a convenient label for diminished performance. "I'm too burned out to think," a staff member tells a sympathetic supervisor. The supervisor who fails to confront such limit-testing is not serving either the individual's or the organization's needs. For supervisors and managers it is most useful to think in concrete, specific terms, that is, to speak of "a person who manifests apathy" rather than "a burned-out person."

Breaking down the process of disillusionment into stages makes it possible to match the type of intervention to the needs of the individual, as **Golembiewski** proposes to do through the use of organizational development techniques. In terms of our own model, since the stage of enthusiasm (attractive as it may appear) is a precursor of later disillusionment, it offers a vital opportunity for intervention before a negative reaction sets in. Teachers, trainers, and supervisors who can temper the high expectations of the enthusiastic novice with anticipatory glimpses of reality in orientation programs and supervision will be acting to preserve that person's effectiveness in the long run (see Cherniss, 1980a, 1980b; **Wilder & Plutchik**).

In the stage of stagnation, intervention focuses on those measures that can restore movement to a stalled career and allow for greater off-the-job satisfaction. It is helpful (where possible) to provide for higher pay, reduced working hours (at least in the sense of less overtime), and educational opportunities with a view toward career advancement as well as personal stimulation. These are, of course, desiderata rather than guaranteed rights, and the individual must take responsibility both for bringing about these changes (with whatever guidance is available) and for coping with the possibility that they will not all be achieved.

The stage of frustration requires a more direct confrontation of dissatisfactions on the job. Here it is necessary to emphasize the normality of the cycle of disillusionment and to legitimize the specific concerns of the discontented worker. Constructive management in this stage entails helping the worker understand the disparity between unrealistically high expectations and real, concrete limitations (see **Pines, Shapiro**). The individual should be encouraged to make constructive use of the energy of discontent by working to bring about changes in his or her job description. This is something that people typically do on their own, whether in a formal or an informal manner, in a creative accommodation to what would otherwise be an impossibly stressful situation.

It is easier to work with a frustrated than with an apathetic person. A frustrated person is aware of being discontented and anxious to do something about it. Consciousness and motivation tend to be lacking in the apathetic person, who is likely to be engaged in denial. It is therefore necessary for the supervisor to be more active in identifying the apathetic individual and in initiating intervention. Furthermore, with apathy a more thoroughgoing intervention is likely to be required.

As a rough benchmark, we might say that the frustrated individual may be able to make use of the strategies of self-care outlined by **Tubesing and Tubesing,** while the apathetic individual more often requires psychotherapy as described by **Freudenberger.** This is, of course, not a hard-and-fast relationship; for example, short-term psychotherapy has helped many people turn frustration into an impetus for change. But it does underline the need for distinct responses, managerial as well as therapeutic, to frustration and apathy.

Ongoing Intervention: Using Day-to-Day Management to Promote Effective Coping

Training sessions mean little unless the principles enunciated are given sustained implementation. A workshop can help participants assume personal responsibility for confronting whatever conditions and whatever choices they face. To deal effectively with burnout, however, management should seek to create (to whatever extent possible) a supportive on-the-job atmosphere. Since the elements of such an organizational climate are detailed by other contributors to this volume **(Pines, Shapiro, Golembiewski, Freudenberger),** our discussion here will be limited to a few key points that tie in with the training program outlined below.

Orientation

It is essential to establish an ongoing dialogue to help workers anticipate the pressures of the job and experience consciously the cycle of disillusionment. The dialogue begins with recruitment, with the avoidance of promises that set up unrealistic expectations (especially of a nonexistent esprit de corps).

Orientation means informing workers about both the limitations they will face and resources that exist for coping, such as supervision and peer "buddy systems." It means providing a map of an unfamiliar environment—the unwritten rules, the lines of power, the key personalities. It means giving at least provisional answers to three questions: "What's the game?" "What are the rules?" "How do I play?"

Such orientation is not meant to slow down the cycle of disillusionment. On the contrary, it may well speed it up, which is all to the good. Situational factors being equal, the more perceptive and sensitive one is, the more rapidly one moves through the stages from enthusiasm to frustration. This rapid movement makes possible more frequent remedial adjustments and makes the slow descent into apathy less likely. This point is often over-looked.

Among the perceptive and sensitive individuals who feel the burnout cycle especially keenly are many who become supervisors and managers. Their frustrations do not cease with promotion to a higher-level position. These individuals can gain insight into the pressures workers feel simply by taking their own experience as a model. Thus, management training is an important ingredient in burnout intervention.

When managers admit their own frustration, they can begin to show subordinates how to deal with theirs. Much of this teaching and modeling is done informally, in one-to-one interchange between supervisor and super-visee. For this reason, "creative supervision" as discussed by **Shapiro** is a key to reducing the damaging effects of the inevitable disparity between expectations and limitations.

Support for the Frustrated or Apathetic Individual

In cases of frustration, the supervisor's stance is one of availability. Intervention is commonly, and appropriately, initiated by the employee. When it comes to identifying the apathetic individual, however, manage-ment cannot rely on self-diagnosis and requests for help. Supervisors should be trained to recognize apathy by observing performance and behavior on the job. The following signs are especially indicative:

- decline in quality or quantity of work
- pattern of absenteeism or lateness
- pattern of personal "emergencies" necessitating leaving work early
- psychosomatic illness
- use of alcohol while on the job
- persistent failure to perform required tasks (such as paperwork)
- acting-out behavior at meetings (silent withdrawal, destructive criticism, rais-ing irrelevant issues, and so on)
- constant denigration of colleagues, together with unwillingness to engage in effective resolution of conflict
- spreading apathetic attitudes among other employees through backbiting, nit-picking, sabotage (beyond the normal level of complaining observable at any workplace)

The most effective way to approach the apathetic individual is through a concrete and detailed critical evaluation of his or her work (see **Shapiro**). The individual should be confronted on behavior, not attitude. Having notified the individual of deficiencies in performance, the supervisor should resist the impulse to interfere with natural consequences. To use the diagnosis of "burned out" as a pretext for protecting someone whose behavior is harmful to the organization is to create a chronic dependency in the place of constructive change. It is necessary for management to set limits and, without being punitive, to enforce them if improvement does not occur within the time agreed upon.

The resources of the organization can be made available in much the same ways to help both frustrated and apathetic individuals. Supervisors should be accessible (within reasonable time constraints) to listen to complaints, advise subordinates concerning work-related problems, obtain needed information from other sectors of the organization, and make appropriate referrals. Psychotherapy, recreation, or special training events may be recommended when called for, and individuals who wish to avail themselves of these opportunities should be supported in doing so. Through an employee assistance program, workers can have access to a professional counselor or therapist employed by the firm (see **Freudenberger**). It is not appropriate, however, to demand anything of a worker besides satisfactory job performance.

What Management Should Not Do

The responsibilities of the organization do *not* include the following:

Psychotherapy or Personal Counseling in the Guise of Supervision. A working relationship is incompatible with a therapeutic relationship. To confuse the two by encouraging supervisors to engage in personal counseling is to compromise the privacy of employees, to dispense an unsatisfactory substitute for professional counseling, and to create more candidates for "supervisor burnout."

"Prescribing" Psychotherapy or Burnout Workshops for Discontented Workers. Resources can be made available, but if participation is to have value, it must be voluntary and self-motivated.

Agency Picnics. Although an agency or firm may hold social functions on occasion, these should not be planned for the purpose of alleviating the symptoms of burnout among the staff. Such manipulated merriment is not only patronizing, but also plainly inadequate to transform the work environment. Social and recreational interventions, crucial as they are, should remain the responsibility of the individual worker to implement during off hours and vacations.

Mental Health Days. Workers should not be given special dispensations (such as extra time off "under the table") on the dubious rationale that

"Nobody has troubles like I (we) do." This "legitimated malingering" (Edelwich with Brodsky, 1980) is unsound for the following reasons:

(1) The idea that the unique stresses of a particular job justify exemption from normal work requirements is patronizing and ultimately disabling to those who are thus favored. Every job, vocation, and career field has its own hardships.
(2) The extra time off is a palliative whose effect will wear off if the need for meaningful long-range interventions is not addressed.
(3) The worker is made to be dependent on the good will of a supervisor whose leniency might not be duplicated elsewhere.
(4) The supervisor or administrator who authorizes the irregularity can be held accountable for its cost.

Although the impulse to make special arrangements with employees regarding time off arises from understandable human and administrative motives, it is recommended that such arrangements be made only under the following conditions:

(1) The time off must be made up (for example, through on-call availability or special services to the organization).
(2) The policy must be applied consistently and equitably to all eligible employees.
(3) The flexible scheduling must be part of a coordinated policy of personnel management rather than a stopgap for the most visibly discontented.
(4) The policy must be implemented in an above-board, administratively defensible manner.

Acute Intervention: Burnout Workshops and Training Programs

Along with agency picnics and legitimated malingering, we can add to the list of unrealistic interventions the "workshop high" (Edelwich with Brodsky, 1980; **Golembiewski**). This is a temporary "fix" that people derive from getting away from the job for a day and venting their frustrations with the encouragement of a dynamic workshop leader. The administrator's version of the workshop high is a blind faith that packing the staff off to a training event will permanently improve the work environment and increase productivity. Actually, many workshops offer merely a "rush" of novelty, entertainment, interpersonal stimulation, and cathartic self-expression (benefits to which some administrators, knowing them for what they are, are still happy to devote a budgetary item for the sake of staff morale). As weeks and then months pass, all that remains is a pleasant but increasingly vague memory.

Yet the workshop format can be used to supplement sound, ongoing management. Is there a kind of workshop that represents a realistic, effective intervention against burnout? It is both more modest and more accurate to say that a well-designed burnout workshop exposes participants to constructive interventions and helps participants devise and discover such interventions for themselves.

To the extent that burnout education for staff members is judged to merit the investment of organizational resources, administrators will have to decide what programs to invest in, whether these should be external or intra-agency events, which employees can benefit from them, and how employee participation is best arranged. This section will present guidelines in the following areas: (1) needs assessment; (2) purpose (as understood by both management and staff members); (3) workshop design, including structural features, procedural features, and substantive features; and (4) evaluation of training.

The substantive recommendations given here apply only to those programs explicitly concerned with burnout rather than to the wider range of training experiences aimed at promoting self-care and self-renewal that are discussed by **Tubesing and Tubesing.** (The two kinds of programs can, of course, be mutually supportive and can usefully be presented in conjunction with each other.) The structural and procedural recommendations, together with those concerning the context of management-staff relations in which the workshops take place, also apply to burnout programs and in some cases are more generally applicable.

Needs Assessment

Needs assessment is not, as may be commonly supposed, a matter of determining which staff members are most severely "burned out" or of measuring the level of apathy of the staff as a whole. Instruments such as the Maslach Burnout Inventory (Maslach & Jackson, 1981b) can be used to target particular problem areas in an organization and to estimate roughly the costs in reduced effectiveness. But it follows from the nature of apathy, as discussed earlier in this chapter, that those who to an outside observer appear most in need of intervention are least likely to benefit from it. As a rule, therefore, it is best to see a burnout workshop as directed primarily not at those caught in the rigidity and denial of apathy, but at those who are engaged (with varying degrees of enthusiasm, stagnation, and frustration) in coping with the dynamics of expectations and limitations.

From this perspective, the assessment of need is reduced to two simple statements: *never* and *always*. "Never" in the sense that the employing agency or firm cannot determine when an individual needs to attend a burnout training event. Management can offer information, opportunities, and recommendations. Management can present programs explaining what burnout is and what resources are available for coping with it. Even if attendance is mandatory, however, the determination of need ultimately is made by the individual, in that an unmotivated individual is unlikely to participate in a meaningful way.

The "always" refers to the fact that it is advantageous for any organization to maintain a constant awareness of burnout—its causes, consequences, and possible remedies—among both management and staff. The realization that burnout is a process rather than some diagnosable malady makes it apparent that it should be dealt with consciously, on a continuing basis, at both the individual and the organizational levels. Training works better as a preventive inoculation than as a cure, and the best times to intervene are in the stages of enthusiasm and frustration. Thus, it makes sense to offer burnout training periodically, both to orient new employees and establish constructive habits of discussion and mutual support within the organization.

Purpose

Administrators should be clear about their intentions and objectives in providing burnout training. Unfortunately, the expectations of those who authorize or plan such training often are either vague or inappropriate. Vague expectations reveal themselves in the image of something analogous to a car wash: "I want you to give my staff a tuneup—plugs, points, lube, and oil—and send them back to the floor good as new." A responsible trainer will not encourage this magical thinking on the part of management, since the value of any workshop lies primarily in what the participants put into it, both during the sessions and after.

To avoid the tuneup fallacy, administrators responsible for presenting burnout training programs need to keep such events in perspective. A burnout workshop exists in the same context of real-world limitations as the job situation it addresses. Too many constraints intervene for even the best trainer to be able to guarantee results. Those individuals who sincerely desire to invest themselves in change will absorb the content of the program and operationalize it. Those individuals who engage in magical thinking and are invested in reinforcing the status quo will persist in those habits. Very occasionally an apathetic person is inspired and reinvigorated by a burnout workshop. But this does not happen enough to justify the expense of training individuals who are identifiably unreceptive.

To make burnout training more productive as well as cost-effective, managers would do well to share its objectives with potential participants and to screen potential participants so as to identify those who are likely to implement the training constructively. Instituting these procedures would have two clear benefits. First, it would compel administrators to clarify the objectives for *themselves* in order to clarify them for participants. Second, it would create a dialogue whereby the decision to have an individual attend the program would be made mutually.

In some situations the responsibility to justify participation, make the necessary arrangements, and/or pay for the training may appropriately lie with the individual; in other situations it may not. In any case, having the individual make some form of commitment instead of having the training be merely a part of the organization's agenda gives worker and management a shared purpose. However, once attendance is authorized, it is the responsibility of management to provide coverage on the job for those who attend and to assure that there will be no adverse consequences for them upon their return.

If the clarification of goals is always a good antidote to vague or unrealistic expectations, it is sometimes needed to counter inappropriate expectations as well. We consider here three common illegitimate purposes or misuses of burnout training (see **Shapiro**)—two on the part of management and one on the part of participants.

First, burnout training should not be used for the purpose of managerial espionage, that is, to ferret out worker discontent in a covert way. No self-respecting trainer can be maneuvered into the role of investigating and reporting to management on attitudes and grievances expressed at a workshop. It is both unethical and counterproductive.

Second, burnout training should not be used to strengthen individuals so that they can be overworked or otherwise abused for a longer period of time before they "burn out." This policy, whatever its short-term convenience, is ethically indefensible and, by misusing the organization's human resources, risks massive turnover occurring at just the wrong time. Of course, management being properly concerned with efficiency and productivity, burnout training programs will be conceived so as to serve the needs of the organization as well as of the individuals of whom it consists. However, the individual's responsibility for confronting reality in whatever forms it may take, rather than chronically complaining about bad working conditions or a stacked organizational deck, does not absolve management of the responsibility of instituting constructive organizational change. Indeed, the worker who accepts organizational reality for what it is will be in a better psychological position to take action aimed at changing the organization.

The third misuse of burnout training occurs when activist zeal on the part of workers is carried to excess. Management may fear that a workshop will incite staff members to tear apart or cripple the organization in the name of stress reduction. In this fantasy there is a bare kernel of truth. The acknowledgement of burnout as an issue to be dealt with in an organization involves a commitment to examine the organization and to consider making changes. Before presenting or authorizing a burnout training program, administrators should weigh the risks involved in having staff members ask questions, raise issues, and take responsibility. These desired outcomes are almost always beneficial for the organization, but there may be some discomfort associated with increased organizational accountability, and there will be circumstances in which management will have reason to want to avoid such strain. However, this process of reexamination rarely takes on dimensions that threaten the stability of the organization. Unfortunately, it is more often the case that a burnout workshop does not have sufficient impact to result in any challenge to the status quo.

The best protection against misuse of burnout training is a prior evaluation of the trainer and the program according to the criteria listed in this chapter. It is advisable to review the content of the proposed training before making any commitments, and to avoid hiring trainers who make ill-considered, impractical recommendations. In the case of the first two misuses of training discussed above, the evaluation is made by the participants. An experienced trainer will begin the presentation in a way that allays fears that he or she is, in a prejudicial sense, an agent of management.

Having considered poorly defined and improper purposes of training, along with the need for management, individual participants, and trainers to arrive at a shared understanding of the actual purposes of a program, we can summarize what those purposes might be. A burnout training program might have the following broad aims (as distinct from the specific behavioral objectives discussed below), presented here in ascending order of ambition:

(1) to lift the spirits of staff members with the temporary diversion of a "workshop high" (a day off in novel surroundings);
(2) to give participants greater insight into their experience of burnout;
(3) to provide motivated participants with tools for coping; and
(4) to establish an improved organizational climate through shared awareness and responsibility and mutual support.

The elements of an effective burnout training program, one designed to have the best possible chance to succeed at all four levels, can be divided into three categories: (1) structural (how the program is set up), (2) procedural (what happens), and (3) substantive (what information is conveyed).

Structural Criteria

Structural criteria are those concerned with the overall coordination of the training program and its relationship to the work organization before, during, and after the presentation itself.

External versus Internal

The choice between running a burnout training program within the organization and authorizing staff members to attend a program elsewhere is in part a matter of practical convenience. Does the organization have the resources (including qualified trainers) to provide the training? What outside programs are available, and how well do they fit the needs of the organization? Can the organization and/or the individual participants afford the cost of an external program?

There are, however, other considerations that give internal training programs a somewhat different character from external programs. A burnout workshop conducted internally can, like any other training session, be scheduled as part of the work day, thus ensuring higher attendance. On the other hand, at an internal program the participants, being employed at the same agency, will miss the creative interchange, the airing of problems and sharing of solutions, with people from different agencies that would occur in an external program and that is so important a part of burnout training. Nonetheless, to have in attendance a high concentration of people who normally work together increases the likelihood of mutually supportive implementation of the content of the training.

Although there are advantages and disadvantages to both the internal and the external formats, there are ways in which the organization can "hedge its bet" on either alternative so as to get some of the benefits of both. An internal session does not have to be a sterile exchange of known views or a gripe session. Rather, it can be used to bring together personnel from different sites or departments (as well as job functions and status levels, as discussed below) who are not normally in contact with one another. With an external program, management can encourage more than one person from the agency to attend at the same time.

Heterogeneous Attendance

Participants may be homogeneous or heterogeneous not only with respect to place of employment, but also with respect to age, sex, experience, status level, and nature of work. Whether a burnout workshop is held externally or internally, it is highly desirable that attendance be mixed with respect to as many of these variables as possible, particularly hierarchical position (line staff, middle management, top management), so that beneficial exchanges of perspective can take place. People need to see that those above and below them have problems, too. Workshop designs can be modified to accommodate heterogeneity.

It is especially valuable for management personnel and front-line staff to attend the same workshop. By their mere presence the managers are making a statement that burnout is an important issue. Moreover, it is when the two groups meet that there is the best chance for administrators to get beyond the belief that workers just go through the motions and pick up their checks, and for workers to challenge their mental image of an administrator waking up each morning and thinking, "How can I sabotage what's being accomplished on the front line today?"

Clearly Defined, Realistic Behavioral Objectives

To have a program that does not claim to do more than it can (or should), it is important to review carefully the objectives by which the trainer articulates what benefits participants can expect to derive from the experience. These may vary greatly depending on the context, but they should clearly delineate outcomes that can be realized and observed behaviorally. The following objectives of actual burnout training programs are intended as models of phraseology and relevant content; they do not form an inclusive or exclusive list for any type of program:

- to identify the stages of disillusionment and the role of intervention at each stage;
- to identify the particular forms of disillusionment that affect various strata of professional and paraprofessional personnel;
- to be able to develop appropriate guidelines for allocation of one's time and energy;
- to have the opportunity to confront problems to the extent that they are capable of solution; and
- to be able to identify and utilize support systems in implementing a chosen course of action.

To an experienced trainer, the distinction between the words "identify" and "understand" is a crucial one. The program objectives should not imply an aspiration to go beyond the realm of behavior to that of inner experience.

Provision for Followup

Provision should be made for follow-up support for participants in implementing what is learned. A burnout workshop should (typically in the course of problem-solving exercises) generate peer support groups, with participants making an explicit voluntary agreement to be in communication at specified times to review with one another their progress in acting on announced intentions. Sometimes a trainer will demonstrate this kind of support by soliciting telephone calls from participants concerning the fulfillment of their commitments.

When it comes to formal support, there is an advantage to having the program presented internally by the firm or agency, since follow-up activities at the job site can then be closely coordinated with the presentation of the training. For workshops of one day's duration or less, an outside trainer generally will not provide follow-up without special arrangements and an additional fee. For a longer program or a series of programs, the trainer may agree to return at a specified time to meet with the administration and perhaps reassemble the participants to review the implementation of problem-solving strategies. Such commitment on the part of the trainer is to be considered a substantial plus in the evaluation of a prospective program.

What management can do, with or without further involvement on the trainer's part, is to enlist those staff members who can be a source of strength for their peers and to provide space and time for these selected individuals to run support groups. Guidelines are essential to keep the groups moving in the direction of realistic communication and problem-solving rather than mere ventilation. One such guideline is that each meeting have an agenda, with specific objectives analogous to those of the burnout workshop itself. The organization may engage the trainer to play a continuing role by teaching the group leaders the techniques of effective group leadership (deflecting gripes and complaints, eliciting specificity of communication, and so on).

Procedural Criteria

Procedural criteria pertain to format, sequence of activities, style of presentation, and management of interaction.

Statement of Intention

Participants should have the benefit of the same kind of clear statement of what the training can and cannot accomplish that management receives in the form of behavioral objectives. In an external or off-hours burnout program where the decision to attend is a voluntary one, the behavioral objectives presumably will have been circulated among prospective participants.

Legitimizing of Concerns

One of the most important messages a burnout training program can get across is that it is not unusual, unnatural, or unjustified for a person to feel frustrated or discouraged on the job. The purpose of such validation is to break through feelings of isolation and self-accusation that exacerbate normal frustrations. It is, of course, essential to distinguish between accepting negative feelings as normal and allowing those feelings or whatever touches them off to serve as excuses for irresponsible behavior.

Opportunity for Participation

A workshop is not a lecture. What participants gain that cannot be found by reading a book on burnout is the opportunity to talk, listen, and compare experiences, both in the group as a whole and in smaller discussion groups consisting of three or four individuals. In such exchanges the speaker can discharge emotionally as well as clarify troubling issues. Listeners can address their own problems vicariously while learning how common those problems are.

Breaking the group down into small discussion groups for some of the exercises elicits active participation and at the same time provides a safe space for those who would not be comfortable standing up and speaking publicly. Even in the small groups, however, participation should be voluntary. In an external training program attended by individuals from more than one organization, it is advisable (in order to minimize the likelihood of inhibition or stale complaining) to change the seating arrangements so that participants will not be speaking only to the co-workers they came with. In intra-agency training, such orchestration is out of place.

Role-playing exercises, both in the small discussion groups and in demonstrations before the group as a whole, can give participants insight into the perspectives of others as well as practice in taking new approaches to difficult situations.

Maintenance of Control

The trainer must structure the experience and continually exercise control so that the airing of concerns takes place in a context of responsibility and engagement with reality. The need for structure and direction is particularly crucial because of the prevalence of "medical students' disease" with regard to burnout, whereby any public discussion of burnout risks becoming a self-fulfilling prophecy.

The more emotionally charged the issue, the more the trainer must project a sense of serious purpose and discipline. "Touchy-feely" workshops on burnout should be avoided. Instead, the trainer must set a tone of concreteness and specificity of communication. Discussion is not about "vibes," but about behavior; not about "personality conflicts," but about particular actions that one finds objectionable.

Substantive Criteria

The content of an effective training program includes not only practical coping strategies, but also an overview of what burnout is and what forms it takes. This broader understanding is by no means of interest only to administrators and theoreticians. Rather, it enables all participants to look at their immediate feelings (however intense) in the context of what others are experiencing as well as what they themselves have experienced and will experience in the course of their careers.

Some major areas to be covered in burnout training are listed here. They are discussed only briefly, since all of them are treated in our book (Edelwich with Brodsky, 1980), in previous sections of this chapter, or in other contributions to this volume:

What Is Burnout?

Is it a syndrome or a process? Are its effects measured in subjective states, physical symptoms, diminished performance, staff turnover, or all of the above? To whom is it likely to happen? Is it contagious? Why is it of concern to the individual worker, the employer, and society?

The Process of Disillusionment

Periodic disillusionment is a condition of existence from which no one is immune. Participants should be cautioned against the belief in some final intervention that will solve their problems. Realistic coping begins with the awareness that each intervention (job change, further education, and the like) begins the cycle anew. The universality of the process also should be stressed. People working at all status levels, including managerial and administrative personnel, in all service occupations (and undoubtedly beyond) are susceptible.

Dynamics of the Process

Participants should be given a "map" of the subjective peaks and valleys that are likely to occur in the course of one's daily work experience, job tenure, career path, and lifetime. The concept of the four stages of disillusionment (Edelwich with Brodsky, 1980) is one example of such a descriptive scheme. The motive force of the process comes from the inherent gap (sometimes wide, sometimes narrow) between expectations and limitations. This disparity between the ideal and the real should be dramatized, along with the critical distinction between acute frustration and chronic apathy.

Identification of Endemic
Sources of Frustration

A range of typical job-related concerns, including those stemming from organizational structure and politics, should be explored through group discussion. Two extremes common in the literature on burnout are best avoided. A narrow, self-absorbed preoccupation with the symptomatology of burnout offers no insight into the realities that individuals must confront in order to manage their frustration. On the other hand, an overemphasis on organizational issues or client behavior takes attention away from the experience of the person providing services, which is the *raison d'être* of the training and is where both the problems and the solutions lie.

Clarification of Responsibility

Although an enlightened organization will take an interest in the problems causing worker frustration and will carry on a dialogue with workers in an effort to resolve such issues, nothing should be allowed to stand between the individual and the realization of his or her responsibility to accept and work with the "givens" of any situation. It is one thing to acknowledge that the actions of the organization or its clients may precipitate worker frustration; it is another thing to hold the organization or its clients responsible for workers' emotional reactions and for any unprofessional behavior that may result.

Measures of Success

A major source of frustration in service occupations is the lack of "hard" criteria for measuring success. An antidote is to develop expectations, goals, and habits of interpretation that enable one's assessment of results to be in line with what can actually be accomplished. Some examples follow:

- Set reasonable goals.
- Focus on the successes, not the failures.
- Focus on the process, not the result.
- Keep a time perspective.
- Do not interpret results self-referentially.

Problem-Solving Methods

The demonstration of a concrete, step-by-step problem-solving strategy is invaluable in helping participants apply the content of burnout training. The technique should include generating alternative solutions, evaluating costs and benefits, choosing a course of action, and making a publicly supported commitment. An example of such an exercise is given in Edelwich with Brodsky (1980: 227-230).

Realistic versus Unrealistic Interventions

Burnout intervention begins with an acceptance of past setbacks and present limitations as "given" and with an exploration of options that can lead from the individual's current "zero point" to a more satisfying future. Participants will benefit from criteria, such as those developed here, for distinguishing between short-term palliatives (such as "mental health days") and interventions that may have a substantial long-term effect, such as further education, expansion of one's personal world, and individual or collective action to change working conditions.

Off-the-Job Interventions

Although changes in working conditions and organizational structure undoubtedly can contribute to increased job satisfaction and reduced frustration, one cannot depend on such fortuitous events to improve one's life. When one is largely dependent on the job for one's sense of satisfaction and personal worth (as enthusiastic novices often are), one tends to be emotionally at the mercy of agency politics, clients' behavior, the appreciation of supervisors, success rates, market mechanisms, and other uncontrollable factors. One can build up an emotional reserve for dealing with disappointment on the job by enlarging the context of one's life and having one's needs fulfilled in other areas (family, friends, interests, recreation). It is, paradoxically, perhaps the single most important intervention in the whole area of job burnout.

Program Evaluation

If program evaluation is to be more than a popularity contest for trainers based on immediate emotional reactions to the experience of the training, the evaluation should be conducted in line with the following criteria:

(1) *Time*. Conduct evaluation at least three or four weeks after the training so as to separate content from sensations ("fun," "good vibes") and to give participants time to act on what they have learned.
(2) *Involvement*. Where possible, replace numerical evaluations with brief essay questions, which require a greater degree of internalization.
(3) *Concrete Application*. Emphasize the operationalizing of goals through specific actions. A sample essay question might be: "State something you learned in the workshop and explain how you are applying it to your life now." Such questions can be adapted to a multiple-choice format as follows: "Which of the approaches listed do you intend to implement?" "How soon?"
(4) *Responsibility*. Have participants "own" their responses by signing the evaluation.

To go beyond even these more disciplined subjective statements to assessments of improved organizational climate and effectiveness is difficult. It can safely be said, however, that a training program or workshop on burnout will have little effect beyond a week's or a month's time (except for isolated individuals) if it does not result in the formation of peer discussion and support groups. These are the visible measures of attitudinal and behavioral change. In other words, the long-term evaluation of the success of a program is inseparable from the commitment to sustained implementation and follow-up on the part of both management and staff.

Summary

Training programs in burnout can be a useful adjunct to (though not a substitute for) sound day-to-day supervision and management. The workshop format can be used to convey information, to provide a forum for the sharing of experiences and concerns by line staff and management, and to develop strategies for intervention. Administrators who must choose from among the many programs offered should look for those with realistic behavioral objectives. A training event is subject to the same limitations, the same "givens," as the work situation itself. It should be seen as a vaccination rather than an antibiotic—not a magical solution for long-neglected problems, but a periodic orientation and reorientation, raising issues for consideration and putting them into perspective. The workshop experience will be little more than a short-lived "high" without ongoing implementation and monitoring at both the individual and organizational levels.

Alternatively, in conjunction with the other techniques discussed in the next five chapters, it can significantly contribute to an overall program to deal with burnout.

9

The Treatment of Choice
Selecting Stress Skills to Suit the Individual and the Situation

NANCY LOVING TUBESING and DONALD A. TUBESING

The placement of this chapter between **Edelwich and Brodsky's** description of individual interventions within the work setting and **Freudenberger's** analysis of professional therapeutic interventions with individuals experiencing burnout provides a perfect backdrop for exploring the resources available to the typical or potential burnout "victim."

We shall focus on the prevention resources and self-care remedies available to the individual who as yet may not have reached the latter stages of burnout characterized by denial, apathy, and total inertia. Those individuals may more appropriately consult **Freudenberger** and his colleagues. So, also, we leave the workplace remedies to **Pines, Golembiewski,** and the organizational development experts. Our emphasis here echoes the major theme of this segment of the volume, strengthening the individual.

Underlying Assumptions

As practitioners and educators who teach stress management techniques to health care and human service professionals, we have formulated our approach to understanding, treating, and preventing burnout based on feedback from thousands of individuals who have shared their experiences with us. Studying this rich data base as well as the literature in the field has helped

AUTHORS' NOTE: This chapter is reprinted, with permission, from *Rx for BURNOUT: A Structured Strategy for Promoting Vitality and Preventing Burnout in the Care-Giving Professions,* © Whole Person Associates Inc, P.O. Box 3151, Duluth, MN 55803.

155

shape some general assumptions about burnout that undergird our intervention attitudes and strategies.

Chronic distress is a causal factor in burnout. We believe that burnout is a stress-related malady with primary roots in the setting where people invest the majority of their time and energy. This is usually the job setting but could just as well be the home. Defining burnout in this way opens the door to applying a wide body of theory, research, and clinical experience concerning stress management to the issue of preferred interventions both on and off the job.

Burnout is a real personal problem. In our experience, professionals at the grass-roots level recognize instantly the symptoms and concepts of burnout and are grateful someone has finally articulated and thereby authenticated their experience. Burnout is not a cop-out, a position we share with **Freudenberger.** Treatment for burnout must take seriously the individual's perception of the problem and the pain it causes. The most important resource for dealing with burnout is the individual whose life it affects. Encouraging the individual to activate his or her own self-care strategies is the first step toward alleviating the problem.

Burnout is a human condition. Organizations do not burn out, although **Carroll and White** disagree. People in organizations burn out. Burnout is a problem for the organization when productivity or service are threatened or when conflict or apathy escalate. Too often managers and supervisors are tempted to intervene for the sake of the organization rather than the individual. If the attitude is one of searching for a technique that the system can use in changing the individual, it is often a fruitless intervention. Whether the issue is performance or morale, people do not change until *they* are ready. Although organizations can promote a climate that minimizes the pressures leading toward burnout, they cannot totally prevent it or cure it once it has occurred.

Burnout is an energy crisis. Many of the symptoms typically associated with burnout suggest a loss of personal vitality. Victims of burnout report fatigue, a reduced energy level, and dampened enthusiasm for life (Maslach, 1976, 1978a; **Pines; Carroll and White).** We might then view burnout as a sort of personal energy crisis with the demand for physical and psychic energy temporarily exceeding the supply, thereby draining the individual's energy reserves. Energy conservation or replenishment then become key issues in a burnout prevention strategy.

Often personal energy spending patterns are themselves part of the burnout problem. If this is the case, repeating the same old remedies will not solve the crisis for an individual. A new approach is needed. A life change, an altered direction, a new attitude, or a humorous twist may well lead to a resurgence of personal energy. Whether such a change in behavior actually solves the perceived "problem" in the external environment may be irrelevant if the individual regains his or her sense of potency, vitality, and enthusiasm through such a strategy.

Burnout affects the whole person. Burnout is a whole-person problem. It affects the intellect, feelings, relationships, and the spirit as well as physical health and job performance. Solutions to the problem may also be found in every dimension of life—and in unlimited combinations. As **Maslach** suggests, these potential remedies need not be from the same levels as the symptoms or the causes of the problem. Even if burnout symptoms are primarily physical (exhaustion, headaches), the best treatment is not necessarily a physical strategy. Making meaningful contact with another person may be just as effective as biofeedback. Values clarification may be more beneficial than exercise.

Looking at some of the underlying assumptions in our definition of burnout, we now turn to the dilemma of developing an approach to burnout prevention and treatment.

In Search of a Treatment of Choice

We believe there is no single, most effective antidote or prophylactic for burnout. Indeed, the most potent force in the burnout equation is the suffering individual whose own internal wisdom can be activated to diagnose and alleviate the symptoms. This single fact is often overlooked in our eagerness to find an effective solution for a difficult problem in society.

It is tempting to look for a cure-all for burnout. We human beings are impatient with the natural healing process. Conditioned by our experience with miracle drugs, we have come to expect dramatic (and speedy) cures. No such remedy has been found for burnout.

The popular literature would have us believe otherwise. Enthusiastic and extremely persuasive proponents of single-answer approaches tout their wares before the public in an endless array of self-help books. Relaxation skills, time management, prayer, physical fitness, diet, assertiveness training, personal freedom, and "joy" are all advertised as the sole prescription for a wide range of maladies. One chain of booksellers carries thirty-five titles on stress management alone. The professional and academic marketplace is no less congested. The Third Annual Symposium on the Management of Stress (1981) featured presentations on stress rehabilitation techniques from acupuncture to Zen, including biofeedback, cryotherapy, diets, herbs, hormones, hypnosis, moxibustion, therapeutic exercise, transcutaneous stimulation, and yoga. Undoubtedly the speakers were experts in their fields, each convinced of the results of their particular remedies and armed with substantial documentation from their research and clinical experience.

We might view the burnout victim as a consumer in this crowded, noisy marketplace of potential remedies, confronted at each display booth with exaggerated and sometimes irresponsible claims about the benefits of each different "cure." This experience not only raises false hopes of speedy resolution, but also lures individuals away from reliance on their own internal wisdom and sense of responsibility for the difficult decisions and behavior changes necessary to halt the progression of burnout.

The other chapters in this volume amply demonstrate that researchers, practitioners, and theorists in the burnout field are actively engaged at different levels in the search for preferred treatment modalities. Perhaps at some future date we will be able to isolate two or three or ten particularly effective personal remedies for burnout and even rank them in some order of efficacy. Unfortunately, our "science" has not yet advanced to the stage of identifying such a select list.

This limitation in the current state of the art may, in fact, provide the key to effective management of burnout: individualized prescriptions. While waiting for **Maslach's** proposed research isolating unique burnout symptoms and specific effective interventions, we are left with the reality that the treatment for burnout must be just as personalized as the life experiences that lead to the problem in the first place. Such an approach challenges individuals to identify the sources of their stress and distress, assess their own strengths and weaknesses, and uncover current blocks to regaining and maintaining vitality. Each individual can then construct a creative self-care and personal nurture plan designed to maximize vitality.

Individualizing Treatment Strategies

The treatment of choice for burnout is *choice*. We need to develop a process in which we as helpers may suggest a wide variety of stress and lifestyle management options that our clients or employees may not have considered. However, we must leave the choice of strategies and the formation and activation of the plan up to the individual. Our intervention is directed toward helping individuals see choices, make choices, and implement choices.

Technology is not yet far enough advanced to present us with data on the relative effectiveness of the options available. This may be no great limitation. Even if it were, our hypothesis is that the focus in planning for treatment should still center on activating the suffering individual's choice-making behavior rather than "selling" our remedies, even if we think we know better.

These options run counter to the traditional medical model of delineating symptoms, isolating probable etiology, and selecting the preferred method of treatment for a "disease" regardless of individual preference and motivation. Although this process often works well for treating physiological disease, the dynamics of "activated expert" and "passive patient" are not likely to be as effective when stress management is the issue and lifestyle adjustment is required.

Our experience in the Wholistic Health Centers project (Tubesing, 1979b) demonstrated that most people, no matter how desperate, have clear ideas about what treatment will be best for them given the circumstances. In what we called a "health planning conference" the individual would sit down with the resource professionals (physician, nurse, pastoral counselor) to assess the total picture of his or her health and health care needs. The final question, when all the diagnosis and brainstorming about treatment options was completed, was addressed to the patient: "Given all this, how can you best take care of yourself?" The answers varied. But following initial surprise at the question itself, every patient, without exception, offered some response. The ideas included, "weight control program," "find a friend," "surgery," "relaxation training," "change jobs," "counseling session," "change my attitude," "take medication," and hundreds of others. Always that internal wisdom came through, and the ultimate treatment was the patient's choice.

Research studies of patient compliance with treatment plans showed that more than twice as many patients completed their treatment plans at the Wholistic Health Centers as did those using other medical facilities. Satisfaction with service was also extremely high (Tubesing & Stroshal, 1976).

We believe the same principles can be applied in the workplace where concerned supervisors and managers are anxious to help their employees deal with burnout. Burnout victims may not know how to get rid of their stress or how to solve the problem that appears to be causing their burnout, but they probably will have some idea of what they need to do next in order to "turn themselves back on again." As likely as not, these ideas will focus on aspects of their life that seem unrelated to the specific problem.

Intervention Principles

The manager or other caring intervener who wants to confront and support the burnout victim without violating personal integrity has five major responsibilities:

(1) to raise consciousness about burnout symptoms and sources, thereby giving individuals permission to authenticate their experience;

(2) to facilitate the individual's assessment process, including identification of coping strengths and weaknesses (*facilitate* it, don't do it!);

(3) to describe stress management alternatives the individual may not see;

(4) to assist the individual in making a plan for revitalization; and

(5) to respect and support the internal wisdom of the individual.

The remainder of this chapter focuses in detail on the third of these responsibilities, expanding the potential repertoire of stress management alternatives. **Edelwich and Brodsky** deal with responsibility, and **Freudenberger** touches on facilitating self-assessment.

Stress Management Strategies

Every person, including the burnout victim, has a wealth of stress management strategies at his or her disposal. These skills have been learned and practiced over a lifetime. Some remedies are used often and for many stress-provoking situations—a hot bath, a long run, a good cry. Others may be saved for major crises—blowing up, full-scale retreat, a values overhaul. Others have been forgotten or have atrophied from neglect—prayer, laughter, deep breathing.

In the case of burnout, people are often out of touch with many of their potential coping resources, having narrowed their typically used options to only a few old standbys that may be out of date, inappropriate to the particular situation, or minimally effective when used repeatedly. One of the major objectives in working with burnout victims will be to help the individual rediscover forgotten skills and develop new skills for managing stress, preventing burnout, and promoting vitality.

The Whole-Person Perspective

In teaching stress management and burnout prevention, we find it important to include not only strategies that reduce physical tension, but also a wide variety of skills from every dimension of life. Stress affects the whole person. Just as symptoms of distress are not limited to the physical realm, so stress management approaches need to be expanded to attend to all aspects of human experience.

Table 9.1 categorizes stress management strategies in the literature according to a whole-person perspective. The literature is full of descriptions

TABLE 9.1   Whole-Person Stress Management

Physical Strategies	Intellectual/Mental Strategies
—Progressive relaxation	—Cognitive restructuring
—Biofeedback	—Systematic desensitization
—Autogenic training	—Stress inoculation
—Visualization	—Covert sensitization
—Sensory awareness	—Thought-stopping
—Deep breathing	—Reframing
—Hot tubs, jacuzzi, sauna	—Values clarification
—Massage	—Paradoxical intention
—Yoga	
—Exercise	
—Diet	
Social Strategies	Emotional Strategies
—Interpersonal skills training	—Catharsis/emotional discharge
—Assertiveness	—Covert assertion
—Support groups	—Self-awareness
—Networking	—Withdrawal
Spiritual Strategies	Environmental Strategies
—Meditation	—Time management
—Prayer	—Problem-solving
—Faith/hope	—Goal-setting
	—Lifestyle assessment
	—Decision-making
	—Conflict resolution

Source: Summarized from Curtis & Detert, 1981; Davis et al., 1980; McKay et al., 1981; Barrow & Prosen, 1981.

and data about physical remedies that interrupt the stress cycle at its end point. They alter the physiological response to perceived stress by stimulating the alternative relaxation response. Physical strategies can also prevent the buildup of physical tension and provide immediate tools to control situational stress reactions.

Intellectual or mental interventions are also well documented as beneficial in interrupting the stress cycle by altering the perception of a specific event as stressful. Social strategies, on the other hand, tend to increase the individual's skill in dealing with potentially stressful situations and offer options for receiving nurture and support from others.

The lists of emotional and spiritual strategies for managing stress are much shorter and are based primarily on clinical observation. The literature has little to say about the value of escape as a coping strategy. Meditation is the only spiritual strategy that has received much attention, although Selye (1976) has argued that the attitude of gratitude is the most healthful life stance. Both spiritual and emotional techniques may be helpful at any stage of the stress cycle.

Environmental strategies help individuals assess and alter the stress-producing aspects of their surroundings as well as change habitual behaviors that tend to disrupt and complicate their environment.

Identifying Personal Stress Skills

This whole-person perspective challenges us to expand our concept of stress management and search all dimensions of life for potential coping resources. Individuals wanting to prevent or ameliorate burnout symptoms have a multitude of personal remedies at their disposal. Which of these remedies is the most effective? In what situations?

We have grouped the plethora of coping techniques (or stress skills) into four major strategies for dealing with life stress: personal management skills, relationship skills, outlook skills, and stamina skills (Tubesing, 1981). Skills from any or all of these groups may be potential components of an individualized plan for preventing burnout and promoting vitality. Each skill is described briefly below with indications for its implementation and suggestions for further reading in the area. Table 9.2 summarizes the twenty stress skills.

Personal Management Skills

Personal management or self-regulation skills help people reorganize themselves in order to take better control of their time and energy expenditure patterns. They maximize efficiency and reduce wheel spinning.

Valuing Skills: the art of choosing between alternatives. This skill is activated when people get in touch with their core values, the center of meaning in their life. Identifying things/people/activities of importance exposes the central worthwhile dimensions of life upon which personal choices are based. Tracking time expenditure also aids in clarifying what is really important to the individual (Simon, 1974; Simon, Howe, & Kirschenbaum, 1972).

Personal Planning Skills: the art of setting goals and making steady progress toward them. Planning prepares people to put their values into action. It's tough to use time and energy to best advantage without a specific goal. Once the goal is clear, planning skills can be used in designing a program for reaching it. This skill is important for putting both long- and

TABLE 9.2   Stress Skills

Overall Strategy	Skill
Personal management: self-regulation skills for organizing time and energy expenditure	*Valuing:* aligning energy investment with core values *Personal planning:* setting goals and progressing steadily toward accomplishment *Commitment:* saying "yes" wholeheartedly *Time management:* setting priorities to spend time effectively *Pacing:* regulating the tempo of life
Relationship: scene-changing skills for altering the environment and interaction with it	*Contact:* forming satisfying friendships *Listening:* tuning into others' feelings and meanings *Assertiveness:* attending to self and boundaries *Fight:* standing firm to effect change *Flight:* retreating from the pressure *Nest-building:* beautifying the environment
Outlook: change-your-mind skills for controlling attitudes and perceptions	*Relabeling:* seeing the promise in the problem *Surrender:* letting go and letting be *Faith:* accepting limits and the unknowable *Whisper:* talking positively to self *Imagination:* using creativity and humor
Stamina: body-building skills to strengthen resistance and relieve tension	*Exercise:* strengthening and fine-tuning the body *Nourishment:* eating for health *Gentleness:* treating self with care and kindness *Relaxation:* cruising in neutral and replenishing resources

short-range goals into perspective (Bolles, 1978; Crystal & Bolles, 1974; Townsend, 1970).

Commitment Skills: the art of saying yes and investing self. Commitment is the courageous act of choosing to pursue certain goals and abandon others. This skill equips people to be pro-active in their lives rather than letting other people or circumstances make their choices. Overcommitment is actually lack of commitment, an unwillingness to say yes wholeheartedly to one option and no to others (Scholz, Prince, & Miller, 1975; Farquhar, 1978).

Time Management Skills: the art of spending time effectively. Sloppy time management habits create their own stress, preventing people from reaching their desired goals. Identifying and eradicating time wasters can add hours to the day. Eliminating unnecessary tasks frees time for the essential or pleasurable ones (Lakein, 1973; Winston, 1978).

Pacing Skills: the art of tempo control. Pacing skills include a whole range of speeds and intensity for a variety of occasions. Pacing is the art of predicting accurately what can be handled, taking on only that amount, and then working steadily toward accomplishment. This skill helps alleviate the crisis mentality that promotes a feeling of always being under pressure (Keleman, 1974, 1976).

Relationship Skills

Relationship or scene-changing skills help individuals control the environment by changing the way they interact with the people and spaces that surround them. Relationships are a primary source of renewal and replenishment.

Contact Skills: the art of forming friendships. People need positive contact with each other; such contact energizes human beings. Conversation skills such as self-disclosure, attention to nonverbal cues, pursuing interesting details, and facilitative questions set the stage for nourishing connections. Contact is a learned behavior, so experimentation and practice are essential to skill-building. Stimulation and support are two potential payoffs in exercising this skill (Zunin & Zunin, 1972; Jourard, 1971; Powell, 1969).

Listening Skills: the art of empathy. Empathy is a special kind of listening that tunes in to the feelings behind the words. Listening skills are probably the most important variable in the development and maintenance of deep relationships. The trust that grows with empathic understanding provides a context for the exchange of love and self/other affirmation. Being unsure of what is "really" being said also wastes energy (Tubesing & Tubesing, 1974; Miller et al., 1975; Gordon, 1970).

Assertiveness Skills: the art of saying no and choosing involvements. Assertiveness begins with tuning in to personal needs, desires, preferences, feelings, and the like. Once awareness is accomplished, the next step is to express these preferences, needs, desires, and feelings without in the process violating anyone else's rights or personhood. Saying no gracefully, forcefully, and respectfully takes practice and persistence (Alberti & Emmons, 1970; Phelps & Austin, 1975).

Fight Skills: the art of standing firm. A fair fight can relieve tension. Fighting can positively influence the environment when done in a manner that clears the air rather than clouding it. Fight skills help individuals determine when issues or situations or challenges or relationships are worth fighting for (Bach & Wyden, 1968; Rubin, 1969).

Flight Skills: the art of retreat. Flight—taking a brief break from pressure—offers the quickest surefire relief from stress. A hobby, a short story, a five-minute vacation, a daydream, a prayer—all offer breathing space for the battleworn. However, flight is a coping skill that is easily misused. Running away can develop into a pattern of avoiding responsibility. Escape into alcohol and drugs creates more stress than it alleviates (Moustakas, 1974; DeMille, 1973).

Nest-Building Skills: the art of beautifying the environment. Both physical and interpersonal surroundings profoundly affect the people who inhabit them. Nest-building skills can be used to create a living or working space that invites relaxation, intimacy, productivity, meditation, healing, or stimulation (Bonny & Savary, 1975).

Outlook Skills

Outlook or change-your-mind skills facilitate healthy changes in attitude by allowing one to view situations from a different perspective.

Relabeling Skills: the art of seeing the promise in every problem. People automatically assign meaning to life events as they occur. Usually this process is unconscious. Relabeling skills make the unconscious perceptual process conscious and allow new meaning choices. When no other method relieves a particular stress, calling the problem something other than a problem (an opportunity to grow? a challenge? an amusing vignette?) may be the trump card (Browne, 1973; McKay, Davis, & Fanning, 1981).

Surrender Skills: the art of letting go. To surrender is not to "give up"; rather it is to "let go" and "let be." Surrender means accepting the present, living with limitations and acknowledging that some forces in life are beyond control. Surrender skills help people accept the inevitable as well as say goodbye to people, places, situations, ideas, or life stages so that their energy is freed to be reinvested in new ventures, to "make lemonade out of lemons" (Westberg, 1962; Friedman & Rosenman, 1976; Tournier, 1962).

Faith Skills: the art of accepting the mysterious and unknowable. Faith supplies the depth dimension to life. Faith skills are the primary resources for dealing with life's mysteries. Why did this child die? What is the purpose of life? Both quiet time and the experience of tragedy stretch faith skills to new levels of depth and strength (Mowrer, 1964; Frankl, 1963; Tournier, 1957).

Whisper Skills: the art of positive self-talk. People are constantly engaged in self-dialogue, telling themselves how they should behave, how they should feel about themselves. One must transform this often negative self-talk into warm affirmations. Since the connection between self-belief and self-talk is so strong and the ultimate message so often disparaging, prompting and practice are important in developing positive whisper skills (Satir, 1975; Davis, Eshelman, & McKay, 1980; Greenburg & Jacobs, 1966).

Imagination Skills: the art of creativity and laughter. Creativity and positive humor share a common root: the ability to visualize the incongruities of life. Creativity and humor are skills of imagination. Laughter heals hurts and releases tension. Creativity energizes. Imagination skills can be fruitfully used to play "ain't it funny" rather than "ain't it awful," separating self from the problem and allowing one to see humor in incongruity (Samuels & Samuels, 1975; Shorr, 1977; Moody, 1978).

Stamina Skills

Stamina skills represent the more traditional approach to stress management, focusing on strengthening the individual physically to stand up to stress and strain.

Exercise Skills: the art of fine-tuning the body. People exercise for a variety of reasons: weight control, muscle development, depression dispelling, personal challenge, invigoration, cardiovascular fitness, solitude. Regular exercise can provide a healthy "high" and dispel muscular tension while at the same time strengthening the body for future stressful situations (Cooper, 1970; Bach, 1973).

Nourishment Skills: the art of eating for health. Proper nutrition habits affect not only the body but the whole person. Developing nourishment skills means designing an eating style appropriate for lifetime use, avoiding sugars and other junk foods, and following sensible nutrition guidelines. A properly nourished body is less vulnerable to stress reactions (Lappe, 1975; Wade, 1970).

Gentleness Skills: the art of treating yourself kindly. The willingness to be gentle with self is a health-giving attitude that reduces wear and tear and conserves energy. Activating the poetic and creative, attending sensitively to body messages and spirit messages, and indulging in playfulness help slow down the tempo of life. Take time to smell the flowers (Hendricks & Wills, 1975; Shealy, 1977; Downing, 1972).

Relaxation Skills: the art of cruising in neutral. There are hundreds of ways to relax: progressive muscle tension and relaxation, yoga, breathing, self-hypnosis, meditation, prayer, music, stretching, visualization, autogenics, massage. Each tension-release method is somewhat different, but all depend on the body-mind connection and all involve a process of letting go. See Table 9.3 for a summary of common relaxation techniques (Curtis & Detert, 1981; Davis et al., 1980).

TABLE 9.3   Index to Common Relaxation Techniques

Technique	Mind/Body Connection
Breathing	Deep rhythmic breathing is the simplest and most reliable relaxation technique. A multitude of special breathing patterns and techniques can be used to combat situational stress and prevent the build-up of tension during the day. Breathing is a primary building block for all other relaxation techniques.
Progressive relaxation	This most common relaxation technique provides a way to identify tension in specific muscle groups and to discriminate between subjective feelings of tension and relaxation. Often the progressive feelings of tension and relaxation of muscle groups is combined with the covert use of relaxing expressions.
Autogenic training (AT)	AT teaches the stressed body and mind to relax quickly on verbal command and to return from an "alarm" state to a balanced, normal state using images of warmth and heaviness to alter respiratory and circulatory functioning.
Self-hypnosis	The self-induced hypnotic trance promotes physical relaxation as well as providing an opportunity to gain control over emotions and to make positive suggestions for change.
Meditation	Meditation may be the most "holistic" of the stress management skills, involving sensory awareness, physical relaxation, surrender of thought processes, and focusing on the life force in breathing and contemplation. This mind-clearing ritual refreshes body, mind, and spirit.

(continued)

TABLE 9.3 (Continued)

Yoga	The underlying goal of yoga is to enable the individual, through self-discipline, to control the body and mind, and thereby the stress response.
Visualization	Visualization skills can be used to refocus the mind on positive, healing images. Individuals may fantasize peaceful, safe scenes or imagine the tension flowing out of muscle groups or painful areas. This technique is often coupled with progressive muscle relaxation or autogenic exercises to maximize deep relaxation.
Massage	Massage provides relief from muscular tension through deep manipulation of tissues, surface stroking, or pressure at certain trigger points that seem to control tightness and energy flow in various parts of the body. Self-massage is an easily accessible tension reducer.
Biofeedback	Biofeedback refers to any objective measurement of biological processes that indicate stress. Whether the particular mechanism records heart rate or skin conductivity or the electrical impulses in muscles, biofeedback gives the individual immediate feedback and monitoring of their stress response. Modifications receive immediate reinforcement.

Source: Summarized from Curtis & Detert, 1981; Davis et al., 1981; McKay et al., 1981; Barrow & Prosen, 1981.

Choosing the Appropriate Skill

The listing of stress skills is clearly representative rather than exhaustive and is intended primarily to raise consciousness about the wide variety of personal resources that could be activated to combat burnout. Given the multitude of options, what criteria might an individual use in choosing an appropriate stress skill? One strategy is to match the coping technique to the situation at hand.

Matching the Skill to the Situation

Personal management or organizing skills are particularly effective for the times when life seems out of control, when the work to be done exceeds the available time, when goals are unclear or values uncertain. Valuing, personal planning, commitment, time management, or pacing might be the skill of choice when organization is the issue.

Relationship skills work best when an individual feels lonely and unsupported, confused or in need of caring, or when the environment is a source of tension. Contact, listening, assertiveness, fight, flight, and nest-building are potential skill resources for these situations.

Both personal management and relationship skills are especially helpful when stress-producing demands of the physical or social environment need to be altered. Assertiveness may help one cope with an inconsiderate co-worker or a persistent salesperson. Personal planning and time management may be essential skills for the harried reporter or dual-career couple. Following a job promotion, contact and listening skills may ensure successs in the new work unit. Values clarification helps people determine what issues, situations, and relationships are worth fighting for. Flight may be the healthiest option when one is powerless to change a destructive situation.

Outlook or attitude-change skills are particularly helpful when a person feels depressed or cynical, when grief over a loss is an important dimension of the discomfort, or when stress comes from self-imposed pressures. Relabeling, surrender, faith, whisper, and imagination are important internal strategies for preventing or coping with such dilemmas. No matter how uncomfortable the situation, changing one's attitude can prevent or alleviate stress. The counselor who feels overwhelmed by an excessive caseload could learn to surrender his or her fantasy of saving the world. The lunch-room monitor may need to exercise relabeling skills in order to view noon-time chaos as youthful exuberance. Imagination skills can help teachers or supervisors who take life too seriously to laugh at themselves.

Stamina skills work well when stress is due to circumstances beyond the individual's control, when people choose to push themselves too hard, or when other stress-reducing lifestyle changes are not yet completed. Exercise, nourishment, gentleness, and relaxation are powerful prophylactic as well as restorative skills. Most stamina skills could be helpful in any stress-provoking situation.

Matching the Skill to the Person

A second natural treatment strategy involves matching the coping technique to the individual, taking advantage of personal strengths and preferences. Individuals with well-developed relationship skills, for example, may be revitalized by joining a support group or by gearing up for a good fight. Relaxation aficionados may prefer to learn some new breathing techniques or incorporate brief tension-reduction exercises into staff meetings or coffee breaks. An individual whose faith is usually a source of strength may want to capitalize on that skill through ritual or meditation at times of crisis.

This principle of skill enhancement may not be so effective for those people who have developed one or two skills to the exclusion of others or those who have focused on only one overall stress management strategy.

A person who relies almost exclusively upon organizational skills, for example, will probably handle certain job pressures (numerous demands, time pressures, tight deadlines, multiple responsibilities) very effectively. That same person may have difficulty responding appropriately to job or personal situations that evoke a grief reaction. The stress and pain of loss simply do not respond very well to getting better organized. In this situation the individual may want to focus on obtaining some personal support (a relationship skill) or practicing surrender (an outlook skill).

On the other hand, a person strong in outlook skills, who easily relabels situations and sees with the wide perspective of the spiritual dimension, may get into trouble by handling excessive task requirements and time demands with a philosophical "fifty years from now who will care?" attitude. The individual might better develop some new skills in the area of personal management and time use.

Periodic assessment of personal stress skills is essential if we are to match the skill to the individual. Which skills are used most often? In what situations? What skills are underdeveloped? Which skills have other positive payoffs? Which skills have been neglected? Which new skills are being developed? Stress management is a dynamic process, and any treatment strategy needs to enhance the uniqueness of each individual's changing resources.

A Vote for Novelty and Diversity

A third coping strategy is based on the principle that stretching and novelty are both intrinsically revitalizing. Instead of attacking the problem head-on or from a position of strength, the most energizing strategy may be to try something new. Anything. This may be the time to daydream, to flee, to fight, to reach out, to set goals, to take on a cause, to change the tempo, to listen, to sit in a sauna—even if it feels awkward and uncomfortable. When people put some of the "old regulars" on the back burner and stretch themselves by exercising and experimenting with underdeveloped skills, they may break out of stress management habits that are no longer effective.

Perhaps the best strategy of all would be for burnout victims to diversify their stress management efforts by creatively combining skills from several areas in devising a personal energy-replenishment and conservation prescription flexible enough to meet a variety of situations.

Stress Management in the Workplace

As a manager or supervisor, how do you decide which stress skills will be most effective for a given individual and situation? You don't! You can only make available as many options as possible and assist those people who really want to change. Respond to their suggestions. Provide both physical space and "time-out" space in the schedule for exercise. Offer instruction in physical self-care, in relaxation techniques, in personal time management. Support support groups. Encourage employees to seek fulfillment in off-the-job activities and involvements. Reinforce assertiveness. Provide relaxation breaks. Hang posters. Do whatever you can to raise consciousness and highlight options for maintaining personal vitality.

The Treatment of Choice Is Choice!

No matter how much you want to help, do not try to make decisions or select preferred methods of treatment for others, lest you fall into the trap of "activated expert" and "passive patient." Your responsibility, as we see it, is to facilitate others' acting on their own behalf. Prod them, support them, listen to them, explore with them, encourage them, and help them to develop plans to take better care of themselves. The rest is up to the individual. The treatment of choice *is* choice.

Perhaps this all sounds like plain common sense. Of course the individual should choose! We have discovered that although the ideas presented here make sense to most people, their application is extremely uncommon. First, it is much easier to implement a single treatment plan, such as autogenic training or aerobic dance, than to facilitate the development of individualized burnout prevention programs. Second, having spent years looking for preferred treatments, it is all too tempting to share our hard-earned expertise with such overwhelming enthusiasm that we inadvertently lose respect for the individual's own expertise and personal preference.

Although we look forward to the time when research and clinical evidence will help us delineate a grid for selecting specific skills to meet personal needs and the demands of a situation, we fully expect that the treatment of choice will remain, as it is now, the personalized prescription written and filled by the individual.

10

Counseling and Dynamics
Treating the End-Stage Person

HERBERT J. FREUDENBERGER

What shall we do with professionals who have reached the end stages of the burnout process? In the overview to this volume, Whiton **Paine** talks about prevention, mediation, and remediation interventions. The other chapters in this and the next section of this volume focus on the first two areas. Remediation, salvage if you would, raises a different set of issues. If Cary **Cherniss** is correct in his analysis of social and other trends, remediation is likely to become far more important in the 1980s than it has been in previous decades. More and more professionals will reach the sixth, seventh, and eighth stages described by **Golembiewski.**

It is difficult to draw a composite picture of a burned-out human being. Such persons exhibit different mixtures of the signs delineated by **Carroll and White** in their Table 3.1. They are alike in their pain, distress, and feeling of hopelessness. This chapter is the first to begin to explicate the treatment resources needed to assist professionals who have completed or are completing the burnout process. It is based on over twelve years' experience with individuals I have worked with, over shorter or longer periods of time, in independent practice as well as within agency, clinic, hospital, and corporate settings.

Typically, these patients were not the type of individuals who flock to lectures and workshops on stress management, and it was unlikely that such techniques as peer groups or the latest relaxation procedure would be particularly effective with this group. They seemed to need more.

Unfortunately they seldom seek counseling and psychotherapy of their own volition. This is not surprising, since many have become accustomed to personal success in work and other settings, a success that frequently is the direct result of their strengths and efforts. They are aware that something is working, often horribly out of kilter, and are frustrated at their inability to understand and influence the process. When they seek help, it is generally because someone else (a spouse, supervisor, the personnel department) has suggested this alternative or has formally referred the individual for diagnosis and treatment.

The remainder of this chapter deals with some of the main remediation issues. Referral network must be understood and strengthened to aid this group of professionals. There also are some treatment techniques that have been particularly useful in working with burnout professionals. Successful diagnosis and treatment involves, in part, the successful separation of work-related and other stressors and understanding of how each contributes to the patient's problems. These are some of the core issues, and others will surface as more counselors and therapists begin to treat this group.

It is useful at this point to state some fundamental conclusions that grow out of ten years of direct clinical experience.

(1) We are not dealing with a mental disorder as that term is usually defined. Sweeney (1981) is correct in seeing burnout as a syndrome, linked to work-related stress.
(2) Many, perhaps most, burnout professionals will respond quickly to a limited number of focused, reality-oriented counseling sessions. Drugs are normally not needed and long-term therapy is unwarranted unless the initial sessions reveal an underlying psychopathology.
(3) Professionals can change even if they are burned out. Given the correct remediation interventions, they can return to their jobs and again become productive. Salvage, in this instance, may be cheaper than the alternative of dismissal and training of a replacement.

Each of these points is discussed in more detail in the remainder of this chapter.

The Referral Network

The sources of referral vary and depend on the referring individual's sophistication and personal awareness, as well as the environment or relationship wherein the burnout predominantly manifests itself. A common source of referral is the physician. After a thorough examination and conversation with the patient the physician may determine that the individual is working too hard, is under too much interpersonal stress, or may be physically and emotionally exhausted. If we are dealing with a physician who has some awareness of burnout, then the referral may be made for that specific complaint (Freudenberger & Richelson, 1980; Freudenberger, 1981a). Other referrals are more vague and include the initial statement, "I think this guy or gal is pushing too hard and is burning himself out; possibly you can be of help. There is nothing wrong with him physically."

Another major source of referral is from an administrator, supervisor or trainer of an agency, clinic, crisis center, nursing school, or drug and alcohol abuse treatment agency. These referrals are usually made in terms of changed performance on the job or a shift in observed attitude or behavior.

The overall impression is that these men and women have, over a period of time, changed in their attitude, demeanor, or relationships to the client, or their overall contribution to the facility in which they are functioning had declined. The shift in job demeanor is observable in excessive absences, illnesses, or the deterioration of the quality of their work.

An interesting source of referrals that has evolved in the past years, have been religious organizations. They may refer a rabbi, minister, priest, or nun who has gone through a number of physical or sometimes psychological evaluations, and questions still remain as to what is happening to this person. Parishioners are also referred.

Parenthetically, I do believe that the number of men and women who have left religious life could have been lessened if there would have been an awareness of the burnout process. Too many left, often significantly disenchanted, not knowing that if someone had understood the process they were going through they might have been able to be helped to remain. This is also true in other work settings.

A fourth source is the corporation, which has become a major avenue of referrals. The referral is usually made through its medical or personnel department and sometimes through a manager or executive within the company. The reasons for the referral vary. Some are referred, as Appelbaum (1981) indicates, because "a personal crisis situation involving marital, family, financial, or legal troubles has been identified, or there is suspicion of excessive alcohol and drug abuse." Other cases are similiar to those referred by the agency administrator. Thus, there are many job-related reasons that executives may require referral (Freudenberger, 1981b).

With the popularization of burnout, more self- or spouse-induced referrals can be expected. For example, high personal and job-related stress as a consequence of transfer are becoming increasingly common reasons for self-referral. The move may bring to the surface previously unresolved family problems that may sometimes require prolonged personal as well as family psychotherapy.

Most of the circumstances preceding a referral are not dissimilar. The individual in question has usually attempted a number of tactics to cope with the changes that are occurring in his or her life. One of the more significant series of responses that emerged in a study conducted by Freudenberger (1981a) was that most persons initially seek to deny that any changes in their mood, attitude, or behavior are taking place. They may work harder, begin to blame the population or environment in which they are functioning, resort to alternative solutions such as alcohol and over-the-counter drugs, or tend to withdraw. Initially they are puzzled about what is happening to them. They appear as strangers to themselves as well as to those around them.

Why this process takes place varies. For some it occurs as a response, as Daley (1979) noted, to a particularly stressful period, say, a project or a deadline. For others, it is a feeling that they have lived with for a year or two, or sometimes longer.

Initial Impressions of the Presenting Symptoms

The symptoms presented cover a variety of personal areas. Many of the symptoms are predominantly in the behavioral, emotional, and cognitive areas. It may also be necessary to refer the individual to a physician for a thorough evaluation of stress-related physical problems. Common symptoms include the following:

(1) Those working within a corporation may suffer from negative thinking and believe that their organization has disappointed them. Their comments are replete with negative, cynical, and depressed overtones.

(2) If they are community workers or have been social activists, they begin to question their motivation and their professional job commitment.

(3) If they are referred by a physician, they suffer from gastrointestinal, dermatological, high blood pressure, or coronary potential symptoms. They usually seek an instant pill cure. They wonder about how long they will need to see me—can I give them "quick relief"? They are worried about what really is wrong with them—are they sick? or are they "having a nervous breakdown"?

(4) As this author has indicated previously (Freudenberger, 1980), the persons who come in overweight often have abused alcohol and drugs; are compulsive shoppers, gamblers, or workaholics; often talk of having lost control of their lives. The loss of control manifests itself in their expressed feeling, which may be an accurate perception, that they are being shunted aside by members of their family or by their company. They no longer think

as clearly as before; their cognitive processes have been intruded upon. Additionally, once their communications break down in the home or at work, they tend to feel even more lonely.

(5) Many also feel that they have been wronged and therefore have a difficult time giving up a deep sense of being victims, pawns, or martyrs.

(6) The burnout process for some has seriously encroached on their attitudes. Where at one time they felt positively about what they were engaged in, they now feel a sense of disenchantment with the tasks, the project, or the relationship. This disenchantment shift some into detachment, depression, and feelings of loss and thoughts of "why bother anymore?" (Maslach, 1976; Marshall & Kasman, 1980).

(7) Often burned-out individuals express overwhelming feelings of guilt, inadequacy, and a real sense of loss and worthlessness. The guilt may be a result of believing that they have not achieved enough; the loss is a feeling of having lost something very precious. They often initially believe that there is no possibility of recovery. Unfortunately, they are sometimes correct.

As indicated, the burned-out professional's major area of diminishing functioning is on the job. It does need to be stated, however, that many professionals also burn out with their families or in interpersonal relationships. They have a way of "using up" and seeking to feed on the people around them, sometimes as a means of buttressing their own diminishing available energies. This leads to concurrent marital and relationship difficulties.

For purposes of clarification, it is also important to point out, in the very strongest of terms, that individuals who are burned out are generally not malingerers, who are using burnout symptoms in order to avoid their responsibilities. Rather, they are often the very people who have given too much. Further, they are neither psychotic, having nervous breakdown, nor mentally ill.

Sometimes there is a tendency to confuse the term "burnout" with depression. They are by no means synonymous. As this writer has indicated (Freudenberger, 1980), "Depression can take many forms and may or may not be connected to burnout. There are differences between a generally depressed state of mind and the form of depression which signifies that burnout is taking place. In nonrelated depression, the condition is prolonged and pervades all areas of a person's life. He may sleep much of the day, have no interest in sex, or desire to eat; there is a general withdrawal. The depression associated with burnout is usually temporary and may be specific to a particular segment of a person's life." Burnout and moderate forms of depression are quite difficult to differentiate on a symptom level. What is essential in the differential diagnosis is to ascertain what were the precipitating causes that promoted the observable symptoms. If they were traumatic, sudden in onset, and dramatic in response, for example, then it is highly probable that it is a form of depression rather than burnout. It is true that depression may accompany burnout, but the terms are not synonymous, nor is one a substitution for the other.

As indicated from my observations, the individuals who are prone to burnout tend to fall into two broad groups. In one group, it is not unusual for them to feel, as children, that they were not equal to others in their neighborhood or their extended family. Sometimes the picture is that of an emotionally deprived child, one whose father is viewed as authoritative, passive, unavailable, cold, and sometimes argumentative. One man talked of his unavailable alcoholic father; others talk of the lack of affection shown by their fathers to them. To these persons, the mothers seem strict, absent, authoritative, unavailable, social climbers, active, and cold. Frequently, these individuals describe themselves as followers, low achievers, overly sensitive, passive, and wanting to be liked.

The second group talks of ambitious, driven, busy, demanding, and active fathers who appeared to serve as models of ambition and achievement for the young person. The mother in this constellation appeared to be helpful, caring, passive, permissive, unpredictable, and soft but not always capable of showing feelings. Members of this group see themselves as sociable, talented, responsive, sometimes frenetic, and high achievers. In both groups, one element emerges rather consistently. A significant number see themselves as having been loners as children as well as in adulthood. They tend to have a difficult time expressing their feelings and being assertive. Susan, a thirty-year-old executive who saw me professionally, seemed to struggle with unresolved dependency needs and to have a strong desire to link up with a company, job, project, cause, ideal , or authority that would gratify her. Along with her felt sense of helplessness as a woman, she hoped to find a certain acceptance in her job and a feeling of competence, adequacy, and "goodness." She had a history of never feeling that she was good enough for her parents. I believe that women who work have the additional problem of often being oppressed as women and having especially to prove themselves at work. This makes them potential candidates for burnout.

Many persons, because of their life experiences, are especially sensitive to disappointments. Because of their loneliness, they tend to invest a great deal in the job to find a sense of fulfillment and identity. The work ethos of competition and achievement serve as values to be emulated. Furthermore, they have a great need to be seen as worthy and good. Initially, they enter the job market full of good intentions—idealistic, hopeful, and somewhat na-ive. They give it their all and more, in order to attain the hoped-for good sense of self. Because of their strong need to be accepted and liked, they have a difficult time saying no. This psychoanalyst has found that many become quite subjective and personalize their evaluations of life situations. This, in turn, interferes with their capability to be objective in their perceptions of what is happening to, and around, them.

They tend to be selfless in giving to the point of being drained, and, because of a seeming need to make sure that they are not perceived as "less than," work extra hard to deny their human frailities. They tend to be lonely people who, when the chips are down, do not believe that they can turn to others for aid. Rather, they believe that in the final analysis they can only rely on themselves.

The needs, personality, and societal values make these persons prone to burning out. This tendency may then be exacerbated by factors inherent within an organization, including the framework of rituals, symbols, sys-tems, and values practiced within that corporation. The burnout process is often heightened by the degree to which individuals perceive themselves as either part of or excluded from the decision process. For the helping profes-sional, the number of cases assigned—whether one is a supervisor or a supervisee, the ward one is assigned to, the chronic or crisis units within which one functions, how close to or distant from the power framework one is—all add to one's sense of authority and personal freedom. Pines (1978) suggests that, in time, an occupational tedium may set in if the individual feels left out and has become routinized. However, within most professional settings, competition, aloneness, moving about from company to company, excelling as an individual, and getting ahead are prized societal values and serve as personal motivations—which can help to do him or her in.

The set of symbols, rewards, and variables built into any organization can also make for an environment that encourages burnout. At risk is the individ-ual who needs to be appreciated, to excel, to compete, and to get to the top. That is the very person who, because of his or her personal history, is likely to become a burnout victim. A related factor is that "uprootness and built-in competitiveness has made the individual more and more of a loner, has decreased the potential support system that a cooperative and congenial group may offer, and over a period of time has forced a person to find [a] major source of gratification within a job setting" (Freudenberger, 1981c). This increases vulnerability because it is in and through the job that many find their one consistent and constant element of life. This one constant, then, serves as the locus wherein the greatest amount of gratification may occur; yet, sadly enough, it is also the very place within which the seeds for the downfall of a human being exist, and where eventually the least amount of gratification may be experienced.

Treatment Approaches to Burnout

Once again, the initial treatment approach ought to be viewed from three perspectives: the personal, the organizational, and that of the society at large. As Bramhall and Ezell (1981) indicate, "treatment with insight therapy is not enough. In order to overcome burnout, both behavioral and situational changes are necessary." Jones (1981a) recently recommended a combination of job redesign, improvement in personal coping skills, and rational emotional psychotherapy. Both are consistent with the ecological framework of **Carroll and White** and the intervention strategy recommended by Paine (1982).

It has been this author's impression that most persons seeking assistance for burnout appropriately expect to reevaluate their behavior within a short-term treatment framework. This seems to be the approach that for the time is most propitious and sensible, whether it occurs within a corporate or an independent practice setting. It is important that the helper offer the professional some short, effective and simple intervention techniques that the client may utilize. (Freudenberger 1976, Freudenberger & Robbins, 1980).

The helper working within a corporate setting must be aware of a number of factors. To protect confidentiality, it needs to be clearly spelled out with administration, personnel, management as well as the professional to be counseled, what may be kept as confidential information and what cannot be treated as such. This is particularly true if the corporation, agency, or hospital is paying the fee or the salary of the one who does the counseling. The realities of the corporate structure, hospital, school, or agency cannot be denied in the treatment process.

Issues that are raised by management concerning a person who is burned out often revolve around such questions as: Can the individual continue to function on the job? Is his or her burnout detrimental to clients or to the performance of other personnel? Does the company need to consider a transfer, a shift of responsibility, or grant a leave of absence, a diminution of job function, or even early retirement or discharge? These are important issues that need to be grappled with by the helper, the professional seeking assistance, and the setting in which the counseling occurs. Counselors must clearly define their roles.

For a manager or a supervisor, the change in a subordinate's behavior becomes a challenge and a real obstacle. Most supervisors hesitate to confront an individual about that observable change. Some commented, in a seminar conducted by this author, that it was none of their business "to butt in." Others correctly stated that they were not psychologists or "junior shrinks" and did not wish to get into something that was over their heads. Their observations are correct. However, there are ways of relating to a burned-out person that may assist in opening a dialogue. Constance **Shapiro** discusses some of these in her chapter on creative supervision.

A manager has certain advantages over a consultant. He or she has a historical work relationship with the individual that may be utilized to evaluate the observed changes in attitude or performance. Furthermore, a manager might have the opportunity to suggest that further conversations take place, allow time for reflection, or recommend articles or books on the problem that the individual might read. If all else fails, a possible referral to personnel or an outside professional might be in order.

In summary, as a manager, supervisor, director, or principal of a school, a good initial approach to a burned-out person is to indicate that the observed change of attitude, behavior, involvement, and motivation is of serious concern.

It is essential that the manager who handles the employee be sensitive and not see the person as a malingerer; he or she should receive some training in how to speak to someone who is burning out. It is also important that the manager be made aware of the danger of projecting his or her own feelings and failing to be forthright with either himself or the employee. As this author has noted (Freudenberger, 1977b), "Above all such conversations need to be handled in a sensitive, empathic, humane and kind fashion, especially if an inhouse or outside referral is contemplated."

Treatment Process

The beginning of treatment is usually an evaluative process. But it is important to convey immediately to the client that what is happening to him or her is not a consequence of personal inadequacy. First, allow the client to ventilate grievances; then, slowly develop and point out what some of the changes in behavior are that have, over a period of time, taken place. During the early contacts it is important to be quite empathetic and seek to alleviate anxiety and fears of mental breakdown. It may also be necessary to diminish some of the more serious impulsive and anxiety-provoking considerations that have occurred to the client in terms of how to solve his or her problem (for example, to leave the job and terminate employment with that firm or in a particular field). The cognitive approach to treatment appears to be most suitable initially. Through this, in time, the client may be helped to develop short- and long-term goals and to understand what may be attended to immediately and what will take time to resolve. For example, Sam, a vice-president of a large conglomerate, reflected on which of his job functions he could sensibly and rather quickly delegate to subordinates in order to diminish his excessive air flights from coast to coast. That was a short-term goal. He also needed to reflect on how he could diminish some of his job responsibilities over the long term. Additionally, the therapist needs to assist the client to reflect on, clarify, and eventually change personal values, dedication, commitment, caring too much, needing to achieve and be on top and so on—that have helped to promote burnout.

Once this has been elicited and established, the next approach is to assist in helping the person to prioritize and evaluate these values: which values are his or her own, which have been imposed by family, and which are a function of the organization and society. During treatment, women in particular may need to be made aware of the necessity of undergoing assertiveness training in order to be able to say no more effectively.

With helping professionals, counseling may need to focus on helping the person to see how a shift in attitudes, such as suddenly finding clients "a drag, boring, intractable," may have very much influenced his or her work behavior. Treatment should also focus on reestablishing a sense of self, gaining control over one's life, and helping to teach or restructure adequate communication with those with whom daily contact has been lost.

We often do not appreciate the degree to which burnout can intrude on cognitive functioning. A person's sense of time for example, difficulty of keeping appointments, overbookings, inflexibility and rigidity—enters into the process. Furthermore, intolerance for ambiguity and unpredictability and the need for excessive control (which in turn impacts on one's ability to think, decide, and be creative) can occur in individuals with this problem. At the beginning of counseling, it is often these factors that make it difficult to reach burned-out persons. They have a strong interest in maintaining a rigid facade, because it is the facade that has enabled them to continue to function. One man put it succinctly when he said his concern had been "left foot, right foot, left foot, right foot—just keep going, and not bother about anything else."

During counseling, a careful evaluation and review needs to be made in order to ascertain whether the burnout was caused by a personal value system alone or in combination with the characteristics inherent within organizations. For example, the job demands of a drug counselor who is on frequent night duty, the nurse on a neonatal unit, the psychoanalyst in independent practice, the manager who works within rigid time schedules—all have built-in burnout potential. Further diagnostic work involves an evaluation of the work setting and the "psychological climate" of the environment. For example, is it an environment, such as a hospital setting, fraught with frustration and hopelessness, or is it an advertising agency within which job security is only as good as the last successful project? Moreover, the issue of appropriate rewards, responsibility in the decision process, and the possibility for advancement all to be considered. Each environment has its own set of factors, rituals, verbalized and nonverbalized expectations. We need to look at individual situations as having similarities with and differences from each other. The individual needs also to be made aware of the negative impacts on his or her lifestyle and physical well-being of increased smoking or drinking, poor nutrition, changed sleeping and eating habits, and other patterns of self-neglect that have subtly crept in.

Another major area that needs to be evaluated during counseling is the impact of burnout on interpersonal and familial relationships. Diminution of contact, poor communication, separation, and social isolation are par for the course. It is important to discuss how to reestablish lines of communication and plan future expenditures of energy and investment in support networks. Sometimes family therapy is called for, and other members of the family will need to be brought in for counseling. Quite often the impact of the burnout victim has been very severe on various members of the family.

Another recent and increasingly effective development is the use of employee assistance programs to impact on burned-out personnel. As Austin and Jackson (1977) suggest, "The role of workmen's compensation laws in the mental health of workers has given a new legal dimension to the development of occupational mental health programs."

As part of this process, in the future there will need to be further clarification and development of the application of employee assistance programs. For example, an issue that has cropped up recently is the need to clarify what is meant by emotional disability and how this, in turn, relates to job stress. In time, legal cases will emerge wherein the clarification of these issues will be necessary. Some of these are discussed by **Minnehan and Paine.** Corporations must understand the impact of burnout as it applies to their employees. The costs and benefits to the corporation to inaugurate employee assistance programs, or bring about changes in major medical benefits packages, will be felt as the years go on. However, corporations will need to acquire support data and be assisted in the development of models for treatment as well as evaluate outcome procedures. Without these accumulated data one cannot readily argue pro or con for the use of employee assistance programs (Paine, 1982). In addition, labor unions and their awareness of these issues have just begun to make an impact on voluntary development of health insurance coverage. Much more will need to be done to incorporate mental health services into union contracts. We are just beginning to learn about stress in the workplace, and now must consider how union members will be affected by burnout and what should be done after damage occurs.

Summary

On the whole, prognosis for burnout recovery is good. The length and depth of the treatment is a function not only of the degree of burnout, but also of the preburnout individual's personality and his or her past functioning. If the person has been personally troubled for a number of years, the removal and understanding of the sources of burnout may only provide symptomatic relief of deeper maladies that require more extensive and intensive therapy.

The overall goal of counseling should be to develop the person's strengths, help him or her to recapture a sense of self, increase confidence, and cultivate his or her ability to be in charge of his or her life once again. Initially, some temporary medication may be necessary to alleviate heightened stress. Further work with a professional may necessitate a serious evaluation of the vocational choice or the firm within which the individual is employed. Counseling may also need to alert the person to other resources. The use of meditation, biofeedback, and other stress management techniques and changes in diet and exercise may need to be introduced. Finally, the person needs to be taught to laugh, use humor, and acknowledge that to err is human and that moderation is a mainstay for balancing one's life.

Conclusions

Burnout is treatable; it may be tended to by the individual alone or in consultation with a family member or a friend. If that does not seem to help, then meeting with a professional may be an answer.

Burnout as a process cannot be separated from the environment in which it occurs. As Carroll and White (1981) indicate, "Burnout is an ecological dysfunction. Its root causes, therefore, must be viewed as stemming from the interaction of both debilitating individual and environmental factors."

Within a corporation, we need to balance productivity and profit-motive values with a concern for human beings and convey that the two sets of concerns are not contradictory. Burnout has come about because we have been using up our people with reckless abandon. We need to come to grips with our seemingly conflicting social values. On the one hand, we pride ourselves on the importance of production; on the other, we refuse to see the price we are paying in terms of people and the anxieties promoted in them (Freudenberger, 1982).

For burnout to be diminished in our environment, we must take many of the steps proposed elsewhere in this chapter:

(1) We must reflect on investing more capital in the training of employees and teaching measures to prevent and lessen burnout among all kinds of helping professionals (Freudenberger, in press).
(2) We must seriously begin to alert corporations to the human and psychic needs of their professional workforce, and that, by tending to human needs, their profits will *not* decrease.
(3) We must increase employee communication and participation in the decision process.
(4) We must consider more team approaches and less of the "every person for themselves" attitude in industry.
(5) We must recognize that the Calvinist ethic of working hard is still determining our work lives.
(6) We must realize that no amount of compassion, caring, helping, understanding, sensitivity, and therapy can act as an adequate substitute for the serious reconsideration that our social and work environments are promoting burnout.
(7) We need to determine, through research, what factors that may promote burnout are inherent in an organizational climate. We also need to evolve legitimate prevention models.

There never will be a sufficient number of effective treatment personnel unless we acknowledge that basic changes are needed, in ourselves as well as within society. Until we do so, we will spend most of our energies writing papers on how to help the burnout victim, who in a larger sense is a victim of the social values by which we all live and function.

PART IV

Changing Organizations

11

Changing Organizations
Is a Work Environment Without Burnout
an Impossible Goal?

AYALA M. PINES

Different work environments can significantly affect the staff burnout rates within organizations (Pines, Aronson, & Kafry, 1981). In our work to date (for example, Etzion & Pines, 1981; Maslach & Pines, 1977a, 1979; Pines, 1981a, 1982; Pines & Aronson, 1980, 1981; Pines & Kanner, 1982; Pines & Maslach, 1978, 1980) burnout is defined as a state of physical, emotional, and mental exhaustion that results from long-term involvement with people in emotionally demanding situations. We have found it to be negatively correlated with satisfaction from work, life, and oneself, and positively correlated with turnover, tardiness, and intention to leave a job. We also have found burnout to be correlated with poor physical health, sleep problems, amount of alcohol drinking, and such on-duty symptoms as headaches, loss of appetite, nervousness, backaches, and stomachaches. And we have found burnout significantly correlated with hopelessness and loss of idealism about work (Pines, 1981c).

This as well as other research reported in this volume indicates that burnout is a very costly phenomenon for the individual, but it is also very costly for organizations. Given the high cost of burnout in terms of lost idealism, turnover, tardiness, absenteeism, poor delivery of services, and the like, organizations have a high stake in trying to prevent it.

Unfortunately, some organizations use the burnout process itself as a screening device, saying, in effect, "Let them burn out and quit; there are three people out there eagerly waiting for each position opening up who will be willing to promise to remain forever both cheerful and grateful." That burned-out professionals most often do not get fired but rather quit their jobs proves the fallacy of this reasoning and strongly suggests that instead of focusing exclusively on weaknesses in the individual that may create a special vulnerability to burnout, a more profitable approach would be to focus more attention on features in the work environment that will prevent burnout-causing tendencies in everyone.

As an example, consider the case of two human services organizations in the San Francisco East Bay Area. This example illustrates the types of job-related stressors that are common to a wide variety of jobs in different types of organizations. Both serve a middle-class, suburban client population, within the boundaries of similar budgets and both use similar therapeutic approaches. They are also similar in structure, organization, and function, and yet are radically different in terms of their levels of staff burnout. The main reason appears to be their very different work environments.

In one organization the turnover was so high that most professionals never had a chance either to really get to know other staff members or to see the impact of their work on patients. The work was very difficult. Professionals were constantly confronted with clients' frustration and antagonism, which was caused in great part by the high turnover of therapists and the clients' repeated need to cope with prematurely terminated therapy. The emotional stress of dealing with clients' anger and frustration was added to the emotional stress inherent in providing psychological help in general, and with time became a heavy psychological burden for the professionals.

In addition to the chronic emotional stress of their work, staff members found themselves isolated in an atmosphere marked by intrastaff hostility. Even students interning in the agency felt inhibited about asking questions, since they were quickly made to understand that asking questions was an indication of inadequacy. Staff meetings were "crocodile sessions" where case presentations were a most dreaded task because of the predictably vicious responses of antagonistic colleagues.

Within a very short time even the most friendly and sensitive staff members became cynical and hostile. Everyone on the staff knew they had no one to rely on for support. The chronic stress of dealing with clients' problems in the absence of support sooner or later became unbearable and eventually resulted in burnout.

In the other organization, turnover was almost nonexistent. Even those who left the area for personal reasons used to come back for what they affectionately called "family visits." The work atmosphere was supportive and exciting, and staff looked forward to their meetings. During those meetings (which usually involved a potluck meal), staff members were able to receive support and counseling from both their colleagues and supervisors, and to give their input concerning the organization's policies.

During one of the case presentations, the director herself presented the case of a multiple-problem family she was working with and felt unsure about treating, asking for the staff's feedback and suggestions. The act had a tremendous liberating effect on the staff, enabling others to ask questions and admit feelings of uncertainty.

In this organization there was always someone ready to cover for a colleague who was under stress and needed a short period of "time out." When a client attempted suicide, his therapist had not only the staff's total support after the fact, but also the knowledge that they approved of the therapeutic approach before the fact. In this organization, when staff members felt the first danger signs of burnout they could explore their feelings with others and deal with those feelings before they reached a critical stage.

The specific negative features of the first work environment, which produced burnout, and the positive features of the second work environment, which reduced burnout, will be discussed at length in the remainder of this chapter.

Work Environment and Burnout

Even very similar organizations can have significantly different levels of burnout. In a study involving 724 employees in fourteen state residential facilities serving the developmentally disabled in eleven different states, it was found that in some facilities burnout was significantly higher than in others ($F[13, 674] = 2.78$, $p < .002$; Weinberg, Edwards, & Garove, 1979). In a study involving 83 staff members from twelve child-care facilities, it was found that there was a significant difference among the centers in job satisfaction ($F = 2.6$, $p < .05$). As the two agencies presented in the introduction illustrate, the crucial element in burnout is often the work environment.

When discussing work environments it is possible to start at a very general level of analysis and thus include such variables as the particular country or culture in which the work environment exists (for example, a special education class in Israel in certain ways is very different from a similar class in the United States); the particular social, political, and economic climate as discussed by **Cherniss** (teaching special education was probably rather different in the 1960s from what it is in the 1980s); the particular location (teaching a special education class in an inner-city ghetto is quite different from teaching such a class in a rich suburban neighborhood); and the particular organization (teaching in a private school is different from teaching in a public school). Memberships in religious communities, the military, the public sector, the private sector or the nonprofit sector can also have a major impact on the work environment and consequently on the perceived stress of the individual.

In addition to the work environment, every discussion of burnout has to include a consideration of both the human service professionals in danger of burning out and the recipients of their services. Just as certain personality or problem-related features of service recipients can make helping them more stressful emotionally and thus more burnout-producing, there are certain personality characteristics that can make some professionals burn out faster than others **(Carroll & White)**.

Yet, even the same person, working with people exhibiting similar problems in two organizations similar in function, location, budget, and sociopolitical environment, may burn out in one and not in the other. The example of the two social service organizations, supported by extensive research, suggests a number of variables in the work environment that play an important role in promoting or preventing burnout. The variables represent four different dimensions of the work environment: psychological, physical, and organizational (see Table 11.1). The *psychological* dimension of the work environment includes features that can be emotional or cognitive in nature. An example of a variable affecting the emotional sphere is the sense of significance and personal growth provided by the work environment. Examples of

TABLE 11.1   Work Environment Features That Are Burnout Correlates

Psychological	Physical	Social	Organizational
Cognitive:	Fixed:	Service recipients:	Bureaucratic:
autonomy	structure	numbers	red tape
variety	space	problems	paperwork
overload	noise	relations	communication problems
Emotional:	Flexibility to change fixed features	Co-workers:	Administrative:
significance		work relations	rules and regulations
actualization		sharing	policy influence
growth		time out	participation
		support	
		challenge	Role in the organization:
			role conflict
		Supervisors and administrators:	role ambiguity
			status disorder
		feedback	
		rewards	
		support	
		challenge	

variables that affect the cognitive sphere are the variety provided by the work environment and the frequency of cognitive overload.

The *physical* dimension of an environment includes, on the one hand, such fixed features as space, architectural structure, and noise, and on the other hand, the flexibility to change fixed features and suit them to one's own tastes and needs. The *social* dimension of the work environment includes all the people coming in direct contact with the individual, including service recipients and administrators. The *organizational* dimension of the work environment includes bureaucratic hassles, administrative features, and the role of the individual within the organization.

Even though some features in Table 11.1 may be misplaced and some other features that should have been included are not, still the table represents four critical dimensions of the work environment that separately and together have a crucial effect on the likelihood of the individual to burn out. A short description of these variables, together with research results documenting their relation to burnout, will now be presented.

The Psychological Dimension of the Work Environment

The emotional and cognitive spheres of people's work have a major impact on their psychological well-being. Emotional and cognitive features can be inherent in the work itself or be a part of the work environment. For example, while the job of a brain surgeon may be inherently more significant than the job of a supermarket checker, different supermarkets can provide the same checkers with markedly different levels of work significance. A member-owned consumer-oriented cooperative, fighting to provide a viable alternative to the large supermarket chains, is probably providing a more significant work environment than most regular supermarkets. It is this environmentally induced sense of significance that is the subject of the present discussion.

The psychological dimension of the work environment includes the cognitive and the emotional spheres. The cognitive sphere will be discussed first. It includes such variables as autonomy, variety, and overload.

Autonomy

The extent to which a certain work environment provides discretion and enables people to decide on their own how to do their work influences their sense of control over that environment. The sense of control mediates against stress and prevents burnout because it is associated with the ability to cope effectively, predict events, and determine what will happen. In one study (Singer & Glass, 1974) the abilities of two groups of workers to tolerate irritating levels of noise were compared. Members of one group worked under noise conditions but were given the option of pressing a button if the noise became too irritating; the other group did not have this option. Most of the people in the first group completed their work without pushing the button. When the work output was compared with that of the second group, it was found that those who worked in the noisy environment without the button made errors on reading tasks and arithmetic problems, showed little tolerance of frustration, and were unwilling to do favors for other people. People in the other group who were under equally adverse conditions, but who did have the option of pressing the button, showed almost none of these effects. The reason for the difference in productivity was the result of the difference between the two groups in perceived control.

Autonomy was found in several of our studies to be positively correlated with job satisfaction and negatively correlated with burnout. That is to say, the more autonomy, the less burnout. For example, in a sample of 198 mental retardation workers, the correlation between autonomy and burnout was $r = -.32$; in a sample of 52 Social Security Administration workers, the correlation was $r = -.35$ (both at $p < .05$).

Variety

All higher organisms actively seek variety in their environment and avoid monotonous environments. After eighteen months in solitary confinement as a suspected spy in France, Christopher Burney (1952) wrote, "I soon learned that variety is not the spice of life; it is the very stuff of life."

A major study made by the University of Michigan's Institute for Occupational Safety (Kaplan, 1975), involving over 2,000 people, found that boredom may produce stress as fast as, or perhaps even faster than, such work conditions as long hours, heavy workloads, and pressing responsibilities. Employees who reported a high degree of boredom in their work were likely to feel that their abilities were not being used well and that the job did not provide as much complexity as they would like.

Variety in the work environment enhances interest and challenge. It has been identified by industrial psychologists as a key factor in employee satisfaction, performance, and attendance. Variety was found in several of our studies to be negatively correlated with burnout: The more variety there was in the individual's work environment, the less likely that individual was to report experiencing burnout. For example, in a sample of 294 psychology students, the correlation between variety and burnout was $r = -.35$; in a sample of 277 professional women, the correlation was $r = -.32$ (both at $p < .05$).

Overload

Overload can be either subjective or objective (French & Caplan, 1973). Subjective overload refers to individual's feeling that he or she has too much work to do or that the work is too hard. Objective overload is the actual volume of work individuals are expected to process per unit of time. The number of telephone calls to answer, people to service, and patients to examine in a day are measurable indicators of objective overload. In this chapter, the focus is on objective overload and on the effect of such objective overload on the individual's strain and burnout.

A work environment can impose two different kinds of objective overload: a quantitative overload and a qualitative overload (Cooper & Marshall, 1976). A quantitative overload is the result of having too many tasks to accomplish per unit of time, while a qualitative overload is the result of having tasks that are too difficult for the individual. An example of a quantitative overload is the case of pediatricians providing primary care in health clinics serving poor and Third World communities. Their overload (and their subsequent burnout) most often result from having to see too many children every single day, even though most children come because of such routine problems as colds and ear infections. An example of qualitative overload is the case of pediatricians in hospital settings providing tertiary care, who feel that they do not have the required skills or knowledge to help a dying child (Pines, 1981a).

Time pressures and deadlines (lines beyond which lies death), exorbitant work demands (tightly scheduled work days, heavy travel, and simultaneous demands), and information overload are among the most stressful aspects of managerial work (Yates, 1979). Overload was repeatedly found in our studies to be a positive correlate of burnout. The more overload in the work environment (both quantitative and qualitative), the more likely were individuals to burn out. For example, in a sample of 52 Social Security Administration workers, the correlation was $r = .30$; in a sample of 725 human service professionals, the correlation was $r = .35$ (both $p < .05$).

Autonomy, variety, and overload all influence the *cognitive sphere* in the psychological dimension of the work environment. The second sphere in the psychological dimension is the *emotional sphere,* which includes such variables as significance, actualization, and growth.

Significance

The myth of Sisyphus describes the punishment inflicted on Sisyphus by the gods, wherein he was eternally condemned to push a large rock to the top of a mountain, whence the rock would roll down again. The gods had determined there could be no more dreadful punishment than futile and hopeless work.

One of the most common reasons for job dissatisfaction and turnover is the belief that the work has no significance, that it is meaningless and futile. Indeed, lack of significance was found in several of our studies to be a major cause of hopelessness, depression, and burnout: The more significance individuals have in their work, the less likely they are to burn out. For example, in a sample of 267 police officers and in a sample of 101 Israeli managers, the correlation between significance and burnout was $r = -.27$ ($p < .05$).

As noted earlier, some jobs are inherently more significant than others, yet within a given job, different work environments can enhance or diminish the individual's perceived sense of significance. In the case of the two home health and family service organizations presented earlier, while in one work significance was diminished by high turnover rates and the staff felt that they were unable to be of real help to clients, in the second, work significance was enhanced by a very supportive supervisor and a network of colleagues who helped reestablish each other's sense of meaning and significance whenever it was shaken by failure.

The area of job enrichment in industrial psychology is concerned with the redesign of work environments to include tasks and activities that promote the psychological involvement of the employees and their sense of significance (**Shapiro**). Examples of methods of job enrichment include giving a worker a whole job with an identifiable end product, allowing the individual or the team the freedom to set targets, and giving them the complete authority and discretion for their unit of work (see Appelbaum, 1981).

Actualization and Growth

"There is in every organism, including man, an underlying flow of movement toward constructive fulfillment of its inherent possibilities, a natural tendency toward growth," wrote Carol Rogers (1961). The human need for self-actualization and growth is a major theme in the writing of humanistic psychologists and several personality theorists (such as Maslow, 1962).

According to Fredrick Herzberg's motivation-hygiene theory, individuals are motivated when they are given opportunities for self-advancement, self-development, achievement recognition, and promotion arising from an interesting and demanding job (Herzberg et al., 1966). Thus, a work environment that enables individuals to actualize themselves and grow professionally is a work environment that should reduce rather than produce burnout. This contention was supported by several of our studies. In all of these studies, self-actualization on the job was negatively correlated with burnout (that is, the more self-actualization, the less burnout). For example, in the sample of 52 Social Security Administration employees, the correlation between self-actualization and burnout was $r = -.40$; in a sample of 205 professionals, the correlation was $-.28$ (both at $p < .05$).

The Physical Dimension of the Work Environment

There is a growing evidence that the physical quality of the work environment can have a major impact on people's mental and physical health (Evans, 1981). We found repeatedly that a comfortable environment at work was negatively correlated with burnout (that is, the more comfortable the environment, the less burnout). For example, in one study the correlation was $r = -.29$, ($p < .05$), while environmental pressures at work such as noise and uncomfortable setting were positively correlated with burnout (that is, the more noise, the more burnout; $r = .27$, $p < .05$). A work environment can be a source of numerous stressors; the ones mentioned most often and thus chosen for discussion in this chapter include architectural dysfunction, crowding, and noise.

Architectural Structure

Craig Zimring (1981), who combines interests in architecture and psychology, views stress as resulting from a misfit between individuals' needs and environmental attributes. The severity of the stress and its long-term consequences for the individual are affected by such things as the importance of the misfit to the individual, the chronic or acute nature of the misfit, and the strategies available to the individual for ameliorating it. According to Zimring, the built environment can stress both directly and indirectly: directly, by supporting or thwarting work-related goals; indirectly, by making desired social interaction easier or more difficult to achieve.

Space

In any given work space, individuals must manage the environment in order to achieve their goals. When other people are a part of that given space, there must be a coordination of everyone's needs for resources, activities, interaction, and space. As the number of people populating a certain space increases, the task of managing and coordinating that environment becomes more difficult and more likely to drain energy that otherwise would be available to attain work goals (Epstein, 1981). Crowded, inadequate space increases the tension and the stress experienced by both service recipients and staff.

Jerome E. Singer and David C. Glass (1974) discuss the important principles that determine how environmental stresses, such as noise and crowding, affect us. They note, for example, that most environmental stressors are not intense enough to cause immediate physical damage. The discomfort is felt immediately; however, the physical impact of the stressors is cumulative and long-range. The social and emotional context of an environmental stressor is as important as the physical propensity itself. When people are on their own turf, crowded and noisy conditions do not have the same impact as when they are on someone else's turf. A noisy and crowded family reunion in one's home is quite different from a noisy, crowded affair in a stranger's home. Particular psychological or social factors can ease or aggravate the effect of an environmental stress such as crowding. All these factors have to be taken into account when studying the relationship between crowding and burnout.

Noise

Noise is a psychological concept and is defined as sound that is unwanted by the listener because it is unpleasant, bothersome, interferes with important activities, or is believed to be psychologically harmful (Kryter, 1970).

Several field studies have artificially increased environmental noise levels and assessed the effects on people's behavior and performance. In one study (Ward & Suedfeld, 1973), highway traffic noise was broadcast outside a large university classroom building. As a result, less student participation and attention were observed when compared to a no-noise control group. Other studies reported a positive correlation between school noise level and the percentage of students scoring one or more years below grade level, and indicated that there are negative effects after the noise exposure is terminated. The cumulative and long-range effects of noise as well as the importance of its social and emotional context are relevant to this relationship with burnout.

Flexibility to Change Fixed Features

In addition to the absolute quality of the fixed features, another crucial element in the physical dimension of the work environment is the flexibility to change those fixed features. Some people are more sensitive to noise than others; some like large open areas while others feel comfortable in small, enclosed areas. In our research, physical environments that were pleasant and designed to meet workers' tastes, needs, and preferences, were found to be negatively correlated with burnout. For example, in the study of 205 professionals mentioned several times earlier, the correlation was $r = -.29$ ($p < .05$). Albert Mehrabian (1976) eloquently explains why the same kind of environment is not good for everyone: "Just as you don't make people wear the same shoe size, you shouldn't make them live and work in the same kind of environment. Working and living spaces should accommodate as much as possible the individual's needs and preferences and be as personalized as possible."

The Social Dimension
of the Work Environment

Most human service professionals, by definition of their occupational choice, are oriented more toward people than toward things and tend to view themselves as caring, sensitive, and understanding. In every burnout workshop I conducted (see Pines & Aronson with Kafry, 1981: Appendix 1), when I asked participants why they chose their particular profession, their listed reasons invariably included such items as "I like people," "All my life people came to me when they needed someone to talk to," "I always wanted to work with people," and "I am a people's kind of person."

Because human service professionals care so much about people, they are particularly sensitive to the social dimension of their work environment. Thus, the social dimension plays a major role in determining their likelihood to burn out: When the social environment is noxious, burnout will occur, even if other things are acceptable; if the social environment is very supportive, burnout will not occur, even if the work itself is extremely stressful. The case of the two home health and family service organizations demonstrates this point well: Even though the organizations were very similar in both function and structure, they were very different in terms of their social environment and consequently very different in terms of their levels of burnout.

The social dimension of the work environment includes all the poeple coming in direct contact with the individual as part of his or her work. For most human service professionals, the social environment includes clients, co-workers, supervisors, and administrators. Each person can, at least potentially, impose certain demands on the individual and provide certain rewards. The ratio of demands to rewards is an important determinant of burnout.

Service Recipients, Customers, Clients

The social and interpersonal dimensions of the workload are important. Working directly with clients, service recipients, and customers is often stressful. There are many different ways in which recipients can influence the physical, emotional, and mental well-being of a service-providing individual. The most straightforward impact results from their number, the seriousness of their condition, and the relationship between them and the service provider.

Numbers. The quality of interactions in many human services is affected by the number of people for whom the professional is providing care. As this number increases—whether it be number of pupils, clients, patients, inmates, or welfare recipients—so does the cognitive, sensory, and emotional overload of the professional. When caseloads are exceedingly heavy, professionals who try not to compromise the quality of the care they provide can get extremely discouraged and frustrated. In a study of mental health settings I did in collaboration with Christina Maslach (Pines & Maslach, 1978), for example, we found that the larger the ratio of mental patients to staff, the more staff members wanted to quit their jobs ($r = .46$, $p = .001$).

Problems. The severity or complexity of the problems presented by the service recipients can have a negative effect on the human service professional, especially when the service involves a prolonged and direct contact. This is also true with customers. The most stressful cases are well known for all those working within a certain occupational field. One of the most stressful work environments for nurses, for example, is the burned children's unit. In mental hospitals, the locked wards are often more demanding emotionally than the open wards. In schools for the deaf and blind, the most difficult cases are those involving kids who are also retarded or otherwise physically handicapped. In business, it is customer relations.

In several of our studies we found that the severity of the problems presented by the service recipients was positively correlated with burnout. For example, in one study involving 52 Social Security Administration employees, it was found that dealing with problem cases was rated as the most stressful activity, an activity much more stressful than just providing information to the public ($\overline{X} = 5.1$ versus $\overline{X} = 3.1$). Similarly, in the study of burnout in mental health settings mentioned earlier, it was found that the higher the percentage of schizophrenics in the patient population, the more burned out the staff was.

Relations. The relations between the staff and customers or service recipients affect the work atmosphere and thus can produce or reduce the staff's work-related stress. In the first home health and family service organization, described earlier, the stress experienced by the professional staff resulted from the added measure of anger and frustration expressed by the clients. In the study of mental health settings (Pines & Maslach, 1978), it was found that the better the staff-patient relations were, the more staff members liked their work ($r = .23$, $p < .05$); the more they were likely to say that self-fulfillment was the reason for their staying in mental health ($r = .60$, $p = .001$); with time, the more positive their attitudes became toward other staff members ($r = .26$, $p = .31$); the more "good days" they had in their work ($r = .25$, $p = .011$); the more successful they felt on the job ($r = .23$, $p = .042$); the more highly they rated the institution ($r = .32$, $p = .006$); and the more positive were their descriptions of the patients.

Co-workers

The differences described earlier between the two home health and family service organizations were mostly due to differences in the relations between staff members. Many different components contribute to the collegial atmosphere of the work environment: for example, work relations, sharing, time out, and support.

Work Relations. The nature of the work relationships can either be a major source of stress at work or a central factor in individual and organizational health. Difficult relationships at work were reported as causing symptoms associated with extensive stress, such as diarrhea, pain in the neck or lower back, anxiety, and insomnia. As Jeree Yates (1979) notes, "Certain associates can *literally* be a 'pain in the neck.'"

In the study of mental health settings mentioned thrice before (Pines & Maslach, 1978), it was found that the better the work relations, the more professionals liked their work ($r = .38$, $p = .001$); the more they felt free to express themselves ($r = .41$, $p = .001$); the more they were likely to be staying in mental health for self-fulfillment ($r = .41$, $p = .040$); the more successful they felt on the job ($r = .31$, $p = .008$); the more "good days" they had at work ($r = .27$, $p = .025$); the more likely they were to confer with others ($r = .27$, $p = .025$); the higher they rated their particular institution ($r = .49$, $p = .001$); and the more consistently positive they were in their descriptions of patients.

Sharing. Sharing and team work can help diffuse many work stresses. For example, in the second home health and family service organization, the fact that the therapist consulted her colleagues about her suicidal patient helped not only her decision about what therapeutic approach to adopt, but also her coping with the extreme emotional stress of his actual suicide attempt. Many psychiatrists, clinical psychologists, and counselors who could have done much better financially in private practice work in a hospital or a clinic setting because they need to share their work stresses and joys with a supportive group of colleagues.

In addition to serving the function of diffusion of responsibility, work sharing can increase challenge, variety, and power. Work sharing was found in every study of ours in which it was measured to be a significant negative correlate of burnout: The more work sharing, the less burnout. For example, in a sample of 87 American managers, the correlation between work sharing and burnout was $r = -.37$; in a sample of 129 social service workers and in a sample of 205 professionals, it was $r = -.28$ (both at $p < .05$).

Time Out. Confinement to work was defined as difficulties in getting away from the job even for a short while, and proved to be correlated with mental stress experienced by personnel in Swedish health care organizations (Wahlund & Nerell, 1977). Almost three times as many persons who were "experiencing frequent stress" felt they were unable to leave their duties for even five or ten minutes. Twice as many of those who said their work was initially strenuous felt they were unable to leave for half an hour, an hour, or a day at short notice. This situation is particularly crippling for individuals involved with a hectic pace, under constant pressure to achieve high productivity, and at the same time responsible for the maintenance of patient care. Perceived mental stress was found in the Swedish study to be related to reluctance to go to work; being too tired after work to engage in anything active, such as hobbies or meeting friends and acquaintances; difficulties in getting one's mind off work during leisure hours; serious consideration of changing jobs, taking drugs, sedatives, and tranquilizers, and smoking; and feeling weariness and fatigue in connection with work.

The availability of time out—which enables individuals to withdraw temporarily from stressful work situations and do some other, less stressful work while others cover for them—is a very important aspect of the social dimension in the work environment. It not only reduces stress at its peak for the individual, but also strengthens ties of trust and commitment between different staff members. The more available time out, we found, the less burnout: In a study involving 277 professional women and in a study of 129 social service workers, the correlation between burnout and the availability of time out was $r = -.27$ ($p < .05$).

Support. One of the most important functions co-workers can provide for each other is support **(Shapiro).** Everyone needs support during times of crisis and appreciation during times of success. These kinds of support and appreciation are most valuable when coming from someone who understands all the intricasies of the work one does, that is, someone who does a similar work. Co-workers can, but do not always, provide each other with support and appreciation. As the example of two home health and family service organizations demonstrated, co-workers determine whether the work atmosphere will be hostile, stressful, and burnout-producing or friendly, supportive, and burnout-preventing.

A supportive network of colleagues is especially crucial when work is emotionally demanding and when it involves making critical decisions that can affect the life and well-being of other people. In a recent study involving 111 elementary school teachers, it was found that the availability of such technical support was negatively correlated with burnout; the more technical support, the less burnout ($r = -.43$, $p < .05$).

Supervisors and Administrators

The relationship between individuals and their supervisors and their supervisors and administrators is another important part of the social dimension in a work environment **(Shapiro).** Several studies focused on the impact of leadership on workers' work stress and satisfaction. One of these studies (House, Filley, & Gujarati, 1971) explored the relationship between individuals' perceptions of their immediate supervisors' behavior and their satisfaction from their work and organization. The data indicated that supervisors' demonstrated consideration for their subordinates was highly correlated with the various indices of job satisfaction. The degree to which supervisors set clear objectives and procedures on the job *with* their subordinates was also positively related to satisfaction (democratic leadership style).

French and Caplan (1972), whose work on organizational stress was mentioned earlier, identified the quality of relation that people have with their supervisors (in addition to peers and subordinates) as a key organizational stance. They defined poor relations as those that involve low trust, low supportiveness, and low interest in listening and dealing with problems. They discovered that poor relations were often the result of role ambiguity, inadequate communication, and role conflict **(Carroll & White).** Once established, poor relations (especially with supervisors) tend to produce psychological stress in the form of low job satisfaction and belief in the existence of job-related threats to one's well-being.

In our studies, relationships with supervisors were found repeatedly to be highly and negatively correlated with burnout. In one study, for example, involving 52 Social Security Administration employees, the correlation between relations with the supervisors and burnout was $r = -.56$, $p < .05$.

There are several ways in which supervisors and administrators can influence the psychological well-being of workers and the general atmosphere in a work environment. Since Constance **Shapiro's** paper deals with those in detail, only brief mention will be made of the most important ones, namely, providing feedback, rewards, support, and challenge.

Feedback. The best feedback is immediate, appropriate, and provided by someone who is in a position to understand the full scale of one's performance, such as a supervisor or an administrator. Feedback about work provides individuals with information about their levels of performance and success and is crucial for their sense of meaningfulness and achievement at work.

Lack of feedback from supervisors and administrators is a damaging organizational stressor. As Jaree Yates (1979: 55) notes, "Nothing seems to bother people more than just being ignored. We appear to prefer any response—even a negative one—to no response at all. Not only are people distressed when they are met with unresponsiveness; they are also discouraged from taking any initiative in the future. . . . Management's lack of responsiveness is always identified as a major stressor—it doesn't seem to make any difference what kind of work the organization is doing or whether it's in the public, private, or not-for profit sector."

The degree to which people received information about their success and performance level was found in several of our studies to be significantly and negatively correlated with burnout. In the sample of 129 social service workers, the correlation between burnout and social feedback was $r = -.36$; in the sample of 198 mental retardation workers, the correlation was $-.32$ (both p at $< .05$). The more feedback received from supervisors and administrators, the less burnout.

Rewards. In addition to providing straight feedback about performance, supervisors can affect organizational morale by adequate distribution of rewards. A reward can be defined as an object, situation, or verbal statement that is presented upon completion of a successful performance of a task and that tends to increase the probability of the behavior involved. Rewards include pay; extrinsic advantages such as benefits, security, and promotional opportunities; and intrinsic advantages such as appreciation and recognition. Lack of rewards was found in several of our studies to be highly correlated with burnout; the less rewards, the more burnout. In a sample of 101 Israeli managers, the correlation between burnout and adequate rewards was $r = -.35$; in the sample of 52 Social Security Administration employees, it was $r = -.47$ (both p at $< .05$).

Unfortunately, in many large bureaucratic organizations the rewards distribution is very slow and inappropriate, resulting in the loss of a very powerful burnout antidote. Even when other job conditions are stressful, if employees feel adequately rewarded for their extra efforts they are less likely to burn out.

Support. Another crucial function for supervisors and administrators is providing their staff and organization with professional and administrative support. This support is independent of the support provided by colleagues and is equally important; in some large bureaucratic organizations it is even more important. In the case of the two home health and family service organizations discussed throughout this chapter, the fact that the head of one of the organizations was extremely supportive of her staff had a major impact on the levels of burnout, job satisfaction, and staff morale in the agency.

Challenge. Supervisors and administrators can enhance significance, learning, and growth by constructively challenging their subordinates. A challenge by a supervisor, like a challenge by a co-worker, needs to be for the benefit of the person being challenged rather than the person doing the challenging. Supervisors who challenge themselves before they challenge their staff can provide a positive role model. An example of such a challenge was provided by the director who, during a case presentation, admitted uncertainty about the difficult case she was treating and thus enabled other staff members to do the same, to the benefit of the staff, the patients, and the organization as a whole.

By utilizing feedback, rewards, challenge, and support appropriately, supervisors can have a major influence on the likelihood of their staff to cope with burnout successfully.

The Organizational Dimension of the Work Environment

The organizational dimension of the work environment and its effect on workers' performance and job satisfaction have been the focus of most writings in the field of industrial and organizational psychology (**Golembiewski**). Variables that are burnout correlates and that are built into the organizational dimension of the work environment include bureaucratic hassles and administrative features as well as the role of the individual in the organization.

Bureaucratic Features

Nowadays, the word "bureaucracy" has acquired a negative connotation as a dehumanizing work environment marked by a rigid hierarchical structure and many unnecessary rules and regulations—a cumbersome and inefficient paper-eating monster.

Most managers and human service professionals, without proper warning and training, end up working within some kind of bureaucratic organization, whether a business, a hospital, a school system, or a welfare organization. By definition of their size and complexity, most of these bureaucratic organizations are slow and unresponsive. They tend to be more self-serving than public-serving and thus to be blamed for causing burnout in idealistic and caring professionals. The problems mentioned most often as burnout-causing among the bureaucratic features of the work environment include red tape, paperwork, and communication problems. All three were found to be significant correlates of burnout. In the study involving 724 human service professionals, the correlation between burnout and such hassles as red tape, paperwork, and communication problems was $r = .26$; in the study involving 101 Israeli managers, it was $r = .40$ (both p at $< .05$).

Red Tape and Paperwork. Many who quit their work in large bureaucratic social service organizations say they are driven out by the frustration of trying to make an inept system responsive to client's needs. Such organizations often generate so much paperwork that workers complain they are shuffling papers instead of treating or serving people. A special federal commission on paperwork, which examined one social service application process, described it as needlessly complex, unduly burdensome, inefficient, inequitable, and unnecessarily costly. The official concern for forms and routines creates special problems for the more caring and idealistic human service professionals, who feel they are becoming clerks instead of professionals. Paperwork is viewed by most of them as a needless waste of their time and emotional energy and as a senseless obstacle to their goal achievement. Ironically, good records are important to effective case handling, supervision, quality control, and management, but they are seldom developed to support the clinical or business process.

Communication Problems. Bureaucratic organizations are often built as rigid hierarchical structures that create communication problems between staff members. Frequently, there are many levels of administrators and many levels of workers in the organization. Caseworkers are monitored by supervisors who, in turn, are monitored by other supervisors. At the top are administrators who may be unfamiliar with the problems of the workers seven steps below. As a result, direction is inadequate and communication difficult. Because of inadequate communication, individuals feel isolated and deindividuated. The problems can be on vertical communication lines—from supervisors and administrators down to and up from the front-line workers—or they can be on horizontal communication lines, between co-workers.

Both kinds are well-known bureaucratic hassles, both are stressful, and both can, and do, enhance the process of burnout.

Administrative Influence

The administrative influence in a certain work environment is often transmitted via rules, regulations, and policy influences. All three when excessive were found in our studies to produce burnout; the more senseless the rules and regulations and the more arbitrary the policy influences, the more burnout. In the sample of 724 human service professionals, the correlation between bureaucratic interference and burnout was $r = .24$; in the sample of 101 Israeli managers, it was $r = .31$ (both p at $< .05$). Another important variable mediating the administrative influence is the perceived level of participation in organizational policy- and decision-making.

Rules and Regulations. When one examines bureaucratic rules and regulations, one often discovers that while some are too vague, others are too detailed. Both excesses serve to frustrate the goal achievement of the individual and thus to enhance burnout. "Every organization of any size has a myriad of rules, policies, and procedures that make sense only to the person who created them," writes Jeree Yates. "There may have been problems that arose because of a lack of a specific procedure, so several procedures and rules were created to cover a situation that probably would occur only with the greatest infrequency" (Yates, 1979: 53).

Policy Influence. In a 1978 investigation of a government service department, it was noted that the work environment in the department was often bewildering to workers (Bacon, 1978). There were frequent alterations of old programs and additions of new programs that created confusion. Just keeping abreast of policies that were forever being revised by Congress, the Department of Health, Education, and Welfare, state legislators, and state and local administrators was an extremely time-consuming task (see **Cherniss** on this problem). While it is usually difficult in any large bureaucracy to identify the source of certain regulations or policy influences, in a government agency it can be nearly impossible. This unclear responsibility keeps workers from effectively stating and correcting their grievances.

In one of our studies, employees in a social service organization were asked to what extent the bureaucracy, administration or organization interfered with their goal achievement. High degrees of administrative interference were correlated with high degrees of burnout ($N = 53, r = .22$). Other studies confirmed the correlation between destructive policy influence and burnout. For example, in the study of 724 human service professionals, the correlation was $r = .24, p < .05$.

Participation. Not having the opportunity to participate in decisions that affect one's work is another organizational stressor and burnout correlate. French and Caplan (1972) summarized the findings of several different studies on the affect of participation. They concluded that of all the stresses they considered, low participation has the greatest harmful effect on job satisfaction and threat. People's psychological well-being is influenced by the amount and quality of their participation in those decisions that have to do with important aspects of their work.

In the study on child-care workers done in collaboration with Christina Maslach (Maslach & Pines, 1977a), it was found that staff members who felt they had more input into the organization's policies liked their job more ($r = .36$, $p = .001$); felt more free to express themselves on the job ($r = .50$, $p = .001$); had more sense of control ($r = .42$, $p = .001$) and more success in achieving their goals ($r = .25$, $p = .030$); and rated their organization higher ($r = .39$, $p = .001$). In addition, the case of the two home health and family service organizations demonstrates how a democratic, high-participation work environment can reduce burnout.

The effect of participation on job satisfaction is related to perceived sense of control and to those studies (some of which were mentioned earlier) in which it was found that the greater the belief in the ability to influence the environment, the lower the reported job strain and the higher the reported work satisfaction.

Role in the Organization

In the previous two organizational features (the bureaucratic and the administrative), the focus was on the organization. In the next feature, the focus is on the individual: an individual whose work environment is characterized by role conflict or role ambiguity, whose career development is adequate or inadequate in terms of such things as promotion and security.

Role conflict exists whenever an individual in a particular role is torn by conflicting demands. The conflicting demands can be imposed by the same source, such as the demand to provide service to a large caseload without affecting the quality of the service provided. And conflicting demands can be imposed by different people, such as a supervisor and an administrator, both demanding, at the same point in time, that different tasks be accomplished. Robert Kahn and his colleagues at the University of Michigan (Kahn, 1978) found that incompatibility of job demands tended to be especially high in positions where the jobholders had the responsibility for dealing simultaneously with some people inside the organization and some outside it.

Role conflict has serious consequences for the individual's subjective experience of stress. In several of our studies it was found that the more conflicting demands imposed by a certain work environment, the more burnout. For example, in two studies, one involving 724 human service professionals and the other involving 87 American managers, the correlation between conflicting demands and burnout was $r = .31$ ($p < .05$).

Role ambiguity exists when individuals have inadequate information about their work roles, the work objectives associated with the role, colleagues' expectations of the work role, and the scope and responsibilities of the job. Kahn and his colleagues found that people who suffered from role ambiguity had lower job satisfaction, higher job-related tension, greater futility, and lower self-confidence. French and Caplan found that role ambiguity was significantly related to low job satisfaction, a feeling of job-related threat to one's mental and physical well-being, and such indicators of physiological stress as increased blood pressure and pulse. Margolis and his colleagues, in a representative national sample involving 1496 subjects, found that role ambiguity was correlated with such stress indicators as depressed mood, lowered self-esteem, life dissatisfaction, job dissatisfaction, low motivation to work, and intention to leave the job. These factors clearly can cause many of the negative experiences identified in this chapter as symptoms of burnout.

Status Disorders. A different set of environmental stressors built into the role of the individual in the work environment is related to status disorders in career development. Career development, according to Cary L. Cooper and Judy Marshall (1976), refers to the impact of overpromotion, underpromotion, status incongruence, and lack of job security. In their literature review of occupational sources of stress, they mention the various physical, emotional, and mental disorders associated with inappropriate career development. For example, they mention case studies of individuals showing behavioral disorders as a result of being either overpromoted (when a person has reached the peak of his or her abilities with little possibility of further development and is given responsibility exceeding his or her capacity) or underpromoted (not given responsibility in accordance with ability level). In each case, the progression of the disorder was from minor psychological symptoms (palpitations, episodes of panic, and the like) to marked psychosomatic complaints and mental illness. In a U.S. Navy research program investigating the effects of status congruence (defined as the matching of individuals' advancement with their experience and abilities), it was found that status incongruency was significant to job dissatisfaction and psychiatric illness (Arthur & Gunderson, 1965).

Status disorders have a negative effect on both the psychological and the social dimensions of an individual's work environment and thus increase burnout.

Positive and Negative Work Features

As the reader has no doubt noticed, some of the work environment features presented in Table 11.1 are positive (such as significance, autonomy, and support) and some are negative (such as overload, red tape, and paperwork). Stress literature has concentrated on the presence of negative conditions as a source of stress and has largely ignored stress reactions that result from a lack of positive conditions. Two studies done in collaboration with Allen D. Kanner (Kanner, Kafry, & Pines, 1978; Pines & Kanner, 1982) emphasize the importance of lack of positive conditions as a source of stress and an antecedent of burnout. Both studies demonstrate that lack of positive work features is significantly correlated with burnout and work dissatisfaction, independently of the presence of negative work features. The implication from these findings for both individuals and organizations committed to the ideal of a work environment without burnout is that working toward such an environmental requires (1) *maximizing positive work features* (such as organizational flexibility, degree of autonomy granted to staff, pleasant work conditions; optimal variety, emphasis on work significance and personal growth, time out during periods of stress, and supportive and challenging colleagial network), and (2) *minimizing negative work features* (such as large ratio of clients to staff, unlimited bureaucratic interference, red tape, paperwork, senseless rules and regulations, role conflict, role ambiguity, and status disorders).

Is a Work Environment Without Burnout an Impossible Goal?

The preceding discussion of work environment and burnout represents a social-psychological perspective. Rather than explain burnout in dispositional terms (the particular vulnerabilities of a certain individual), it focused attention on situational factors (those environmental features that cause burnout). The social-psychological approach does not deny the importance of individual traits, characteristics, and disposition; rather, it suggests that burnout has a major environmental component.

It was suggested that in addition to such general variables as historical trends, culture-specific influences, and political considerations, every work environment has four dimensions: psychological, physical, social, and organizational. Throughout the chapter, data were presented in an attempt to demonstrate the effects of a variety of environmental factors within those four dimensions. However, it is important to note that in addition to their specific effects, independent of each other, these environmental variables also interact with and affect each other. Thus, for example, high levels of participation in the organizational dimension are likely to have a positive effect on perceived autonomy in the psychological dimension. Again, good relations with co-workers in the social dimension can reduce negative impacts of noise and crowding in the physical dimension. If the preceding discussion convincingly made the point that each of the twenty-eight individual variables presented has an effect on burnout, that effect is even greater when all the intercorrelations between variables are taken into consideration.

Does that mean that a work environment without burnout is a possible goal? Unfortunately, the answer is a qualified no, because the discussion does not take into account the individuals in the particular work environment—their personal histories, physical and emotional makeups, strengths, weaknesses, and strategies for coping with burnout. Yet, as the research presented throughout the article strongly suggests, in spite of all individual differences, the work environment has a crucial effect on burnout. While individual differences may determine how soon one will burn out, how extreme the experience will be, and what will be its consequences, the work environment determines the likelihood of burnout across the board. If a totally positive work environment does not assure a complete lack of burnout, a totally negative work environment will most definitely cause it, even in the most energetic and highly committed individuals. Thus, both the individual and the organization interested in preventing burnout cannot err by focusing their attention on the work environment. Achieving a work environment without burnout requires a conscious and well-coordinated effort of both the individual and the organization to maximize positive and minimize negative work features, so that the work environment will prevent rather than produce burnout.

12

Creative Supervision
An Underutilized Antidote

CONSTANCE HOENK SHAPIRO

Most work on burnout focuses on individual stress management techniques (**Tubesing & Tubesing**) as the main antidote for burnout. Thus, since the term "antidote" conjures up images of medicinal cures for individual ailments, it is important to concur with **Carroll and White** that the origins of burnout lie not only in the individual or solely in the environment, but, rather, in the interaction between them. Creative supervisory practices operate directly to facilitate healthy interaction between the individual and the work setting.

For example, supervisors can have a profound influence on many of the on-the-job characteristics correlated with low staff burnout. These include:

- leadership that provides support, structure, and information;
- communication that is timely, appropriate, and accurate;
- an environment that is planful, efficient, and orderly;
- rules and policies that are explicit;
- workers who have freedom to be self-sufficient and make their own decisions;
- room for staff creativity and innovation;
- support and nurturing from supervisory staff;
- manageable job pressure; and
- peer networks of friendship and support among staff.

Such characteristics have been subject to research on burnout in child abuse and neglect agencies (Berkeley Planning Associates, 1977) and have been mentioned in articles on burnout in many other organizational settings. Given that sensitive and high-quality supervision can mitigate inherently stressful work conditions and, further, can promote some conditions known

213

to reduce burnout, it is appropriate to scrutinize the role of the supervisor in the organization as a potential antidote for burnout.

Background

Supervision at its best is far broader than the assignment of work and the monitoring of its completion. Efforts to enhance work-related skills, to promote self-esteem, to encourage peer support, and to maintain clear channels of communication are important for supervisors in any organizational setting, including industry, hospitals, jails, schools, religious organizations, the military, and social service agencies.

Historically, the identification of burnout is a relatively recent phenomenon. The roots of burnout can be discerned in research on occupational tedium (Pines & Kafry, 1978), job satisfaction (Weinberger, 1970; Locke, 1976), high staff turnover (Kermish & Kushin, 1969; Podell, 1967), overload (Frankenhaeuser & Gardell, 1976), and organizational stress (French & Kaplan, 1972). As the literature on burnout has proliferated and research directions have evolved, a variety of professions have been identified as vulnerable to burnout. Lawyers (Maslach & Jackson, 1978), police (Maslach & Jackson, 1979), child-care and day-care workers (Freudenberger, 1977a; Mattingly, 1977; Maslach & Pines, 1977a), child protective workers (Martin & Klaus, 1979; Daley, 1979; Shannon & Saleebey, 1980), mental health professionals (Maslach & Pines, 1977b; Pines & Maslach, 1978a), medical professionals (Fox, 1980; Patrick, 1979; Gray-Toft, 1980), and educators (Walsh, 1979; Hendrickson, 1979; Reed, 1979) are among the professionals whose work places them at risk with regard to burnout. Other resources can be found in the consolidated references at the end of this volume.

The situation in the helping professions is of particular interest because, as Hayes (1981) points out:

> These professions make heavy demands upon workers who perform services that deal with people's problems day in and day out. The workers are constantly confronted with the reality of human suffering and the seemingly limitless number of persons in need.

Much of the current literature on burnout emphasizes the psychological and emotional impact of the helping relationship as predominant in the burnout syndrome. A few studies (Hayes, 1981; Pines & Kafry, 1978) focus on the organizational context in which burnout occurs. It is apparent from these two perspectives that a systems or ecological approach can shift the focus from the individual's ability to cope with a demanding situation to the individual in the context of his or her environment. Such a perspective highlights the interlocking and interactive components that persons experience in the work setting; assumes that a change in one part of the system will generate changes in other parts; and recognizes that systems strive to establish a dynamic equilibrium. Utilizing a systems perspective allows one to appreciate that any behavior in the work setting, whether facilitative, abrasive, or passive, will have an impact on other components of the system. The ability of a supervisor to detect such influences and to intervene at appropriate opportunities can greatly influence how individuals in the system feel about one another and about their work.

Organizationally, supervisors are in an ideal position to influence internal and external characteristics found in the work environment. Not only can they serve as advocates for their staff by addressing bureaucratic sources of burnout, but they can also influence, on an interpersonal level, staff who may be experiencing symptoms of burnout. In a report on child protective demonstration projects, Berkeley Planning Associates (1977) found that those projects in which workers reported inadequate supervision had the highest incidence of burnout. This is probably also true in other work settings, since supervisory functions are largely generic.

Supervisory Functions

At the interface between the individual and the organization, supervisors need to utilize specific skills in order to reduce the impact of burnout on their staff. Unfortunately, many persons are promoted into supervisory positions by virtue of competence in their professional roles, not by virtue of supervisory knowledge and skills.

Supervisors are at risk of having divided loyalties until they establish their roles and demonstrate their levels of competence in the organizational setting. Once role clarity is achieved and the supervisor feels equal to the task of moving beyond administrative routines to creativity, he or she can serve a crucial function in reducing stress. Such stressors as communication barriers, unclear expectations, lack of flexibility within the job structure, and inadequate or inappropriate training opportunities are ones the creative supervisor should address in efforts to reduce the potential for burnout in the work setting. These are discussed below.

Facilitating Communication

Clear communications reduce stress. In this context, supervisors facilitate communication with supervisees, create opportunities for peer support, and effectively utilize formal organizational channels. All three functions require a comprehensive view of the importance of open communication in the total work environment, an understanding of common problem areas, and a refusal to engage in disruptive interactions.

Reducing Organizational Games

For example, the imbalance of power and authority often causes supervisors and supervisees to engage in a series of games with one another in an effort to equalize or redistribute power (Hawthorne, 1975; Kadushin, 1968). Berne (1964) defines games as "an ongoing series of complementary ulterior transactions—superficially plausible but with a concealed motivation." Games can take many forms, but the one aspect all games have in common is the need for two players in order for one person to achieve a payoff. A supervisor who is alert to the game phenomenon is in an ideal position to refuse to be a partner and, further, to elicit for discussion the issues that precipitated gamesmanlike behavior by a supervisee. However, supervisors are, themselves, vulnerable to initiating games in which they expect their supervisees to be willing partners.

Hawthorne (1975) identifies supervisory games as falling into the categories of abdication and power. The payoff of both categories is avoidance of a clear definition and exercise of supervisory authority. Hawthorne describes games of abdication as occurring when the supervisor deliberately relinquishes authority, manipulates the circumstances so that he or she is unable to exercise authority, projects the responsibility elsewhere, or uses inappropriate kinds of authority. Games of power, on the other hand, are characterized by supervisory strategies that convey such messages as "Remember who's boss," "I'll tell on you," "Father (or mother) knows best," and "I know you really can't do it without me."

The energy and mutual frustration expended on games can contribute to the emotional exhaustion that leaves a staff member vulnerable to burnout. Strategies for combating the misguided energy spent on games can vary, depending on the readiness of supervisor and supervisee to communicate more forthrightly. A primary strategy is for the supervisor to examine his or her behavior for evidence of gamesmanship. If certain behaviors are engaged in with the explicit purpose of abdicating responsibility or maintaining a power imbalance, the supervisor must come to terms with his or her need to exercise control by covert strategies. Ceasing to play games when they are recognized as ploys is one way of bringing supervisory communications to a more open and honest level. The refusal of a supervisee to play a game initiated by a supervisor could have the same effect of interrupting the dynamics before both parties become entrenched in supervisory ploys.

Supervisees initiate games too, often as a way of avoiding dependence, defending against feelings of inadequacy, and reducing the power disparity within the supervisory relationship. A supervisor who short-circuits a staff member's efforts to play games will automatically stop the game. It is to be hoped that the supervisor will follow interruption of a game by exploring the need for gamesmanship in the supervisory relationship. Once the staff member acknowledges feelings of inadequacy, competition, and loss of control that motivate the need to initiate and play games, it may be possible for both supervisor and supervisee to deal openly in their work together with the issues at hand, rather than expending energy on elaborate and time-consuming games.

The use of assertive behavior in the supervisory relationship holds potential promise for accomplishing the goal of open and straightforward communication. Lange and Jakubowski (1976: 38) define assertion as "standing up for personal rights and expressing thoughts, feelings and beliefs in direct, honest and appropriate ways which respect the rights of other people." Goals in assertiveness training may include the expression of negative feelings, such as anger and resentment, as well as facilitating the expression of positive feelings, such as affection or praise. Shapiro (1981a) reports that social work students who were taught assertiveness techniques were able to generalize assertive responses to a range of hypothetical supervisory situations. Such should be included in professional training **(Wilder & Plutchik)** and in the continuing education of both staff and supervisors.

Clarifying Work Expectations

Another aspect of the need for clear supervisor-supervisee communication is in the orientation to the job and the work setting for new staff members. Clear expectations regarding work roles, learning goals, and evaluation criteria should characterize the earliest contacts between supervisor and supervisee.

Supervisees will want to know what is expected of them in their work. Formal expectations are defined in various places in each work setting. A knowledge of agency rules and regulations, bureaucratic channels, policies, and procedures provides a reassuring amount of concrete information for the new staff member. In addition, more informal expectations, such as use of autonomy, exercise of initiative, collaboration with other staff, definition of professionalism, and observance of ethical issues, will need to be explored by the new staff member, both through supervision and in interactions with other staff.

Enhancing Work-Related Skills

Although many persons view supervision as an opportunity for guidance on specific work-related tasks, the creative supervisor will also view it as an opportunity to increase the supervisee's competence through encouraging the application of theoretical knowledge to practice situations. Clearly, the first step in this process is to ascertain the existing knowledge base of the supervisee. Subsequent discussion should focus on what skills or theoretical knowledge the supervisee would like to master, with the supervisor identifying what learning opportunities exist on the supervisee's workload for applying new theoretical knowledge and skills. A portion of each supervisory session should be devoted to discussion of progress toward specific learning goals, so that both supervisor and supervisee have a sense of forward motion in learning, even though work responsibilities may be tedious, routine, frustrating, or discouraging.

One method of specifying learning goals is through the use of an explicit *contract* between supervisor and supervisee. It is not unusual for professionals to use contracts with clients in helping relationships; inasmuch as supervision is a model of a helping relationship, the positive experience of utilizing a contract in that context may encourage the staff member to use contracts in other aspects of his or her work experience as well. Contracts have been found to reduce anxiety that is an inherent aspect of many beginning relationships as well as to mitigate any existing power imbalance. Contracts can help the parties involved to prioritize issues and thus to gain a sense of direction for their work together.

Maluccio and Marlow (1974) characterize contracts as having four essential components: mutual agreement, differential participation in the intervention process, reciprocal accountability, and explicitness. Because of the focus of contracts on the mutual roles of participants, they are especially well suited to use within the supervisory relationship. Expectations for involvement from both supervisor and supervisee emphasize the mutual responsibility for movement toward agreed-upon learning goals. This approach is also applicable to industrial settings.

Evaluation

The specter of evaluation is often a threatening one to staff members who view it as an opportunity for a dissatisfied or vindictive supervisor to wield power unfairly. Also stressful are those evaluations written by supervisors who give little thought or attention to the achievements or ongoing need for improvement of their supervisees. Ideally, evaluation should be incorporated into the supervisory function of education, with periodic evaluation conferences serving as benchmarks in the ongoing educational process of the supervisee. Kadushin (1976) outlines specific desirable evaluation procedures that ideally should maximize the supervisee's participation while conveying the supervisor's appraisal of the staff member's total functioning on the job over a specific period of time. Kadushin's guidelines include the following:

(1) Evaluation should be a continuous process rather than an occasional event.
(2) The supervisor should discuss the evaluation procedure in advance with the supervisee.
(3) The evaluation should be communicated in the context of a positive relationship.
(4) The evaluation procedure should be a mutual, shared process, with the supervisee contributing a self-evaluation or a critique of the supervisor's evaluation.
(5) Evaluations should be made with some recognition and consideration of reality factors that might be determinants of the worker's performance.
(6) The principal, if not the exclusive, focus of evaluation should be the work performance of the supervisee rather than the evaluation of the worker as a person.
(7) The evaluation should review both strengths and weaknesses, growth and stagnation, and should be fair and balanced.
(8) A good evaluation should be more than a listing of good and bad performance, being instead an analysis of why certain behaviors and procedures are desirable and effective and why others are not.
(9) The evaluation should suggest tentativeness rather than finality and focus on modifiable aspects of the worker's performance.
(10) Evaluations should be formulated with some consistency. The supervisor needs to apply the same standards in the same way to all of his/her supervisees who have approximately the same education and experience.
(11) It is desirable for the supervisor to indicate a willingness to accept evaluations of his/her own performance from the supervisee.
(12) Involvement of staff in establishing evaluation criteria is likely to ensure the selection of more relevant criteria, to intensify commitment to the evaluation process, and to clarify expectations with regard to evaluation.

Relatively few agencies and organizations view evaluation in its broadest dimension as an integral part of the educational process of supervision. Administrators' concerns regarding evaluations focus on issues of accountability and personnel procedures. The danger in such a narrow perspective is that evaluation becomes routinized, depersonalized, and expedient. Insensitive evaluation procedures could be viewed as one factor contributing to staff burnout, inasmuch as a person's creativity, eagerness to learn, and skills are ignored or categorized into predetermined measures of work achievement.

Decreasing Job Pressures

A major contributing factor to burnout is a workload that is perceived as overwhelming. Supervisors can counter this in several ways. First, new staff members need to build up to their full workload gradually, with an orientation period designed to make them more competent in the tasks they undertake. Second, in addition to regular supervisory sessions, new staff members are often appreciative of having a peer with similar responsibilities available as a consultant on routine matters. Building a "buddy system" into the staff member's initial experiences also sets the tone for collegial interaction and peer support as familiarity with the work continues to build.

Third, to the extent that the staff member and supervisor can identify initial competencies, the beginning workload can represent a mixture of the familiar and the new, with a gradual adding of more complex and demanding tasks as the staff member develops increasing knowledge and skill. To the extent that the supervisor can help the supervisee to exercise some control over the balance in work responsibilities, feelings of being overwhelmed are less likely to contribute to burnout.

A fourth strategy the supervisor can use to help the supervisee is to prioritize work responsibilities. Initially, new staff members have little perspective from which to judge the relative urgency of assigned work. Staff may need help in developing a system for responding to routine tasks, crises, out-of-the-office travel and visits, dictation, and consultation with other professionals. One caution against an undue emphasis on time management techniques is that a preoccupation with scheduling one's work can lead to depersonalization in interactions with staff and with clients. Time management must never be viewed as an end in itself but, rather, as a technique for gaining some control over multiple and competing work responsibilities.

In order for the supervisee to consider supervision to be a serious and worthwhile undertaking, the supervisor must set a reasonable pace and serve as a favorable role model. Supervisors who are available only to consult on problems, who cancel supervisory sessions without rescheduling them, who allow interruptions of supervisory conferences, and who demonstrate no planful response to their supervisees' learning needs should not be surprised when their supervisory efforts are disregarded or avoided. Supervisees are entitled to expect of supervisors a preparedness for sessions, dependability in setting aside or promptly rescheduling meeting times, the ability to individualize needs, and a sense of continuity in the helping relationship wherein there is a sense of progress toward specific goals and a mutual recognition of mastery in new areas.

Creating Channels of Peer Support

Just as helping professionals encourage their clients to reap maximum benefit from natural helping networks (friends, family, religious leaders), so should supervisors help their staff members to meet one anothers' supervisory needs. The tutorial model of supervision, in which the supervisor is presumed to impart knowledge to his or her supervisees, is only one of several potentially useful approaches. To the extent that supervision is regarded as preparing staff members for more autonomous functioning in the work setting, the tutorial model may prove dysfunctional for more experienced workers.

Peer support has been identified as one factor that can serve to reduce burnout. Recognizing the importance of socioemotional bonds in the work group, the effective supervisor can utilize a variety of strategies to promote peer learning and friendship. Watson (1973) writes of alternative models of supervision that rely on peer support rather than on an exclusive relationship with one's supervisor. These peer relationships occur informally in many work settings, but their potential for purposeful learning needs to be sanctioned and encouraged by supervisory staff.

Consultation

Consultation can be provided by an agency staff member or by someone outside the agency with expertise in a particular area. A consultant should be provided with the specifics of the case, either orally or in writing. It is the consultant's task to review the situation presented, to offer a point of view with respect to the situation, and, in the course of the consultation, to explain to the staff member the basis for his or her opinions. The value of case or problem consultation rests on the staff member's freedom to initiate sessions at his or her own discretion. Consultation is most appropriate when it is used by experienced workers who possess a solid knowledge base and a motivation for self-directed learning.

Group Supervision

Group supervision represents an extension of the tutorial model to a group of staff members and, like the tutorial model, is most effective with inexperienced supervisees. Ideally, the supervisees in the group will have comparable levels of training or experience, so that they can identify shared learning needs. Content for group discussion focuses on common issues and concerns experienced by staff, the supervisor playing a strong role as educator.

Peer Group Supervision

In peer group supervision, all members of the group participate as equals. Since such participation depends on significant contributions by the members, experienced staff members are preferable participants in this supervisory model. The role of leader in the group can be rotated or it can be assumed by one person. The role of the leader is not to supervise, but to moderate discussion of an agenda agreed upon by the group. The group is used as a sounding board for individual staff members' issues and concerns.

Team Supervision

The concept of team supervision can be found in the literature (Watson, 1968, 1973) and appears applicable to a variety of work settings, including productivity circles in industry. Through the use of group process, team members arrive at decisions. Ideally, team members contribute diverse knowledge bases to the team, so that issues and cases discussed will be considered from many perspectives. Although the team leader does not function as a supervisor, the leader's task would be to help the team arrive at a group decision regarding the situation under discussion. Because of the need for viable contributions from each team member, this model is most suitable for those staff members with a solid knowledge base and considerable experience. The often intense interpersonal relationships within work teams can generate a certain level of stress among staff members. Unless team members are willing to identify and to work through their differences constructively, group contagion can result in disruption of peer relationships.

The various methods of supervision should be introduced as an appropriate response to staff members' learning needs. Workers may choose to begin with one supervisory model and move into another model as knowledge and experience increase. However, an organization needs to be flexible in the use of models and not assume there is a fixed progression through which all staff members must move. No model should be viewed as better than any other; rather, all models have the potential to fill a perceived supervisory need in a given setting.

One special consideration in the use of multiple models is the importance of maintaining mechanisms to achieve accountability and linkages in communication. Since supervisory models differ in the extent to which a staff member's performance can be evaluated and discussed, the evaluation component should be built into each model to assure staff members that their gains will be recognized and their learning needs will be addressed.

Dealing with Employees' Personal Problems

When a staff member's work performance seems to be affected by personal problems, it is important for the supervisor to avoid adding role conflict to the worker's difficulties. As Stiles (1963) says, "A supervisory relationship contains an implicit contract: the worker is responsible for attempting to maximize his performance and continuing his professional development; the supervisor is responsible for helping him achieve these goals."

In order to avoid role confusion or role conflict, the supervisor who encounters inadequate work performance by a staff member with personal problems must remain focused on work expectations in supervisory discussions. If, despite attention to areas needing improvement, the staff member seems unable to meet the stated expectations, the supervisor could suggest appropriate resources for the worker to utilize, including those discussed by **Freudenberger.** Such resources could include counseling, a medical checkup, or whatever other intervention is deemed advisable by the supervisor. The choice of whether to utilize the resource rests with the worker. Subsequent supervision should remain focused on the staff member's efforts to grow and change professionally.

Kadushin (1976: 159-160) emphasizes the organizational ramifications of shifting from educational supervision to psychotherapy:

> To accept the supervisee for psychotherapy requires a modification of work standards. The criteria for a decision regarding enforcement of agency standards become the therapeutic needs of the supervisee-client rather than the needs of the agency. Exercise of administrative sanctions required in maintaining adequate standards may be antitherapeutic for the supervisee-client. The supervisor cannot at the same time be a psychotherapist to the supervisee and guardian of agency standards.

In actuality, few supervisors and supervisees are interested in developing a psychotherapeutic relationship. In a survey of 469 social work supervisors by Kadushin (1974), less than 1 percent checked "helping supervisees with their *personal* problems" as a source of satisfaction. Similarly, the statement of dissatisfaction in supervision least frequently checked by the 384 supervisees surveyed was "My supervisor tends to become too involved in my personal problems." Recognizing the professional and organizational dangers inherent in therapist-supervisor role confusion, supervisors should strive to identify alternative sources of support for troubled staff.

Maximizing Organizational Flexibility

Another area of supervisor role performance involves the extent to which flexibility exists or can be introduced into the job, as discussed by **Pines.** The concept of flexitime has particular importance for persons needing to balance personal and professional aspects of their lives. If the standard workweek can be shifted so that staff members can distribute their forty hours in other ways than the eight-hour day, burnout may diminish as autonomy and initative are respected. Since many agency settings can serve clients best by making early-morning, evening, and weekend hours available, flexitime can benefit clients and serve consumers at the same time it allows staff increased choices in scheduling their work.

Flexibility in workload is another aspect for the creative supervisor to utilize whenever possible. By varying the kinds of responsibilities of each workload, the supervisor helps the staff member in several ways. First, work will not appear too routinized, and tedium can be alleviated by concentration on different sets of tasks demanding different skills and levels of involvement. Second, for staff members involved in stressful jobs, a regular respite or change of pace afforded by other work responsibilities can reduce the intensity to manageable proportions. Third, a variety of tasks helps staff members to gain a sense of ongoing mastery of new learning. Ultimately such a diverse knowledge and skill base could prepare staff members for promotions within the organization, for entry into further academic pursuits, or for service as consultants or advisers both in and outside of the agency setting. To the extent that staff members can enhance their sense of contribution to the workplace and their sense of career development or professional identity, a varied workload may reduce burnout at the same time it contributes to productivity. Ironically, the task of supervision becomes particularly challenging when flexibility and variety are introduced into staff workloads.

Variations in workload can be accomplished in several ways. The tendency in many work settings is to assign certain kinds of tasks to staff who have exhibited skill or talent in particular areas. Not only does this reduce the opportunity for other workers to gain familiarity and skills with tasks exclusively channeled into a specific person's workload, but the "chosen" staff member may begin to experience burnout. Use of similar skills with no incentive to expand a limited knowledge base soon begins to outweigh the initial advantages of being the agency "expert" in a particular area. In order to avoid such typecasting of staff, a supervisor must encourage supervisees to utilize the experts in different areas as consultants, rather than overloading the experts with responsibilities that do not provide the opportunity for continued learning and development.

If varying responsibilities on staff workloads is not feasible, perhaps the supervisor can periodically rotate workloads among staff. In settings where continuity is less important than a fresh approach brought by a staff member new to various tasks, this option reduces the tedium that contributes to low productivity, high error rates, and decreased staff morale.

Sharing responsibilities among members of a team has the advantage of peer support built into a structure that encourages the pooling of expertise. To the extent that certain decisions to be made carry heavy responsibility, it is more reassuring for a staff member to share such responsibility with other members of the team. The decisions reached by the team are more likely to represent a variety of perspectives or to include a variety of options if the initial decision proves unworkable or inappropriate. The availability of the team to reassess decisions is preferable to an individual staff member reaching his or her limits in responding to a complicated task.

Staff members need supervisory help to view resources beyond the work environment as accessible and fruitful. Encouraging meetings and conferences on common areas of concern can establish cooperative community ties as well as add to the skill and knowledge base of persons who participate. In addition, client service can be maximized by the efficient use of interlocking community services. Duplication and gaps in service delivery can best be addressed when strong working relationships with other agency staff are promoted.

The supervisor's encouragement of staff creativity also can reduce the sense of tedium and enhance staff members' sense of competence. Whether utilizing new technology, new models for serving clients, new methods of streamlining tasks, or new interpersonal styles of working cooperatively with others, staff members need encouragement to identify creative ways of meeting a variety of challenges in the work setting. Supervisory reinforcement of creativity and organizational flexibility can contribute to a sense of ongoing vitality and receptivity to staff-initiated ideas.

The Supervisor's Role in Continuing Training

Training has the potential to contribute to the career advancement of staff or, conversely, to invite cynicism and resentment. As **Edelwich and Brodsky** indicate, the manner in which the supervisor initiates and responds to training opportunities can make the difference between positive and negative staff reaction. Supervisory input to content, reinforcement of content and its applicability in the work setting, and evaluation of learning acquired through training sessions are all integral aspects of encouraging continuity in learning for staff.

Given that the supervisor and the trainer will be in close contact regarding learning goals and course content, it is logical for the supervisor to encourage a focus on the applicability in the work setting of the material being taught. Trainers are likely to be more effective in their work if they create between-session opportunities to apply new learning. The supervisor may need to offer suggestions to the trainer for ways in which such applications can be utilized, given the variety of responsibilities that staff members may have.

Likewise, awareness by the supervisor of content learned in training sessions can be utilized during supervisory sessions with each staff member. The supervisor should help staff to conceptualize issues along the lines of new content being learned. When staff are encouraged to make links between theory and practice, they will be less likely to view training sessions as mere diversions from the challenge of their workloads. Positive reinforcement by a supervisor of staff utilization and application of new knowledge also will encourage staff to expand their repertoire of theoretical bases and practical skills. In addition to supervisory input and encouragement, other staff can encourage one another to utilize new learning. The supervisor should encourage staff to remind one another of ways in which applications of new knowledge can be achieved. Modeling by the supervisor of respect for education's function in the workplace can enable staff to apply new learning both in their work responsibilities and in peer support situations.

Training can serve to invigorate staff by providing ideas of new, different, more sophisticated, or more advanced ways of performing work responsibilities. The supervisor who initiates contacts with community educational resources and who follows through by helping trainer and staff identify learning needs, anticipates that training can be a valuable preventive intervention against burnout.

Whither Supervision?

How long should supervision continue? Do experienced workers gain the same benefits from supervision as fledgling staff? Should supervision be interminable? How can supervisors reduce staff stress without increasing their own?

Certainly, the range of supervisory options available in a given work setting helps staff to appreciate that their learning needs can be met in a variety of ways. Just as learning styles differ among individuals and in the same individual over time, so needs of staff for supervision rarely can be met by one model alone. The challenge is for organizational administrators to recognize that supervisors may need encouragement to move away from the styles in which they were supervised and into new models of meeting staff learning needs.

The benefits of creative supervision are not limited to staff alone. The energy the supervisor expends in responding creatively to challenges in the work environment can be an investment against supervisory burnout. Inasmuch as creativity can generate positive administrative feedback, high staff morale, increased productivity, and a heightened sense of personal competence, the creative supervisor receives psychological refueling from many sources in the organization.

The issue of helping supervisors to enact their roles with increasing competence also relates to how they supervise senior staff members next in line for supervisory positions. Once competence in work responsibilities has been demonstrated, some advanced and experienced staff members may need only occasional consultation in performing their work roles. However, in order to keep these workers from burning out, new input and fresh ideas must be provided from some source in the work setting.

One option might be to encourage experienced staff to begin grooming themselves for supervisory positions. Reading materials, university courses, institutes, workshops, and in-service training sessions can provide a knowledge base in supervision. Opportunities to supervise students or interns in the organization allow the experienced staff member to put into practice the theoretical knowledge on supervision and to identify areas of competence and professional limitations. Experienced staff members may also be encouraged to serve as consultants to persons in other organizational settings, to present papers at professional meetings, and to author articles for journals in their fields.

The challenge of providing creative supervision includes helping the novice staff member develop investments in work responsibilities, enhancing the competence of advancing staff, and encouraging experienced staff to develop their own styles of supervision and consultation. Creative supervision does not originate with the supervisor alone, just as burnout does not originate with the individual staff member. The interface between the organization and the individual is where scrutiny must be applied in detecting conditions that favor or thwart burnout.

Summary

The organization plays a vital function in sanctioning certain practices that serve to prevent or reduce burnout. Organizations must take into consideration that satisfactory completion of work responsibilities is only one aspect of a staff member's motivation for growth and development. Other motivations for remaining invested in the organizational setting include the expectations that ongoing learning needs will be met with appropriate opportunities, that supervisory styles can be utilized differentially as learning styles evolve and change, and that an organizational climate will promote respect for new learning and encourage educational involvement from academic and community resources. Supervisors face a challenge in responding to staff needs, but organizations carry an equally weighty responsibility. The organization must give priority not only to stability, but to the growth and change that come when staff and supervisors are vitally involved in shaping a responsible work environment that discourages burnout while it encourages creativity.

13

Organizational Development (OD) Interventions
Changing Interaction, Structures, and Policies

ROBERT T. GOLEMBIEWSKI

This chapter approaches the amelioration of psychological burnout through the value-directed technology usually called organization development or, more conveniently, OD (French & Bell, 1973, 1978; Golembiewski, 1979; Huse, 1980). Conventional components can be described briefly and with certainty. In the context of a relatively specific set of values that in effect seek to increase satisfaction of individual needs while relating to organizational requirements, OD, in one popular definition (French & Bell, 1973: 15) is seen as

> a long-range effort to improve an organization's problem-solving and renewal processes, particularly through a more effective and collaborative management of organization culture—with special emphasis on the culture of formal work teams—with the assistance of a change agent, or catalyst, and the use of the theory and technology of applied behavioral science.

Broadly, OD designs can influence interaction, structures, and policies or procedures that should "go all around the world"; that is, they can develop systems with congruent and reinforcing interaction, structures, and policies. However, the earliest and most frequent OD experience has been with inter-action-centered designs, while structures and policy have received more recent and less attention.

What do OD theory and praxis imply for reducing burnout via designs that impact on interaction, structures, and policies or procedures? Three foci preoccupy a response to this central question:

- the developments in OD associated with the early recognition of and response to a specific kind of burn-out—that among intervenors or change agents;
- the things that OD seems to do that can, on balance if usually indirectly, reduce burnout conceived as a consequence of the accumulation of stressors at work; and
- the special class of problems raised for OD theory and praxis if burnout is conceptualized as a set of progressive stages or phases.

"Doctor, Heal Thyself":
Burnout Among OD Intervenors

In one basic sense, OD specialists have been in a strategic position to recognize and respond to burnout. Simply, the phenomenon surfaced quite early among OD intervenors as one of the problems associated with their activities, and some reasonably effective ways to anticipate and moderate its effects have been developed over time. OD intervenors are the "catalysts" for the application of behavioral science theory and methods featured so prominently in the above definition of OD.

This section can help establish the legitimacy of proposing a role for OD in burnout. Specifically, OD intervenors have recognized related phenomena among themselves—more vitally, *in* themselves—and have also done some constructive things in response to that recognition.

Seven Adaptations to Early
Identification of Burnout

By the late 1960s, various aspects of the burnout phenomenon became quite common subjects in OD conferences and symposia, although basically as shoptalk rather than as foci for research (see Mitchell, 1977). These early sightings tended to be reported in colorful but quite general terms. Thus "flame-out" tended to be the term that described the syndrome, not "burn-out"; and the associated verbiage tended toward the spectacular.

These robust metaphors did not trigger any substantial research, but reasonable ameliorative adaptations have been made by OD intervenors to early warning signs. Seven points must suffice here to suggest the range of these adaptations.

First, however global and general, the talk and some writing among OD professionals had the major effect of legitimating the subject.

Second, greater sophistication has developed concerning the cross-pressures of the intervention situation, a sophistication reflected in both shoptalk and the developing literature that socializes intervenors (Golembiewski, 1972, 1979; French & Bell, 1980; Huse, 1980). Highlighting the wickedness of these cross-pressures (Argyris, 1970: 128-176) has multiple effects. For example, consider the intervention setting in terms of role demands. Thus the OD intervenor came to be seen as a "boundary spanner," who played a role described in terms of "marginality" (Gardner & Whyte, 1945; Ziller, Stark, & Pruder, 1969). Marginal roles like boundary-spanning require an individual to function in two or more collectivities, with the potential for serious incongruence between the values and goals of the multiple settings.

Third, this sophistication about intervention loci has induced a number of guides for praxis. For example, co-consultation variously moderates the potential for misperception and miscalculation.

Fourth, a greater knowledge has developed about what will "work" under conditions that can be specified with increasing precision. Success rates seem substantial. In 574 cases, these rates varied from 70 to over 80 percent, approximately, depending on the specific OD design in question and the specific criterion of success (Golembiewski, Proehl, & Sink, 1981).

Fifth, a greater tethering and clarification of expectations has developed over the years, which gets reflected in, for example, the contracting that occurs between intervenor and host (Percarich, 1974).

Sixth, OD intervenors are encouraged—as by their capstone accrediting agency, now Certified Consultants International and earlier called International Association of Applied Social Scientists—to participate in personal-development experiences that can reduce burnout. Such experiences can be of four kinds, often mixed:

- periodic meetings with fellow professionals, peaking in periodic peer review, to exchange information and support, to give perspective on ethical concerns, and so on;
- cognitive or skill-building experiences, which can affect competence or mastery and hence self-esteem;
- those experiences focusing on the explicit direction of one's life, such as career planning (Shepard and Hawley, 1974), or clarification (Kirschenbaum, 1977), which can—often in combination (Isgar, 1980)—help reduce or manage stressors that can lead to burnout; and
- learning designs focused on the recognition and management of personal stress (Adams, 1978, 1980a), which typically include skill practice with activities that can help one cope with stress: meditation, deep breathing, large-muscle exercise, and so on.

Note also that a following section of this chapter reviews the senses in which OD, overall, can be viewed as stress-reducing and hence as inhibiting burnout.

Seventh, and perhaps paramountly, OD intervenors have been very creative in developing support systems that can do multiple duty in inhibiting burnout as well as in dealing with its consequences. Such support groups serve stereophonic purposes, whose saliency is best reflected in the enormous energies associated with the twice-yearly meetings of the OD network, supplemented by periodic meetings of many local ODN clusters throughout the world.

OD and Burnout Approached Indirectly: Some Major Things OD Does to Reduce Stress

How does OD reduce burnout, in general, and why? Briefly, many OD designs have as a prime (if general) consequence the alleviation of a broad range of stressors. For example, interaction-centered designs can improve communication and hence reduce stress between people; and structure-oriented interventions can make jobs less frustrating. Hence if—and this seems a very big if—burnout is conceived as the additive or cumulative product of such stressors and stresses, as discounted by the coping skills of individuals, OD can be said to inhibit the development of burnout in two distinct if related senses: It can help reduce or eliminate the stressors, and it can help individuals cope with the stresses.

A simple model underlies this overall characterization of OD. Attention is directed first at the multiple ways in which OD designs deal with both stressors and stresses (A); then the focus will shift to sketching the senses in which the OD process can have stress-inducing features (B). In OD, in sum, A − B is typically greater than zero, even though B should never be neglected.

OD Processes as Generally Stress-Reducing

Let us take two approaches to OD as stress-reducing, one focusing on a particular kind of learning and the other seeking to provide an overview of OD praxis.

The Generic Approach via Stress Management Workshops

OD's focus on stress-reduction is most sharply reflected in that class of experiential learning designs most often described as "stress management workshops" or given some similar title. See **Edelwich and Brodsky** for details of workshop designs.

The empirical literature concerning the efficacy of such workshop experiences seems both slim and conclusive. Consider only three conclusivities. First, an effective program of stress management involves a huge realm **(Tubesing and Tubesing).** Following Adams (1978), stressors may be placed in four categories:

- Type I includes stressful and recent events at work—major changes in work demands, or in policies, procedures, and structures—each having some "rebound" or readjustment value (Naismith, 1975).
- Type II includes such stressors as a serious illness or death of a family member (Cochrane & Robertson, 1973).
- Type III includes on-the-job pressures, the most prominent of which include work on role overload, interdepartmental squabbles over jurisdiction or resources, a "crisis management" atmosphere, and feedback that is usually negative and punitive (see French & Caplan, 1972).
- Type IV includes off-the-job stressors, which may cover a broad range: environmental pollutants, financial concerns in an inflationary economy, worries about children or friends caught up in criminality or the drug culture, marital problems, and so on.

Second, although workshop experiences can begin to make inroads into this phenomenal expense, they are profoundly limited. The essential point can be framed conveniently, if perhaps oversimply, in terms of three summary propositions. To begin, Dickinson (1981: 4) concludes that the "literature on stress management tends to be dominated by micro-level responses . . . , that is, solutions which are instituted with the individual rather than the organization." Among these micro-level exemplars are relaxation techniques, meditation, biofeedback, hypnosis, exercise, or proper sleep and special diets (Furst, 1979; **Tubesing & Tubesing**). The same bias gets dramatic emphasis even in a major—indeed, perhaps even the singular—organizational effort to deal with stress at work in a hospital. Adams (1978: 259) reports these protective/preventive measures help employees armor themselves against destructive stress:

(1) Current health physicals will be supplemented with more comprehensive blood work and appropriate counseling.
(2) A counseling and/or referral service will be developed.
(3) Managers will be taught to identify stress symptoms in self and others.
(4) Managers will be required to take vacations.
(5) Regular vigorous exercise will be encouraged and classes will be held.

(6) Education concerning nutrition and exercise will be programmed.

(7) Organization levels of stress will be monitored periodically by surveys.

However, ample reasons imply that this micro-bias has strict limitations, despite its obvious value. For example, Payne (1980: 269) isolates major classes of stress-related problems that "are not responsive to individual coping responses. Coping with these may require interventions by collectivities rather than by individuals." Payne's view has much support (see French & Caplan, 1972: 61-64), but the program outlined by Adams implies how difficult it is to deal directly with organizational sources of stressors, even in an otherwise well-mounted effort. Similarly, on-the-job stressors tend to get little attention, for example, despite the common perception that they are both central in inducing burnout and in managing or alleviating it **(Pines)**.

In sum, then, the typical stress management workshop emphasizes individual far more than organizational development, and more out of necessity than preference. This generalization holds in several senses that in combination imply sharp limits on the efficacy of the stress workshop in combatting burnout. To be sure, individuals may learn coping skills that can transfer to other arenas, such as work. But the stress-inducing potential of such loci typically remains undisturbed, since the "context of stress" at work seldom gets focal attention. Relatedly, the "management of stress" suffers from the unavailability at work of the support systems so commonly provided temporarily in the stress workshop. Indeed, if major stressors inhere in organizational interaction, structure, and policies or procedures, workshops may be tragically counterproductive. The "workshop high" may only raise expectations, which would then be dashed on return to a recalcitrant work site, with a consequent deepening of despair **(Edelwich & Brodsky)**.

Organizational Approaches via Conventional
OD Designs That Can Claim
Stress-Reducing Effects

Even though OD has seldom mounted a direct assault on stress and hence burnout (Adams, 1978), the news is not all bad. Far from it, in fact. Much OD theory and praxis contributes to that objective.

Three major themes help establish the ways in which OD influences burnout, even if indirectly, without specific targeting. The themes emphasize, in turn:

- three panels of OD designs, among whose effects one may credibly count reduction of many stressors, with consequent amelioration of burnout conceived as an accumulation of stressors that have outstripped the coping capabilities of individuals;

- a sketch of some evolving theoretical networks that provide reasonable crosswalks between OD designs and stress reduction; and
- an inventory of organizational policies, practices, and structures that are at once common in OD applications and illustrate *in vivo* ways of energizing the theoretical networks referred to above.

Three Panels of OD Designs That Can Reduce Stress. Table 13.1 provides broad if only illustrative detail on the first major theme. The table is built around three broad classes of work-site stressors, which are usefully distinguished, even if interacting. These stressors relate to interaction, structure, and policies or procedures, and are described briefly in the left column. The center column of the table seeks to distinguish classes of stress reducers. The right column describes OD designs or interventions appropriate to various classes of stress reducers.

Table 13.1 also summarizes a range of useful OD designs, "useful" in terms of an experienced and anticipated general balance of positive versus negative effects in numerous settings. Consider the structure-centered section of the table, for example. Few organizations have gone whole hog in restructuring in accord with OD values. However, typical organizational structures generate fragmented and balkanized specialties and tend to induce autocratic managerial styles and defensive climates or atmospheres. The amalgam tends to induce low satisfaction and low productivity. The demonstration seems equally convincing at the most lofty managerial levels (Chandler, 1962), where the principles prescribe departmentation by "function" such as research or manufacturing, as well as at lower levels (Golembiewski, 1965; Lawrence & Lorsch, 1967), where tasks or processes determine departmentation. Nonetheless, the "principles" do have their attractions, especially under certain more or less specific conditions (Perrow, 1970). And the shift toward untraditional structural modes can be costly (Davis & Lawrence, 1977).

Granting the power of interaction-centered designs, they need to be reinforced by a range of complementary structures and policies or procedures. At times, indeed, preoccupation with interaction-centered designs can be self-defeating (Golembiewski, 1979: Part 2), a growing awareness that has not yet overcome the common myopia. Hence, Table 13.1 also emphasizes several designs related to two other panels of OD designs, so as to lessen the dilemma posed when organization members have internalized a set of values and attitudes for interaction that are not reinforced by—or may even be at cross-purposes with—practices rooted in structures and policies.

(text continued on p. 243)

TABLE 13.1 Three Panels of OD Designs That Can Serve as Work-Site Stress Reducers

Work-Site Stressors	Classes of Stress Reducers	Applicable OD Designs
1. Perceptual distortions and uncertainties	Skill- and attitude-building for avoiding fight/flight responses	Historically, the T-Group was the dominant vehicle for such learning. In the last decade or so, attention has shifted to a range of designs with more specific foci: —giving and receiving effective feedback (Golembiewski, 1979 Part 1, pp. 59-64) —enhancing "process analysis" (Schein, 1969) Of special management significance, this shift in design-of-choice implies a profound shift in targets: from putative equals in a T-group to individuals at different hierarchical levels, from the impact of personal style to concerns about a supervisor's managerial style, etc.
2. Ineffective feedback and disclosure linkages between people, which create low-quality data that induce decisions which create new problems while seeking to solve the old	Building supportive or nondefensive atmospheres or climates	"Team-building" is no doubt the dominant mode here. The focus may be affective or instrumental in diverse combinations, but the common focus is on creating a specific kind of social order that emphasizes openness, owning, and learning from experience in nondefensive ways. Variant team-building designs have been developed for organization phases (such as start-up and phase-out), as well as for distinct types of crises (Dyer, 1977).

3. Conflict between pairs, e.g., between peers or between a superior and subordinate due to the former's supervisory style	Building conflict resolution skills	Third-party interventions are appropriate here (Walton, 1969), but several other design variants (e.g., Filley, 1975) have been developed consistent with values underlying OD
4. Intergroup conflict	Building conflict resolution skills	Various confrontational modes have been used widely—three-dimensional images (Golembiewski, 1979: Part 2, 168-175), mirror designs (Fordyce & Weil, 1971: 101-105), etc.
5. Climate or atmosphere that induces risk, as well as low levels of trust, openness, and owning	Commitment-building	Commitment plays a central role and is the intended consequence of participation → involvement → meeting needs. The "target of change," in effect, approximates the "agent of change," thereby reducing threat, resistance to change, and defensiveness. Typically, OD efforts involve broad ranges of employees, so resulting commitment can be unusually broad and deep.
6. Norms or local values that induce #1-5 above	Integrative norm-building	Norms constitute a significant element in all interaction-centered designs. Typically, they get expressed at least as the values that will guide interaction and problem-solving—specific degrees of openness and so on. Such normative development also can be variously more explicit, as in a work unit designing its intended character, expounding its "managerial credo," or developing a statement of "mission and role" (see Harrison, 1972)
7. Normlessness that induces #1-5 above	Integrative norm-building	

(*continued on the following page*)

TABLE 13.1   (Continued)

Work-Site Stressors	Classes of Stress Reducers	Applicable OD Designs
Structure-Centered		
1. Jobs that are variously need-depriving	Need-responsive job designs	Such designs seek to develop jobs consistent with a more or less specific model of individual needs (e.g., Herzberg et al., 1959). Such OD applications may be classified as static or dynamic, depending on the degree of autonomy and self-control for individuals. Static applications emphasize job rotation or job enrichment, with the latter seeking to build positive motivators into a job (e.g., Ford, 1969). Dynamic applications involve the development of poly-specialists, who are paid not for the specific task they perform, but for their range of competencies, which they provide as the changing situation requires (e.g., Elliott, 1953).
2. Roles that create mismatches: overloads or underloads between work demands and individual skills/attitudes; sharp incongruencies between authority and responsibility; etc.	Role clarification	Applications here can focus on the specific content of roles (Huse, 1980: 292-294), or they can involve a broader mix of content and relationships, as in role negotiation experiences (Harrison, 1972).
3. Objectives that are unclear, incomplete, incongruent, or even contradictory	Objective-setting	This central but often-neglected activity can be approached via such process-oriented designs as value clarification or goal-setting (Kirschenbaum, 1977), or it can be institutionalized in broader

238

		programs such as Management by Objectives, or MBO (Golembiewski, 1979: Part 2, 168-175).
4. Win-lose competition, mistrust, and conflict between units of organization contributing to a common flow of work	Intergroup conflict resolution	Common fragmenting tendencies at work can be approached in at least three ways: —facilitating communication between units, as via Three-Dimensional Image Designs (Golembiewski, 1979: Part 2, 138-152). —via boundary-spanning devices, such as an "integrator" between two or more functionally specialized units (Stumpf, 1977) or via "project management" overlays (Thamhain & Wilemon, 1975). —by basic structural change (see #5 below)
5. Basic structures for organizing—such as functional or bureaucratic structures—that induce problems for both people and productivity, e.g., —long communication chains and centralized decision-making —fragmented flows of work —low personal commitment to and involvement in work	Organizational integration	A range of OD efforts can respond to such structural effects: —managing the consequences by providing periodic ventilation sessions (e.g., Fordyce & Weil, 1971: 89-130) —providing opportunities for greater decision-making at many levels of organization (e.g., Bernstein, 1980) —developing norms that seek to inhibit the development of consequences like low trust and closedness, despite the continued existence of structures inclined to generate such consequences, as in much team-building (Dyer, 1977) or in linking line/staff officials (Dyer et al., 1976)

(continued on the following page)

TABLE 13.1 (Continued)

Work-Site Stressors	Classes of Stress Reducers	Applicable OD Designs
		—developing broad philosophic systems—such as "self-forcing, self-enforcing" systems (Sayles & Chandler, 1971)—to "fill in the cracks" between major units of organization —basic structural change (Golembiewski, 1979: Part 2, 33-94) at various levels of organization, e.g., • "autonomous work teams" at lower levels (Walton, 1977) • integrative structural models at top levels (Carew et al., 1977)
Policies or Procedures		
1. Practices or benefits perceived as variously unattractive: low or inequitable salaries and wages, arbitrary or casual performance appraisals, poor supervision, etc.	Self-evaluation and renewal	The goal is to create organizations aware of, and responsive to, their own consequences. Commonly, relevant designs systematize data-gathering—whether by interviews, "sensing groups" that are level-homogeneous but functionally heterogeneous (e.g., Cash & Minter, 1978), or opinion surveys (e.g., Golembiewski & Hilles, 1979). Data are fed back into the system for action-planning at multiple levels. The focus may be quite specific, a broad "quality of working life" program, or anywhere between.

	Responsiveness to different and changing individual needs	Various designs consistent with OD values can be applied in response to different or changing individual or family conditions
2. Practices or benefits that are fixed and hence nonresponsive to many individual situations, which include: —different macrodevelopmental stages for adults as they age —short-cycle physiologic or psychological variations experienced by all people —phases in roles, such as in parenting		—from changing stages of adulthood (e.g., Horton, 1975) to the changing distribution and ages of children in the family that could impact on policies such as those concerning relocation —a broad range of policies and procedures—such as "cafeteria benefits" (Tavernier, 1980)—can be designed so as to be adaptable to variations in individual or family conditions —career planning can be useful in the long run, as well as at specific life stages or points of transition (e.g., Shepard & Hawley, 1974) —policies such as flexible workhours can permit some adjustment to short-run variations in energy level, need, and even whim (Ronen, 1981) —policy innovations can relate to emerging lifestyle differences—e.g., "job sharing" (Seybolt, 1979: 18) for husband-wife pairs, or various "permanent part-time" arrangements—in ways that meet individual and organization needs

(continued on the following page)

241

TABLE 13.1 (Continued)

Work-Site Stressors	Classes of Stress Reducers	Applicable OD Designs
3. Practices or benefits related to major real or potential conflicts of needs and interests: termination, demotion, discipline, etc.	Seeking a greater balance of individual and organizational needs in extreme cases	Growing experience exists with approaches to OD values under difficult conditions, so as to minimize adverse effects for both individuals and their employing organization, as in —demoting a batch of managers due to market conditions (Golembiewski et al., 1972) —closing a plant (Slote, 1977; Taber et al., 1979) —increasing output during periods of negative or slack economic growth so as to preclude layoffs or shut downs (Donovan & Wilkes, n.d.)

Theoretical Networks Underlying the Stress-Reduction Claim. What theoretical networks underlie the several classes of stress reducers in Table 13.1? Readers can consult convenient sources (for example, French & Bell, 1978; Golembiewski, 1979; Huse, 1980).

But this treatment would be remiss if it failed at least to sketch some major theoretical supports for the position that the designs in the table can be reasonably claimed to reduce stressors, despite the general failure of OD applications specifically to target such an effect. Three foci will provide the sparse illustration here: social support, control over the environment, and individual variation.

Social support as central, even paramount, in reactions to stressors. "Primary among situational factors suggested as mediators of the effects of life stress," Sandler concludes (1979: 218), "is a broad range of social relationships conceptualized as providing social support." Numerous observers (such as Cobb, 1976) have described how the availability of individuals providing social or emotional support can moderate the effects of numerous stressors—bereavement, job loss, and so on.

"Social support"—or the existence of "support systems"—includes, but refers to more than, the mere presence of others. That "mere presence" can have significant effects is implied by research both recent and hoary with age (for example, Triplett, 1898), but Handy's (1978) warning seems appropriate. Not every collectivity is a support group, and some collectivities can be socioemotional millstones. Rogers (1957: 96) describes one special kind of support system—an idealized therapeutic relationship—as characterized by an empathic understanding and by "unconditional positive regard." And Cobb (1976) stresses the sense of networks—of communication and of mutual obligations—that rest on loving and caring, on the participants being mutually valued and esteemed.

The OD designs in Table 13.1 variously seek to build and maintain the kind of support systems that research has clearly associated with the reduction of stressors and stress (Beehr, 1976). The point is no doubt clearest in the case of interaction-centered designs, and especially the T-Group or sensitivity training group. Narrowly, the security of a support system seems a major element in encouraging openness and owning in interaction-centered designs; hence, OD intervenors carefully attend to the development and maintenance of group relationships. Globally, indeed, perhaps the ultimate OD goal is the creation of an appropriate social order and culture at work—a widely accepted set of values and attitudes, with reinforcing skills, to meet individual needs, to improve problem-solving, and to enhance problem-solving capabilities that facilitate choice or change (see Winn, 1968).

Inducing appropriate social support systems rests on substantial theory and experience. Generally, interaction-centered designs seek to meet individual needs as well as organizational requirements (see Golembiewski & Carrigan, 1970). Success rates for several interaction-centered designs permit substantial confidence about attaining expected effects (Golembiewski, Sink, & Proehl, 1981).

Two major boundary conditions limit this optimism about interaction-centered designs. As one goes down the hierarchy and as work is more mechanized and routinized, first, the usefulness of structural and policy interventions usually increases. Unless suitably reinforced, in fact, interaction-centered designs may be seriously counterproductive in such cases. Job enrichment or flexible work hours are included in the family of useful designs under the stated conditions. Second, where the risks to participants implied by interaction-centered designs may be unacceptably high, intervenors might well decide to recommend various structural or policy initiatives. Such initiatives can approach OD values and serve a broad range of personal and organizational goals (Ronen, 1981), while they do not expose participants as would interaction-centered designs.

Environmental control as a major moderator in reactions to stressors. Ample evidence from multiple sources implies that environmental control can serve in significant ways to buffer the individual from stressors (Lefcourt, 1973). Indeed, the perception that control is possible may be sufficient, even though it is never exercised (Glass, Singer, & Friedman, 1969). Here the central dynamics might involve a diminished potential for frustration, whose avoidance explains the general attractiveness of the family or organizational approaches that permit control over aspects of the environment (Golembiewski, 1962: 125-148).

Confidence in the relationship between controllability and stressfulness gets useful reinforcement from a range of associated ideation and research, as in the tendency of uncontrollable conditions to generate "learned helplessness" in organisms (Seligman, 1975; Sweeney, 1981). The bare notion of learned helplessness has received substantial empirical support which reinforces the centrality of controllability as a moderator of reactions to stressors.

The OD designs in Table 13.1 fit comfortably with this theoretical mini-network involving control over stressors. The watchwords of OD interaction-centered designs, for example, prominently include "participation," "involvement," and "ownership." These terms of intent clearly relate to the enhancement of control over events by participants in OD designs, as well as to the choice of which aspects of the environment are relevant to the specific sets of actors. The latter point is critical, although often neglected with serious consequences for both theory and research design, as Stokols (1979: 39-43) convincingly argues. Similarly, OD structural and policy interventions also seek to increase participants' control over the work site. The designs can vary: Flexible work-hours programs clearly have the intent of increasing employee control over one aspect of work (Ronen, 1981), and structural designs such as those for "autonomous groups" extend this intent over many dimensions (Golembiewski, 1979: Part 2, pp. 33-94).

Whatever the design, the common expectation can be phrased in such terms: that an exchange process will be engaged, with a resulting mutual empowerment. As participants increase their mutual control, to sketch the nature of the exchange, so also might their commitment to common objectives increase, various resistances might be reduced, the willingness to engage one another as problem-solvers might grow, and a normative consensus could develop concerning a desirable quality of working life as well as specific objectives and projects. An acceptable balance has profound payoffs for both individuals and their organizations, a point also made by **Shapiro.** Both must obviously surrender some elements of value, but the exchange permits aspiring to a work site that neither party could induce independently—one that is productive and satisfying.

Individual variation as conceptually/practically key in reactions to stressors. Any theoretical network involving reactions to stressors must include individual differences and variability, to conclude our brief catalogue. Bare illustration should suffice. Consider the work on controllability, which reflects a dominant tendency. But as Stokols (1979: 36) appropriately notes, "the joint utilization of the controllability *and* salience dimensions will yield a more adequate conceptualization of human stress than do existing models based on the controllability dimension alone." And whence derives "salience"? It clearly resides in differential individual experiences and preferences (see Cooper & Marshall, 1980: 97-101).

Although the implications of the crucial point are unevenly appreciated, the OD designs in Table 13.1 variously accommodate to individual differences and variability. In that sense, again, OD designs can be said to help moderate reactions to stressors and to inhibit the development of burnout. For some details, consult Edelwich with Brodsky (1980) and Cherniss (1980b). The case is clearest with flexible work hours, perhaps, a strategy that seeks to relate to widely remarked differences between people—to allow for the fact that some are "early starters" while others are not, that we all face situations that make it awkward to start and stop work at a definite time each day, and so on. Similarly, "cafeteria benefits" (which include some fixed fringe benefits as well as some that can be allocated variably by different individuals) permit organization members to respond to their specific and changing life situations. Relatedly, but in far more complex ways, interventions like career planning (Cooper & Marshall, 1978: 91-92) also relate to individual differences and reflect the value to individuals and to their employing organizations of responding to such differences.

Organizational Features Associated with Stress Reduction. Despite OD's lack of specific focus on burnout, to review the immediate argument, Table 13.1 rests on two broad assumptions that require testing. Thus, the table proposes that typical OD designs can affect a broad range of stressors that might reasonably encourage burnout. In addition, it proposes that OD theory and results can be said to constitute the essential base from which an aggressive and organizationally rooted attack on burnout could be launched.

Consult the entries in the table's right column, "Applicable OD Designs." That inventory is illustrative and sketchy, but it serves to suggest the large and growing range of relatively tested approaches to the several idealized conditions at work that also seem appropriate for managing and limiting burnout viewed as deriving additively from a range of stressors in organizations. See also **Shapiro** in this volume.

OD Processes as Stress-Inducing in Some Particulars

There is no silver lining without a dark cloud; so it is with the preceding analysis. Put directly, OD processes also may be viewed as stress-inducing in specific senses, even as their overall impact is stress-reducing.

Table 13.2 conveniently reflects the general argument underlying this point, by outlining important stress producers likely to be energized by OD efforts. The exhibit basically speaks for itself, although its cumulative impact on occasion has been disregarded by some OD enthusiasts.

How to raise the probability that stress reduction will be greater than production in OD efforts? No magic bullet exists. The ethical OD intervenor should raise early the issue of the range of pleasant/unpleasant consequences, so as to avoid later surprises. Beyond that, OD theory advises intervening where the trauma is great enough to motivate change as well as to ease participants over the inevitable rough spots until major effects begin to show up.

OD and Burnout Approached as a Specific Target: Some Conceptual and Practical Problems

Although OD does tolerably well in the general case, a direct attack on burnout must overcome significant conceptual and practical problems. How

TABLE 13.2   OD Stress Producers and Their Effects

Stress Producers	Stress Effects
Long-range change	Substantial periods of change can be highly stressful and disruptive to needs for security and stability.
Uncertainty	Uncertainty about the effects of an OD program on one's position, role, status, and future may be anxiety-producing. Uncertainty about the program is also common because of uncontrollable variables that may affect the program.
Changes in organizational culture	Adapting to change organizational norms and values may be difficult or even impossible for some organizational members.
Problem-finding and -solving	Identifying problems may involve considerable risk to some organizational members, and solving problems may require difficult decisions and considerable demands on time.
Confrontations	The open confronting of issues characteristic of OD may create awkward and stressful situations for persons unaccustomed to confronting or being confronted.
Conflict	OD may expose conflicts that now must be confronted and resolved.
High stakes	The stakes in OD can be high, since OD includes high-risk activities such as individual, group, and intergroup interventions and possible major changes.
Threat	OD can be very threatening to organizational members who are insecure about their jobs, their performance, or their ability to handle feedback.
Time demands	Devoting the necessary time to make OD work while performing one's regular duties can create time pressures.
Pressures for results	OD can be expensive and time-consuming [and these claims for resources often will be made at the very time that] the pressure for measurable results is increasing.

Source: Reprinted from Warwick (1981: 38). Copyright 1981, Training and Development Journal, American Society for Training and Development. Reprinted with permission. All rights reserved.

so? Three points significantly contribute to the key conclusion that serves to introduce this section:

- OD has not been strong in accommodating specific individual differences.
- Little is known about individual predispositions to burnout, or individual precursors of it, which largely limits even consciously targeted OD efforts to a remedial rather than a preventive mode.
- Burnout does not yet refer to a definite domain that can be measured validly and reliably.

It will seldom be possible to say much that is either brief, simple, or unqualified about these three themes, but they do highlight one direct conclusion. The conceptual and practical problems with mounting organizational efforts that specifically target burnout, in sum, imply the usefulness of efforts to strengthen individuals in their management of stressors and stress. Other chapters in this volume provide useful perspectives on this strengthening of individuals, fortunately, so this discussion can single-mindedly pursue its organizational focus.

OD's Mixed Response to Individual Differences

The OD literature has Janus-like qualities with regard to individual differences. On the one hand, OD rests conceptually in the interface between individual needs and organizational demands, with the goal of increasing the congruence between the two. That puts OD in the business of individual differences, definitely but only generally.

But the OD literature remains far less definitive when it comes to acknowledging classes of individual differences, both up front, in the choice of a specific design, and in the interpretation of data gathered during such an OD design as survey/feedback. Consider only the significance of burnout differences in choosing among alternate OD designs. Burnout seems to vary quite regularly with differences in self-reports concerning twenty-two measures of work-site characteristics. They include the six facets of the Job Descriptive Index, or JDI (Smith, Kendall, & Blood, 1969); the ten component measures of the Job Diagnostic Survey (Hackman & Oldham, 1980); and variables measuring job tension, willingness to disagree with supervisor, participation at work, job involvement, and trust in fellow employees as well as several levels of supervision. The higher the burnout, crudely, the worse the work-site profile (Golembiewski, Munzenrider, & Phelen, 1981)—"worse" defined by self-reports of lower degrees of participation, involvement, and satisfaction with many facets of work, as well as by higher tension at work. What to treat, then? The easy answer would seem: Improve the work-site characteristics *and* ameliorate the burnout. However, the two sections below imply this obvious solution is simplistic; and those sections also imply that working on one of these tasks can be at cross-purposes with the other.

Unhelpful Demographics of a Ubiquitous
but Unevenly Distributed Target

Demographics contraindicate an easy solution to the covariance of differences in burnout and individual perceptions of a work site. Generally, the data suggest that burnout does not correspond conveniently to demographic differences. Measured burnout within work units will vary significantly; and conventional demographic categories account for very small percentages of common variance between burnout and demographics, as the review by Golembiewski and Scicchitano (1981) establishes. Moreover, only scattered evidence of burnout covariance with demographics was found in a study that utilized a broad range of variables and two alternative ways of measuring burnout—one an additive measure, and the second based on progressive phases or stages of burnout (Golembiewski & Scicchitano, 1981). Finally, questions can be raised as to the adequacy of the usual additive ways of measuring burnout, as will be done in the section below.

There may be a long-run way out if precursors of burn-out can be isolated. Type A behavior (Jenkins, Zyzanski, & Rosenman, 1979) seems a likely candidate, based on the construct's properties as well as on a corpus of research on topics with at least a kinship to burnout (see Chesney & Rosenman, 1980; McMichael, 1978: 133-138). An ongoing study by this author tests directly for an association of Type A with burnout, but results are not yet available. If such precursors can be found, they could be used for training and career-planning purposes, with the goal of inhibiting future burnout.

Finally, short of a breakthrough re precursors, the existence of significant individual differences urges that priority be given to OD designs that provide major opportunities for tailoring to, and by, specific persons. Flexitime constitutes one such option. It can be used or not—individuals decide—with real but relatively restricted impact on others in the organization (Ronen, 1981). Conveniently, flexitime also seems to covary with a range of effects broadly congruent with organizational purposes, such as high morale and high productivity, in both business (Nollen, 1979) and public (Golembiewski, 1980) organizations. Few available OD options fit the flexitime prototype, however.

Phases or Stages of Burnout

Not only may burnout be difficult to ameliorate once identified and located, to make a critical if neglected point, but we are still substantially removed from a reliable and valid way of measuring whatever it is (see **Maslach**). This deficiency has major costs. In large organizations, it makes identification of targets difficult. Far more significantly, this lack also inhibits the development of a theoretical network encompassing the interaction of individual behavior and organizational structure and policies, which network alone will support the kind of comprehensive approach necessary for dealing with the precursors and consequences of burnout in both remedial and preventive modes. Indeed, approaches to burnout may perforce need to be highly individualized and clinical in orientation, and hence limited in both reach and grasp. Witness the typical focus on ameliorating the personal effects of burnout by individual counseling or by sending individuals to stress management workshops.

But despair does not yet seem appropriate, for real progress has been made toward measuring burnout. Two significant if incomplete lines of progress deserve attention, in fact. First, the Maslach Burnout Inventory (Maslach & Jackson, 1981b), or MBI, seems to apply to a broad range of settings. Maslach reports many applications in people-helping settings (Maslach & Jackson, 1978, 1979). Others (Golembiewski, Munzenrider, & Phelen, 1981) have shown that the MBI also seems to apply in a commercial setting involving a broad range of specialties. Basically, the MBI seems to tap three phenomenal domains, each defined by responses to a number of opinional items:

- Depersonalization, or the tendency to see persons as things or categories;
- Personal Accomplishment, or the sense of working effectively on worthwhile tasks; and
- Emotional Exhaustion, or the perception that a respondent is at the end of his or her psychological rope.

The instrument also seeks to tap a Personal Involvement domain. For various technical reasons, neither Maslach and Jackson (1981a) nor others (Golembiewski, Munzenrider, & Phelen, 1981) have been successful in extracting such a domain from MBI items.

Second, although most observers fixate on additive measures of burnout, analytic considerations (see Edelwich with Brodsky, 1980; **Edelwich and Brodsky**), and some evidence (Golembiewski, Munzenrider, & Phelen, 1981) suggest the usefulness of conceptualizing burnout as a set of progressive phases or stages. Specifically, by dichotomizing the distribution of scores around the mean for each MBI dimension, eight phases of burnout can be distinguished, given the assumption that Depersonalization represents early signs of burnout while Emotional Exhaustion characterizes advanced cases:

	I	II	III	IV	V	VI	VII	VIII
Depersonalization	Lo	Hi	Lo	Hi	Lo	Hi	Lo	Hi
Personal accomplishment (a reversed scale)	Lo	Lo	Hi	Hi	Lo	Lo	Hi	Hi
Emotional exhaustion	Lo	Lo	Lo	Lo	Hi	Hi	Hi	Hi

Percentage of Employees
from one organization
classified   18.0 8.8   12.8   16.9   9.3   13.2   9.3   16.9

These eight phases or stages generate both vocabulary and central issues-for-testing about burnout, and the phase model has numerous properties that differ markedly from additive approaches. The specific argument can get byzantine, quickly. So here note only that the phase model has a specificity beyond that of the total MBI score, and provides far more information than separate subscale scores. For example, total MBI scores probably would not differ significantly for individuals classified in Phases II, III, and V; but there seem ample reasons to insist on differentiating persons in those stages, as the following discussion should establish.

Preliminary work implies the usefulness of the phase model (Golembiewski, Munzenrider, & Phelen, 1981). A half-dozen or so variant tests of the phase model agree in two major particulars. Thus, twenty-two work-site descriptors reveal expected differences in all cases, twenty of which achieve the .05 level on the overall F test. The more advanced the stage of burnout, the "worse" the self-reports of respondents about a variety of facets of the work site: satisfaction, participation, involvement, tension at work, and so on. Moreover, depending on the MBI dimensions included and the Hi/Lo cutting-points, as many as 50 percent of the work-site descriptors attain the .05 level in tests of paired comparisons of all phases on each variable.

Implications of Phases for OD Praxis

The phases above have four major implications for OD practice related to managing or inhibiting burnout. First, initial evidence implies that, at the very least, one must sharply distinguish additive burnout scores from a phase model (Golembiewski & Munzenrider, 1981). Provisionally, the several phases might reflect different causes or precursors of burnout.

Second, distinguishing phases of burnout could help target ameliorative designs for specific individuals. For example, HiLOLO individuals would seem responsive to the broad range of interaction-centered OD designs: sensitivity training, process-oriented team building, and so on. In contrast, such interaction-centered designs might only contribute to stimulus overload for HiHiHi individuals, and perhaps LoHiHi and LoLoHi. Such individuals might better respond to designs that "structure" life somewhat more for them, as in designs for job redefinition or restructuring, for role negotiation, or similar approaches. These contrast with designs that "free up" or "unfreeze" individuals, or that variously rely on heightened confrontation or stimulation.

"Standard practice" does not respect these implications of a phase model. Several observers (such as Freudenberger, 1975, 1977b) note that interaction-centered designs were often prescribed, as in encounters that "talk cold turkey" and "lay out the bare facts." This might be reasonable advice for Phase II, or HiLoLo. But the prescription seems inappropriate for those— perhaps LoLoHi, and more probably in HiLoHi, LoHiHi, and HiHiHi— who seem already overloaded with intense and negative stimuli, who might be suspicious if not paranoid, who might be more prone to blame and to assign responsibility to others rather than to self, and so on.

Much the same holds for one of today's popular burnout remedies: the reduction of the amount of time the helper works directly with clients during a day, a year, and a career (Kahn, 1978; Maslach & Jackson, 1978). This prescription could, as Edelwich notes (Edelwich with Brodsky, 1980: 243), merely highlight for some the dilemma of "having to give up direct client contact for the sake of career mobility." The prescription might be appropriate in advanced burnout Phases VI and VIII, but it could evade the point where Depersonalization or lack of Personal Accomplishment are at issue, as in II, III, and IV. There the basic issues may inhere less in contact overload than in awkward structure, policies, and procedures—work so organized as to inhibit effective performance (Carew, Carter, & Gamache, 1977), creating low-power roles for individuals that inhibit task performance while encouraging a need-depriving work site (Kanter, 1977: 245-249) and perpetuating inflexible policies with regard to status, pay, and schedule.

Third, and obviously, knowledge of phases would permit directing timely attention to those persons in early stages of burnout so as to arrest or reverse their tragic progression. This represents an attractive strategy. It could involve work-site changes in structure and policy, but would probably emphasize interaction-centered designs.

Fourth, progressive phases or stages of burnout also challenge much of what is accepted as "good practice." Advanced burnout may well be initially induced by deficits in the facets of work, for example, while it is also *not* reversible by mere improvements in those deficits. In sum, awesome implications inhere in the finding that progressive phases of burnout are associated with a worsening profile by survey respondents on many facets of work (Golembiewski, Munzenrider, & Phelen, 1981). Given such a "bad" profile, orthodox prescriptions in the behavioral sciences urge job enrichment, expanded responsibilities and opportunities for growth, enhanced opportunities for participation, and so on. However, these orthodox prescriptions poorly suit advanced stages of burnout, which imply the need for rest rather than additional stimulation, relief from responsibility rather than the enlargements thereof, and so on.

Conclusion

A brief scorecard suffices to indicate the thrust of this review of how Organization Development, or OD, can contribute to the amelioration and management of burnout. Three points do the job:

- OD has done a good job in working toward amelioration/prevention of burnout in intervenors.
- OD presents a growing body of theory and experience generally related to reducing stressors at work, overall, and hence can reasonably be viewed as constituting a base for the specifically targeted amelioration of conditions that can lead to burnout, despite the paucity of documented direct and frontal attacks.
- OD faces major challenges in exploiting the approach to burnout via phases or stages, which gives some promise of greater specificity in targeting particular ameliorative designs to specific individuals.

PART V

The Future

14

Beyond Burnout
Obstacles and Prospects

JOHN-HENRY PFIFFERLING and FRED M. ECKEL

The preceding chapters present an overview of burnout in 1981. As Whiton **Paine** indicated in the overview to this book, these efforts detail the strengths, the weaknesses, and the hopes of a rapidly developing area. They appropriately concentrate on the present and the near future, but it is also useful to look somewhat further ahead. The following are some thoughts on the obstacles and prospects that need to be considered as burnout becomes a more formal field of inquiry.

Ideally, the next ten years will see planned interventions for the reduction of burnout and its sequelae, and these interventions will be evaluated carefully. Job stress will also begin to be approached from a cross-cultural perspective. For example, American industry will look at productivity and changing gross national products and discover that the context of a worker's relationship to his or her company does have a relationship to morale, productivity, absenteeism, sabotage, and loyalty. Worklife and its relationship to personal values of security, life satisfaction, and dysfunctional coping will be seen as intimate relatives, and these links will be widely recognized and other links forged.

Job dissatisfaction, tedium, anomie, and a host of negatively valued work-related feelings have become incorporated into the working term, "burnout." Researchers must now tease apart folk definitions from clinical and empirical definitions in a complex arena that combines social, individual, and ecological frustrations related to dysfunctional coping. The tools needed for a careful disentanglement must be borrowed from various methodologies, including both social and person-centered disciplines.

There are many obstacles that may prevent appropriate interventions from decreasing the prevalence of the burnout stress syndrome. They include the following.

Professional educational practices incorporate a world view that sees educational training as both necessarily hard and prone to dependency and debilitation. Rituals of passage are erected that allow the graduates to feel that they are part of an elite and that they have earned their status. Professional cultures share a vision that sees competitiveness, prestige gained by criticizing others, and credential dominance as paramount. The personal aspects of the professional are perceived as hampering this process of professional values development and clarification.

The corporate workstyle also reinforces competition between individuals, negative feedback, qualified friendships, and an incongruence between personal goals and corporate goals. Shared values including interpersonal openness, constant receptivity to alternative modes of enhancing productivity, interworker interdependence, and a shared organizational vision are downgraded by the structured ethos of most American companies. The legacy of the 1960s, "work should be meaningful," is a new worker right that finds resistance in traditional segregation of personal and professional or work selves.

Academic bickering about the appropriate discipline "owning" the burnout issue serves to prevent interdisciplinary research, definitions, and evaluation projects. Each discipline sees burnout as either an extension of its "natural" interest—occupational stress, worker satisfaction, social alienation, psychological insecurity, anomie, reality shock—or as an intrusion of pop psychology into legitimate inquiry. One of the advantages of this volume is that the authors were purposely selected from diverse disciplines and were able to recognize their common interests.

Careful assessment of the validity of the burnout construct, and purported interventions that make a difference in reducing the harmful consequences of burnout, need long-term, carefully designed studies. Obstacles to these projects come from a variety of sources. Potential critics see burnout interventions as possibly seditious: One may cite the fear that employees, sharing grievances, will attribute them to management. Expectations for undeliverable, idealistic work environments may aggravate crises of failed expectations. Semantic and discipline differences may cause experts to disagree about the essential components of the burnout phenomenon. Intervention advocates will cite anecdotal and empirical data to verify their favored intervention and degrade competitors' strategies. Most seriously, funding sources must be identified that see both basic and applied research in this area as legitimate and thus worthy of support.

Many potential contributors to the field will shy away from involvement because of its pop psychology and popularized connotations. Their own elitism may be so caught up with identifying exotic issues that they disregard the most common causes of dissatisfaction and the pervasiveness of the phenomenon.

Resistance may be strongest from those in higher education, who may perceive burnout researchers as pointing the finger of blame at a faulty educational system that allows reality shock, unrealistic expectations, and mythical values to predispose their graduates to crises of confidence. Additionally, they will prevent researchers from carefully assessing curriculum interventions that may add some needed joy to professional training. **Wilder and Plutchik** should be read carefully here.

Cultural Considerations

Increasingly, American companies will look at other styles of management, most notably Japanese models, and discover that a more integrated vision of company-employee relations helps the company succeed. Taking the initiative is rewarded in Japanese managements, and individuals are not discouraged from trying. This prevents some environmental variables relevant to the burnout-prone setting. As American companies discover the relevance of "vision" management, which allows shared visions of company goals to permeate the workforce, the uniqueness of each person's strengths becomes a corporate asset. If one works in an environment where one's assets are emphasized and one's deficiencies appropriately addressed, the context of work as stress is reduced. This is one aspect of **Shapiro's** creative supervision.

Japanese models of corporate concern for the impact of the work role on the personal growth of the individual are already beginning to influence American corporate style. Professional culture and professional education may be slower to focus on the efficacy of person-centered management, because they allow rigid interpersonal behavior to dominate. Professional training reinforces the separation of the person from the professional role, creating disvalue for the person of the professional or trainee. These habits become coping styles that allow contagious critical teaching and competitiveness to maintain themselves. As teachers in professional schools reduce their counseling role, we needlessly reinforce cynicism and paranoid attitudes. Interdependence and cooperation are not modeled in professional schools; thus, emulation of professional egos that display closure and defensiveness is perpetuated. This problem will worsen as "tenured in" departments burn out.

The epidemic of burnout attests to our neglect of our human needs. American culture has distanced itself from information indicating that constant giving must deplete itself. Thus, we have predisposed a generation of professional help givers to deny their own varied needs for renewal. Physicians see resiliency and strength every day, but their medically ethnocentric world view denies the reality of optimism. Lawyers have a vision of adversarial relationships, thereby removing themselves from counseling, cooperative and harmonious legal models. Simple justice is an altruistic model, but law schools support little training and few rewards for students that are mediation- or counselor-oriented. Their human resources are needlessly undernourished.

Ecological Considerations

We can borrow from economics the notion of the zero-sum society and gain some insight into professionals' predictable reactions to their burnout. Professionals, as a result of accepting the prevalence of burnout problems, will begin to demand greater rights. Doctors, pharmacists, social workers, teachers, and others will less easily be trapped by their training ethic into denying their needs for support and positive reinforcement. Patients' rights issues coming from the 1960s will evolve into professionals' rights issues because of the publicity given the burnout syndrome. As society dumps its dirty laundry on helping professionals, they will begin to retaliate to cut their losses. The burnout syndrome is a synergistic issue combining high expectations, a vulnerable personality, and an environment that is not geared for personal vulnerability. It is interesting that almost all of the initial research on job burnout is derived from studies of helping professionals who fought for their clients' rights.

Cherniss's (1980a, 1980b, 1981) conceptual framework for thinking about burnout and Carroll and White's (1981) ecological perspective aptly reinforce this view. **Cherniss** sees burnout as a product of the historical moment: (1) a reflexive consciousness that sees job satisfaction as a partial right, (2) a legacy of the 1960s that reinforces both provider accountability and client power, (3) a decline of community assistance for those in need of human services, and (4) a set of professional expectations that are unrealistic and prepare the professional for a crisis of failed expectations, including definitions of what is "real" work and what is oppressive. Cherniss sees the cumulative impact of these factors as setting the stage for disillusionment, reality shock, and the burnout syndrom. Many of these factors will become more acutely disturbing in the 1980s.

Carroll and White see burnout as a useful label that explains why some workers rather than others develop a progressive behavioral pattern that manifests itself in a reduced qualitative and quantitative work output. They see the individual's coping repertoire as inadequate for a successful work environment, with the co-equal relationship of environmental and personal variables producing the burnout phenomenon. The signs of burnout, to these authors, always represent ecological dysfunction; thus, corrective action must come from multiple sources, a point also made by **Paine.**

Burnout is a holistic concept reflecting a failure in many sectors of an individual's defense networks. To these authors, burnout is contagious and conceptually possible in organizations as well as individuals. Burnout is an interacting phenomenon needing stressful work conditions, a predisposed individual (commonly with unrealistic expectations), and a nonwork environment that is not sufficiently vitalizing to counteract the stress situation.

As these variables in the ecosystem surrounding the target individual transect, they produce an appropriate setting for the burnout process. As **Golembiewski** and **Paine** indicate, interventions must be designed to change many of the unbalanced inputs. However, if one views burnout as a reflection of societal dysfunctions, it is clear that some of the planned interventions must impact on society in general, at least in the short run, and that they will be stressful to the status quo. An evaluation of the costs and benefits of these interventions must include the costs to society.

As **Maslach** points out, this expansionistic view of burnout may gain publicity, but it reduces fine-honed analyses of the phenomenon. Thus, the greater the household use of the term, the more difficult it will be to measure its specific effects and causes. This is one of the dilemmas of the burnout phenomenon: As more researchers begin to conduct careful studies of its prevalence and similarity to related issues (job dissatisfaction, tedium, and so on), its popularity confuses the specificity of the "syndrome." This will become even more confusing as burnout becomes linked with the stress literature discussed by Sweeney (1981).

Critics of the popularized burnout field will see it as a misused justification for decreased quality of work and will use its breadth to downgrade serious attempts to look at environmental, individual, and societal factors predisposed to dysfunctional stress responses. This backlash is already beginning, as critics decry "cop-out" and defend old conceptions of worker responsibility and as researchers and treatment specialists defend present turf. These positions will become less terrible as burnout's "bottom line" becomes clearer **(Minnehan and Paine).**

As research progresses to a more refined assessment of burnout symptoms, etiology, and prevalence, and as interventions begin to tease apart the aggravating factors, the phenomenon itself will be redefined. Working with people—in particular, dealing with people in crises—seems to be a core agent of burnout manifestations. However, we do not know the protection factors that preserve committment by helping professionals. Are there particular personal and interpersonal factors that protect some individuals from a burnout-prone environment? Are there coping styles that can be reinforced by an agency or office that protect against the negative attitudes that accompany burnout cases? As is the case in medicine, one's need to be in control and to be in a caring role often sows the seeds for reduced morale when client gratification is absent and resources are inadequate; and what will we do with the increasing numbers of end-stage cases discussed by **Freudenberger?**

Certainly, individuals who regularly assess their work goals, set realistic expectations, and identify factors that impede or promote those goals that are under their control can more realistically reward themselves. Sophisticated training resources in these areas are increasingly available (**Edelwich and Brodsky**). Coping styles that promote flexibility and affirmative communication about work roles reduce the sense of hopelessness so prevalent in an overburdened setting. As the congruence between an individual's expectations for his or her work role, its significance, and potential for growth match the actuality, we would expect greater satisfaction (see **Pines**). Individuals who perceive that they have some sense of control over space, noise, vacation, and new policies seem to be protected from morale crises.

In our work with health professionals, we have stressed two strategies as basic. To reduce unrealistic expectations by the professional, other workers, and the recipients of his or her services, we ask them to formulate a Principles of Practice document. This document is a dynamic formulation of what you expect your practice to accomplish, how it will be evaluated, and what your definition of your role is. Physicians, for example, will write their definition of medicine. These premises and principles are shared with those around them—particularly their patients. All sides benefit from clarifying expectations (See Pfifferling, Blum, & Wood, 1981).

In addition, we suggest that individuals avail themselves of materials on enhancing coping options. The best book we know of on nonchemical coping skills is written for medical students (Virshup, 1982). It describes the context of stressful activities for medical students and then addresses each unmet need with specific exercises. If one's needs for attachment, nurturance, creativity, identity, and physical health are repeatedly frustrated, anxiety and burnout feelings develop. As one's repertoire of coping options is enlarged, one is less apt to resort to dysfunctional coping tactics and more able to confront the stressors creatively. The **Tubesings** suggest a similar approach.

The prevalence of the specific set of factors that commonly accompany those experiencing burnout syndrome has not been carefully described as to specificity for particular demographic subgroups of professionals—that is, by gender, ethnicity, profession, career changes, years since graduation from professional school, and so on. A host of epidemiological factors need to be measured against a defined set of burnout symptoms or in the context of the phases of burnout. These studies have not been conducted as yet, and will conflict with the general reluctance of professionals to study themselves.

If loss of self-esteem is commonly associated with burnout, then how do individuals with street savvy ("survivor") attitudes fare when placed in a burnout-prone environment? The recovered drug addict/counselor seems to do poorly, but the reason seems to be the lack of upward mobility associated with a lack of credentials. Alternate reward systems may be a treatment modality for this population. Middle-class professionals present different problems, as their value systems are confronted by their burnout state, and they need different interventions.

The subcultural characteristics of each population at risk must also be articulated, so that intervention modalities fit the value system of the workers in a particular stressful environment. Just as different career expectations predispose an individual to either frustration or satisfaction, so different expectations for success in a helping environment predict comfort or frustration. We need to understand why certain worker-client relationships protect against and others precipitate such crises as client suicide (see **Shinn** for some potential antidotes). Long-term studies in comparable populations with defined differences exposed to purported relief interventions need to be measured. The tools of anthropology, long-term immersion by participant observation, and the tools of social epidemiology seem optimal for high-quality studies of the burnout problem. Why haven't they been tried?

Most indices of burnout reflect symptoms with health indicators, but few have studied diagnosed burnout patients with specific physical health problems. Why hasn't occupational health looked at the "disease" of burnout and collected rates of hypertension, back pain, gastrointestinal disorder, and the like? Subtle measures of physiological reactivity, for example, could possibly be used as predictors of burnout-proneness, but many data must be collected and analyzed.

If burnout is to be studied and considered a legitimate phenomenon, then primary physicians need to be looking for its symptoms in their patients. It is interesting that neither primary care medicine nor psychiatry includes burnout as an entity. As an entity derived from folklore (worker labeling) and social psychology (via self-assessment of helping professionals), it will be interesting to see the relative acceptance that burnout has within orthodox medicine. Will psychiatry see the burnout epidemic as a legitimating crisis for massive infusion of funds into preventive mental health programs? Will the administrators of employment assistance programs see burnout as their territory and use its prevalence as a vehicle for their programs' healthy growth?

As burnout becomes accepted as a pervasive "phenomenon" preventing workers from delivering quality work, interventions will become better funded and, ideally, well-studied. The quality of the work environment and its negative consequences, particularly the costly ramifications of burnout (tardiness, sabotage, absenteeism, incomplete care, and so on), may become a *cause célèbre* of the 1980s. The inextricable links between personal and professional well-being will be reinforced by such a focus. Loyalty, company commitment, and employee support may need to be reinforced as essential protective factors in preventing poor care and poor performance.

Cross-cultural analyses of work environments with increased and decreased burnout may serve as useful models for U.S. interventions. Studies that demonstrate regional variations, or variations based on size, complexity, company spirit, and the like, must be conducted so that the tendency to focus individually or even professionally can be balanced by a more community-oriented approach. Just as occupational medicine has shown that 10 percent of most workers have 80 percent of most sicknesses, in the workplace we must conduct epidemiological studies to see which environments, social contexts, and occupations have the greatest prevalence of burnout. Those environments with the least burnout, assuming a uniform definition, should offer us insight into protective mechanisms that reduce or even prevent burnout. A testable set of environmental factors (modified from Levin, 1980) might include the following (assigning one point to each, a score of three or more indicates a work environment that is burnout-prone):

- continuously high stress levels
- norm of constantly "giving to others"
- encouragement of hierarchical staff interaction
- constant demands for perfection
- minimal receptivity for sharing of worker grievances
- expectations for extra effort with minimal rewards
- no reinforcement for suggestions on improving morale
- repetitive work activities
- minimal additional resources available for extra-effort tasks
- lack of encouragement for professional self-care
- discouragement of mutual participation
- evangelistic or psychotheological leadership styles
- policy changes showing little direct relation to problem priority
- policy changes that are too frequent to be evaluated
- rigid role typing for workers

- playfulness is unprofessional
- pervasive "isms" (ageism, sexism, nepotism, and so on)
- emphases on past successes
- constantly shifting of ground rules for policy
- minimal emphases on positive feedback
- minimal priority on comfortableness of environment

These are some of the obstacles and prospects facing professionals, decision makers, researchers, and practitioners in the 1980s. As resources decline and the problems grow, it will become increasingly difficult to turn obstacles into opportunities. But this must be done to avoid the serious personal, social, and economic costs of widespread burnout. Ultimately, burnout will take its place among the ongoing concerns of educators, personnel specialists, managers, stress researchers, trainers and consultants, treatment specialists, public servants and others concerned with job stress and productivity. It is hoped that this volume will hasten that process.

Epilogue

Question:
How many workers are needed to change a light bulb in a high stress, high frustration work environment?

Answer:
A minimum of ten:

- two of whom did not make it in to work (one was sick and the other took a mental health day);
- one who was too hung over and another who was too depressed to notice the bulb was out;
- two who wouldn't do it because they were arguing over who didn't do it last time;
- one who broke an arm attempting to change the bulb (that was after another dropped the new bulb);
- finally the bulb was changed by an exasperated supervisor with high blood pressure, prior to her heart attack.
- the tenth is a reader of this book concerned about the plight of the other nine.

Good luck,
For yourself, and
For the others
You may help
Study, avoid, reduce, eliminate
Burnout and job stress

Bibliography

Adams, J. D. Improving stress management: An action-research based OD intervention. In W. W. Burke (ED.), *The cutting edge*. La Jolla, CA: University Associates, 1978, 245-261.

Adams, J. D. Groundrules for survival: Or, how to stop being a victim. *OD Practitioner*, February 1980; *12*, 4-6. (a)

Adams, J. D. *Understanding and managing stress*. San Diego: University Associates, 1980. (b)

Albee, G. W. *Mental health manpower trends*. New York: Basic Books, 1959.

Alberti, R. E., & Emmons, M. L. *Your perfect right*. San Luis Obispo, CA: Impact, 1970.

Albrecht, K. *Stress and the manager*. Englewood Cliffs, NJ: Prentice-Hall, 1979.

Applebaum, S. H. (Ed.). *Stress management for health care professionals*. Rockville, MD: Aspen, 1981.

Argyris, C. *Intervention theory and method*. Reading, MA: Addison-Wesley, 1970.

Arthur, R. J., & Gunderson, E. K. Promotion and mental illness in the Navy. *Journal of Occupational Medicine*, 1965, *7*, 452-456.

Auerbach, J. S. *Unequal justice: Lawyers and social change in America*. New York: Oxford University Press, 1976.

Austin, M. J., & Jackson, E. Occupational mental health and the human services: A review. *Health and Social Work*, 1977, No. 1, 93-103.

Babbie, E. R. *Survey research methods*. Belmont, CA: Wadsworth, 1973.

Bach, G., & Wyden, P. *The intimate enemy (How to fight fair in love and marriage)*. New York: Avon, 1968.

Bach, L. *Awake, aware, alive*. New York: Random House, 1973.

Bacon, D. Mess in welfare—The inside story. *U.S. News and World Report*, February 20, 1978.

Bales, R. F. *Interaction process analysis*. Reading, MA: Addison-Wesley, 1950.

Barrow, J., & Prosen, S. S. A model of stress and counseling interventions. *Personnel and Guidance Journal*, 1981, *60*, 5-10.

Baum, A., Singer, J. E., & Baum, C. S. Stress and the environment. *Journal of Social Issues*, 1981, *37*, 4-35.

Baum, M. C. *The short-term, long-term and differential effects of group versus bibliotherapy relationship enhancement programs for couples*. Doctoral dissertation, University of Texas at Austin, 1977.

Bean, R. B. *Sir William Osler: Aphorisms*. Springfield, IL: Charles C Thomas, 1961.

Beck, A. T., Weissman, A., Lester, D., & Trenxler, L. The measurement of pessimism: The hopelessness scale. *Journal of Consulting and Clinical Psychology*, 1974, *42*, 861-865.

269

Becker, H.S., Geer, B., Hughes, E.C., & Strauss, A.L. *Boys in white: Student culture in medical school.* Chicago: University of Chicago Press, 1961.

Beehr, T.A. Perceived situational moderators of the relationship between subjective role ambiguity and role strain. *Journal of Applied Psychology,* 1976, *61*(1), 35-40.

Beehr, T.A., & Newman, J.E. Job stress, employee health, and organizational effectiveness: A facet analysis, model, and literature review. *Personnel Psychology,* 1978, *31,* 655-699.

Behavior Today. Career burnout—Or, inhumanity in the human services. October 6, 1980, p. 5.

Beit-Hallahmi, B. Ideology in psychology: How psychologists explain inequality. In R. Solo & C.H. Anderson (Eds.), *Value judgments and income distribution.* New York: Praeger, in press.

Belsky, J. Child maltreatment: An ecological integration. *American Psychologist,* 1980, *35,* 320-335.

Berberian, R.M., Gross, C., Lovejoy, J., & Paparella, S. The effectiveness of drug education programs: A critical review. *Health Education Monographs,* Winter 1976.

Berkeley Planning Associates. Project management and worker burnout. In *Evaluation of child abuse and neglect demonstration projects, 1974-1977* (Vol. 9). Springfield, VA: National Technical Information Service, 1977.

Berne, E. *Games people play.* New York: Grove Press, 1964.

Bernstein, P. *Workplace democratization.* New Brunswick, NJ: Transaction, 1980.

Bishop, J.E. The personal and business costs of "job burnout." *Wall Street Journal,* November 11, 1980, p. 1.

Blair, E.H. *Reference guide to workmen's compensation law.* St. Louis: Thomas Law Book Co., 1975.

Bledstein, B.J. *The culture of professionalism: The middle class and the development of higher education in America.* New York: Norton, 1976.

Bloom, S.W. The process of becoming a physician. *The Annals of the American Academy of Political and Social Science,* March 1963, 346.

Bloom, S.W. The sociology of medical education. *Milbank Memorial Fund Quarterly,* April 1965, *43.*

Bolles, R.N. *The three boxes of life and how to get out of them: An introduction to life/work planning.* Berkeley, CA: Ten Speed Press, 1978.

Bonny, H., & Savary, L. *Music and your mind.* New York: Harper & Row, 1975.

Borgen, F.H., Weiss, D.J., Tinsley, H.E.A., Dawis, R.V., & Loiquist, L.H. The measurement of occupational reinforcer patterns. *Minnesota Studies in Vocational Rehabilitation* XXV, Bull. 49, 1968. (a)

Borgen, F.H., Weiss, D.J., Tinsley, H.E.A., Dawis, R.V., & Loiquist, L.H. Occupational reinforcer patterns. *Minnesota Studies in Vocational Rehabilitation* XXIV, Vol. 1, 1968. (b)

Boss, R.W. Time-extended intervention with a law enforcement team. In R.T. Golembiewski, *Approaches to planned change,* Part 1. New York: Marcel Dekker, 1979.

Bowers, D.G. OD techniques and their results in 23 organizations: The Michigan ICL Study. *Journal of Applied Behavioral Science,* 1973, *9,* 21-43.

Bowers, D.G., & Hausser, D.L. Work group types and intervention effects in organizational development. *Administrative Science Quarterly,* March 1977, *22,* 76-94.

Bradford, L.P., & Bradford, M.J. *Coping with emotional upheavals at retirement.* Chicago: Nelson-Hall, 1978.

Bramhall, M., & Ezell, S. How burned out are you? *Public Welfare,* Winter 1981, 23-27.

Brenner, M.H. *Mental illness and the economy.* Cambridge, MA: Harvard University Press, 1973.

Bronfenbrenner, U. Toward an experimental ecology of human development. *American Psychologist,* 1977, *32,* 513-531.

Browne, H. *How I found freedom in an unfree world.* New York: Avon, 1973.

Browne, P. J., Cotton, C. C., & Golembiewski, R. T. Marginality and the OD practitioner. *Journal of Applied Behavioral Science,* October 1977, *13,* 493-506.

Bucher, R., & Stelling, J. G. *Becoming professional.* Beverly Hills, CA: Sage, 1977.

Burney, C. *Solitary confinement.* New York: Coward, McCann, 1952.

Burke, W. W. (Ed.). *The cutting edge.* La Jolla, CA: University Associates, 1978.

Burke, W. W., & Hornstein, H. (Eds.). *The social technology of organization development.* La Jolla, CA: University Associates, 1976.

Cammann, C., Fichman, M., Jenkins, D., & Klesh, J. The Michigan Organizational Assessment Questionnaire. In S. E. Seashore et al. (Eds.), *Observing and measuring organizational change: A guide to field practice.* New York: Wiley-Interscience, in press.

Campbell, D. T. From description to experimentation: Interpreting trends as quasi-experiments. In C. W. Harris (Ed.), *Problems in measuring change.* Madison: University of Wisconsin Press, 1963.

Campbell, D. T., & Stanley, J. C. *Experimental and quasi-experimental designs for research.* Chicago: Rand McNally, 1966.

Caplan, R. D., Cobb, S., French, J.R.P., Jr., Harrison, R. V., & Pineau, S.R., Jr. *Job demands and worker health* (HEW NIOSH No. 75-160). Washington, DC: U.S. Government Printing Office, 1975.

Carew, D. K., Carter, S. I., Gamache, J. M., Hardiman, R., Jackson, B., & Parisi, E. M. New York State Division for Youth. *Journal of Applied Behavioral Science,* July 1977, *13,* 327-339.

Carrington, P., Collings, G.H., Jr., Benson, H., Robinson, H., Wood, L. W., Lehrer, P. M., Woolfold, R. L., & Cole, J. W. The use of meditation: Relaxation techniques for the management of stress in a working population. *Journal of Occupational Medicine,* 1980, *22*(4).

Carroll, J.F.X. Staff burnout as a form of ecological dysfunction. *Contemporary Drug Problems,* 1980, *8,* 207-225.

Carroll, J.F.X., & White, W. L. Understanding burnout: Integrating individual and environmental factors within an ecological framework. In W. S. Paine (Ed.), *Proceedings of the First National Conference on Burnout,* Philadelphia, November, 1981.

Cartwright, D., & Zander, A. (Eds.). *Group dynamics.* New York: Harper & Row, 1968.

Cash, W. B., Jr., & Minter, R. L. Concern meetings: A useful OD tool. *Training Directors Journal,* March 1978, *32,* 44-45.

Chandler, A. C. *Strategy and structure.* Boston: MIT Press, 1962.

Cherniss, C. Personality and ideology: A personological study of women's liberation. *Psychiatry,* 1972, *35,* 109-125.

Cherniss, C. *Professional burnout in human service organizations.* New York: Praeger, 1980. (a)

Cherniss, C. *Staff burnout: Job stress in human services.* Beverly Hills, CA: Sage, 1980. (b)

Cherniss, C. Trends to watch: Historical, political, social and economic. In W. S. Paine (Ed.), *Proceedings of the First National Conference on Burnout,* Philadelphia, November 1981.

Cherniss, C., & Egnatios, E. Participation in decision-making by staff in community mental health programs. *American Journal of Community Psychology,* 1978, *6,* 171-190.

Chesney, M. A., & Rosenman, R. H. Type A behavior in the work setting. In C. L. Cooper & R. Payne (Eds.), *Current concerns in occupational stress.* New York: John Wiley, 1980, 187-191.

Cobb, S. Role responsibility: The differentiation of a concept. *Occupational Mental Health,* 1973, *3,* 10-14.

Cobb, S. Social support as a moderator of life stress. *Psychosomatic Medicine,* 1976, *38,* 300-314.

Cochrane, R., & Robertson, A. The Life Events Inventory. *Journal of Psychosomatic Research,* 1973, *17,* 135-139.

Coe, R. M., Pepper, M., & Mattis, M. The "new" medical student: Another view. *Journal of Medical Education,* February 1977, *51.*

Coelho, G. V., Hamburg, D. A., & Adams, J. E. (Eds.). *Coping and adaptation.* New York: Basic Books, 1974.

Cohen, J. Weighted kappa: Nominal scale agreement with provision for scaled disagreement or partial credit. *Psychological Bulletin,* 1968, *70,* 213-220.

Cohen, S., & Weinstein, N. Nonauditory effects of noise. *Journal of Social Issues,* 1981, *37,* 36-70.

Connis, R. T., Braukmann, C. J., Kifer, R. E., Fixsen, D. L., Phillips, E. L., & Wolf, M. M. Work environment in relation to employee job satisfaction in group homes for youths. *Child Care Quarterly,* 1979, *8,* 126-142.

Coombs, R. H. *Mastering medicine.* New York: Free Press, 1978.

Cooper, C. L., & Marshall, J. Occupational sources of stress. *Journal of Occupational Psychology,* 1976, *49,* 11-28.

Cooper, C. L., & Marshall, J. Sources of managerial and white collar stress. In C. L. Cooper & R. Payne (Eds.), *Stress at work.* New York: John Wiley, 1978, 81-105.

Cooper, C. L., & Payne, R. (Eds.). *Stress at work.* New York: John Wiley, 1978.

Cooper, C. L., & Payne, R. (Eds.). *Current concerns in occupational stress.* New York: John Wiley, 1980.

Cooper, K. *The new aerobics.* New York: Bantam, 1970.

Cowen, E. L. Baby-steps toward primary prevention. *American Journal of Community Psychology,* 1977, *5,* 1-22.

Crystal, J. C., & Bolles, R. N. *Where do I go from here with my life?* New York: Seabury Press, 1974.

Curtis, J. D., & Detert, R. A. *How to relax.* Palo Alto, CA: Mayfield, 1981.

Daley, M. R. Burnout: Smoldering problem in protective services. *Social Work,* 1979, *24,* 375-379.

Davis, M., Eshelman, E. R., & McKay, M. *The relaxation and stress reduction workbook.* Richmond, CA: New Harbinger, 1980.

Davis, S. A. Organic problem-solving method of organizational change. *Journal of Applied Behavioral Science,* January 1967, *3,* 3-21.

Davis, S. A., & Lawrence, D. *Matrix.* Reading, MA: Addison-Wesley, 1977.

Dean, A., & Lin, N. The stress-buffering role of social support. *Journal of Nervous and Mental Disease,* 1977, *165,* 403-417.

DeMille, R. *Put your mother on the ceiling (children's imagination games).* New York: Viking, 1973.

Dickinson, D. F. *Coping with burnout: The Georgia DYS experience.* Unpublished manuscript, University of Georgia, 1981.

Donovan, J. M., & Wilkes, W. The production team increases productivity at Honeywell. St. Petersburg, FL: Honeywell Aerospace Division, n.d.

Downing, G. *The massage book.* New York: Random House, 1972.

Dressel, P. *Professional burnout: Sociocultural and sociopolitical perspectives.* Unpublished manuscript, Georgia State University, 1980.

Dunette, M. D. (Ed.). *Handbook of industrial and organizational psychology*. Chicago: Rand McNally, 1976.

Dunn, W. N., & Swierczek, F. W. Planned organization change: Toward grounded theory. *Journal of Applied Behavioral Science*, April 1977, *13*, 135-158.

Dyer, W. G. *Team-building*. Reading, MA: Addison-Wesley, 1977.

Dyer, W. G., Maddocks, R. F., Moffitt, J. W., & Underwood, W. J. A laboratory-consultation model for organization change. In W. W. Burke & H. Hornstein (Eds.), *The social technology of organization development*. La Jolla, CA: University Associates, 1976.

Edelwich, J., with Brodsky, A. *Burn-out: Stages of disillusionment in the helping professions*. New York: Human Sciences Press, 1980.

Edelwich, J., & Brodsky, A. Expectations versus limitations: Linking training interventions to needs on and off the job. In W. S. Paine (Ed.), *Proceedings of the First National Conference on Burnout*, Philadelphia, November 1981.

Einsiedel, A. A., Jr., & Tully, H. A. Methodological considerations in studying the burnout phenomenon. In J. W. Jones (Ed.), *The burnout syndrome*. Park Ridge, IL: London House Management Press, 1981.

Elliott, J. D. Increasing office productivity through job enlargement. *Office Management Series*, No. 134. New York: American Management Associates, 1953.

Ellis, A., & Harper, R. A. *A new guide to rational living*. North Hollywood, CA: Wilshire, 1975.

Epstein, Y. M. Crowding, stress and human behavior. *Journal of Social Issues*, 1981, *37*(1), 126-144.

Eron, L. D. Effect of medical education on medical students' attitudes. *Journal of Medical Education*, October 1955.

Eron, L. D. Effect of medical education on attitudes: A follow-up study. *Journal of Medical Education*, October 1958.

Etzion, D., & Pines, A. *Burnout and coping: A cross-cultural cross-sexual comparison*. Paper presented at the International Interdisciplinary Conference on Women, Haifa, Israel, 1981.

Evans, G. W. (Ed.). Environmental stress. *Journal of Social Issues*, 1981, *37*(1).

Everly, G. S., & Girdano, D. A. *The stress mess solution*. Bowie, MD: Robert J. Brady Co., 1980.

Everly, G. S., & Rosenfeld, R. *The nature and treatment of the stress response: A practical guide for clinicians*. New York: Plenum, 1982.

Extein, I., Pottash, A.L.C., & Gold, M. S. Relationship of thyrotropin-releasing hormone test and dexamethasone suppression test abnormalities in Unipolar Depression. *Psychiatry Research*, March 1981, *4*, 49-53.

Farber, B. (Ed.). *Stress and burnout in human service professions*. New York: Pergamon, 1982.

Farquhar, J. W. *The American way of life need not be hazardous to your health*. Stanford, CA: Stanford Alumni Association, 1978.

Filley, A. *Interpersonal conflict resolution*. Glenview, IL: Scott, Foresman, 1975.

Ford, R. N. *Motivation through work itself*. New York: American Management Association, 1969.

Fordyce, J. K., & Weil, R. *Managing with people*. Reading, MA: Addison-Wesley, 1971.

Fox, A. Burnout . . . really hit home. *American Journal of Nursing*, 1980, *80*, 226.

Frankenhaeuser, M., & Gardell, B. Underload and overload: Outline of a multidisciplinary approach. *Journal of Human Stress*, 1976, *2*, 36-46.

Frankl, V. E. *Man's search for meaning*. New York: Pocket Books, 1963.

Freidson, E. *Profession of medicine*. New York: Dodd, Mead, 1970.

French, J.R.P., Jr. Person-role fit. *Occupational Mental Health,* 1973, *3,* 15-20.

French, W., & Bell, C.W., Jr. *Organization development.* Englewood Cliffs, NJ: Prentice-Hall, 1980.

French, J.R.P., Jr., & Caplan, R.D. Organizational stress and individual strain. In A.J. Marrow (Ed.), *The failure of success.* New York: AMACOM, 1972.

Freudenberger, H.J. Staff burn-out. *Journal of Social Issues,* 1974, *30,* 159-165.

Freudenberger, H.J. The staff burn-out syndrome in alternative institutions. *Psychotherapy: Theory, research, and practice.* 1975, *12*(1), 35-47.

Freudenberger, H.J. *The staff burn-out syndrome.* Washington, DC: Drug Abuse Council, 1976.

Freudenberger, H.J. Burn-out: Occupational hazard of the child care worker. *Child Care Quarterly,* 1977, *6,* 90-99. (a)

Freudenberger, H.J. Burn-out: The organizational menace. *Training and Development Journal,* July 1977, *31,* 26-27. (b)

Freudenberger, H.J. How to survive burnout. *Nation's Business,* December 1980, 53-58.

Freudenberger, H.J. *Burnout of professionals.* Unpublished survey, New York, 1981. (a)

Freudenberger, H.J. Burnout syndrome. *Registered Representative,* April 1981, 25-34. (b)

Freudenberger, H.J. Executive burnout. *Harvard Business Club Published Lecture.* New York: October 1981. (c)

Freudenberger, H.J. The burned out professional: What kind of help? In W.S. Paine (Ed.), *Proceedings of the First National Conference on Burnout,* Philadelphia, November 1981. (d)

Freudenberger, H.J. Coping with job burnout as a law enforcement officer. *Law and Order,* 1982, *30*(5).

Freudenberger, H.J., and North, G. *Situational anxiety.* Garden City, NY: Doubleday, 1982.

Freudenberger, H.J., & Richelson, G. *Burn-out: The high cost of high achievement. What it is and how to survive it.* Garden City, New York: Doubleday, 1980.

Freudenberger, H.J., & Richelson, G. *Burnout: How to beat the high cost of success.* New York: Bantam, 1981.

Freudenberger, H.J., & Robbins, A. The hazards of being a psychoanalyst. *Psychoanalytic Review,* 1980, *6*(2), 273-296.

Friedlander, F. The primacy of trust as a facilitator of further group accomplishment. *Journal of Applied Behavioral Science,* December 1970, *6,* 387-400.

Friedman, M., & Rosenman, R.H. *Type A behavior and your heart.* New York: Fawcett, 1976.

Furst, L. *Stress for success.* New York: Van Nostrand Reinhold, 1979.

Gann, M.L. *The role of personality factors and job characteristics in burnout: A study of social service workers.* Unpublished doctoral dissertation, University of California, Berkeley, 1979.

Gardner, B.B., & Whyte, W.F. The man in the middle. *Applied Anthropology,* 1945, *4*(2), 1-28.

Garfield, C.A. (Ed.). *Stress and survival: The emotional realities of life-threatening illness.* St. Louis: C.V. Mosby, 1979.

Gaylin, W., Glasser, I., Marcus, S., & Rothman, D. *Doing good: The limits of benevolence.* New York: Pantheon, 1978.

Gendlin, E.T. *Focusing.* New York: Everest House, 1978.

Girdano, D.A., & Everly, G.S. *Controlling stress and tension: A holistic approach.* Englewood Cliffs, NJ: Prentice-Hall, 1979.

Glass, D.C., Singer, J.E., & Friedman, L.N. Psychic cost of adaptation to an environmental stressor. *Journal of Personality and Social Psychology,* 1969, *12,* 200-210.

Glasser, W. *Reality therapy.* New York: Harper Colophon Books, 1975.

Goldenberg, I. I. *Build a mountain: Youth, poverty, and the creation of new settings.* Cambridge, MA: MIT Press, 1971.

Golembiewski, R. T. *Small group.* Chicago: University of Chicago Press, 1962.

Golembiewski, R. T. *Men, management and morality.* New York: McGraw-Hill, 1965.

Golembiewski, R. T. *Renewing organizations.* Itasca, IL: Peacock, 1972.

Golembiewski, R. T. Managing the tension between OD principles and political dynamics. In W. W. Burke (Ed.), *The cutting edge.* La Jolla, CA: University Associates, 1978, 27-46.

Golembiewski, R. T. *Approaches to planned change* (Parts 1 and 2). New York: Marcel Dekker, 1979.

Golembiewski, R. T. Public-sector productivity and flexible workhours. *Southern Review of Public Administration,* December 1980, *4,* 324-339.

Golembiewski, R. T. Organizational development interventions: Limiting burnout through changes in policy, procedures and structure. In W. S. Paine (Ed.), *Proceedings of the First National Conference on Burnout,* Philadelphia, November 1981.

Golembiewski, R. T., & Carrigan, S. B. Planned change in organization style based on laboratory approach. *Administrative Science Quarterly,* March 1970, *15,* 79-93.

Golembiewski, R. T., Carrigan, S. B., Mean, W. R., Munzenrider, R., & Blumberg, A. Toward building new work relationships. *Journal of Applied Behavioral Science,* March 1972, *8,* 135-148.

Golembiewski, R. T., & Hilles, R. *Toward the responsive organization.* Salt Lake City: Brighton, 1979.

Golembiewski, R. T., & Munzenrider, R. Social desirability as an intervening variable in interpreting OD effects. *Journal of Applied Behavioral Science,* July 1975, *11,* 317-332.

Golembiewski, R. T., & Munzenrider, R. Efficacy of three versions of one burn-out measure. *Journal of Health and Human Resources Administration,* 1981, *4,* 228-246.

Golembiewski, R. T., Munzenrider, R., & Phelen, D. *Phases of progress burnout and their worksite covariants: Critical issues in OD research and practice* 1981. (Mimeo)

Golembiewski, R. T., Proehl, C. W., Jr., & Sink, D. Success of OD applications in the public sector. *Public Administration Review,* 1981.

Golembiewski, R. T., & Scicchitano, M. *Some demographics of psychological burnout.* Unpublished manuscript, 1981.

Goodstadt, M. S. Alcohol and drug education: Models and outcomes. *Health Education Monographs,* Fall 1978.

Gordon, T. *Parent effectiveness training.* New York: Wyden, 1970.

Gray-Toft, P. Effectiveness of a counseling support program for hospice nurses. *Journal of Counseling Psychology,* 1980, *27,* 346-354.

Grayson, M., Nugent, C., & Oken, S. L. A systematic and comprehensive approach to teaching and evaluating interpersonal skills. *Journal of Medical Education,* November 1977.

Greenberger, R. S. How burnout affects corporate managers and their performance. *Wall Street Journal,* April 23, 1981, pp. 1; 22.

Greenburg, D., & Jacobs, M. *How to make yourself miserable: A vital training manual.* New York: Random House, 1966.

Gross, R., & Osterman, P. (Eds.). *The new professionals.* New York: Simon & Schuster, 1972.

Gurman, A. S., & Kniskern, D. P. Enriching research on marital enrichment programs. *Journal of Marriage and Family Counseling,* April 1977.

Hackman, J. R., & Oldham, G. R. *Work redesign.* Reading, MA: Addison-Wesley, 1980.

Hampden-Turner, C. M. An existential "learning theory" and the integration of T-group research. *Journal of Applied Behavioral Science,* October 1966, *2,* 367-386.

Handy, C. The family: Help or hindrance? In C. L. Cooper & R. Payne (Eds.), *Stress at work*. New York: John Wiley, 1978, 107-125.

Harris, C. W. (Ed.). *Problems in measuring change*. Madison, WI: University of Wisconsin Press, 1963.

Harrison, R. Research on human relations training: Design and interpretation. *Journal of Applied Behavioral Science*, January 1971, *7*, 71-86.

Harrison, R. Understanding your organization's character. *Harvard Business Review*, May 1972, *50*, 121-123. (a)

Harrison, R. When power conflicts trigger team spirit. *European Business*, Spring 1972, *9*, 55-57. (b)

Harrison, R. Person-environment fit and job stress. In C. L. Cooper & R. Payne (Eds.). *Stress at work*. New York: John Wiley, 1978, 175-207.

Hartings, M. F., & Counte, M. A. An administrative and curricular model for behavioral science teaching. *Journal of Medical Education*, October 1977.

Hartunian, N. S., Smart, C. M., & Thompson, M. S. *The incidence and economic costs of major health impairment*. Lexington, MA: Lexington Books, 1981.

Harvey, J. Eight myths OD consultants believe in . . . and die by. *OD Practitioner*, February 1975, *7*, 1-5.

Hasenfeld, Y., & English, R. A. (Eds.). *Human service organizations: A book of readings*. Ann Arbor: University of Michigan Press, 1974.

Hawthorne, L. Games supervisors play. *Social Work*, 1975, *20*, 179-183.

Hayes, M. *The organizational context of burnout*. Paper presented at the Annual Program Meeting. Council on Social Work Education, 1981.

Heckman, S. J. *Effects of work setting, theoretical orientation, and personality on psychotherapist burnout*. Unpublished doctoral dissertation, California School of Professional Psychology, Berkeley, 1980.

Hendricks, C. G., & Wills, R. *The centering book*. Englewood Cliffs, NJ: Prentice-Hall, 1975.

Hendrickson, B. Teacher burnout: How to recognize it; what to do about it. *Learning*, 1979, *7*. (a)

Hendrickson, B. Teachers combat burnout. *Learning*, 1979, *7*. (b)

Herzberg, F., et al. *The motivation to work*. New York: John Wiley, 1959.

Holahan, C. J., & Spearly, J. L. Coping and ecology: An integrative model for community psychology. *American Journal of Community Psychology*, 1980, *8*, 671-685.

Hollingshead, A. B., & Redlich, R. C. *Social class and mental illness*. New York: John Wiley, 1958.

Horton, R. *Life-style transitions: Mid-career crises and career changes*. Paper presented at the annual meeting of the Association for Humanistic Psychology, Estes Park, Colorado, August 1975.

House, R. J., Filley, A. C., & Gujarati, D. N. Leadership style, hierarchical influence and the satisfaction of subordinate role expectations: A test of Likert's Influence Proposition. *Journal of Applied Psychology*, 1971, *55*, 422-432.

Huse, E. G. *Organization development and change*. St. Paul: West, 1980.

Isgar, T. Quality of work life for consultants. *OD Practitioner*, October 1980, *12*, 1-8.

Jackson, S. E., & Maslach, C. After-effects of job related stress: Families as victims. *Journal of Occupational Behavior*, 1982, *3*. (a)

Jackson, S. E., & Maslach, C. After-effects of job-related stress: Families as victims. *Journal of Occupational Behaviour*, 1982, *3*, 63-77. (a)

Janis, I. L. Group identification under conditions of external danger. In D. Cartwright & A. Zander (Eds.). *Group dynamics*. New York: Harper & Row, 1968, 80-90.

Janis, I. L. *Groupthink*. Boston: Houghton Mifflin, 1972.

Jenkins, C. D., Zyzanski, S. J., & Rosenman, R. H. *Jenkins Activity Survey*. New York: Psychological Corporation, 1979.

Johnson, J. H., & Sarason, I. G. Moderator variables in life stress research. In I. G. Sarason & C. D. Spielberger (Eds.), *Stress and anxiety*. New York: Halstead, 1979, 151-168.

Johnson, J. H., Sarason, I. G., & Siegel, J. M. *Arousal seeking as a moderator of life stress*. Unpublished manuscript, 1978.

Jones, J. W. *The Staff Burnout Scale: A validity study*. Paper presented at the 52nd Annual Meeting of the Midwestern Psychological Association, St. Louis, 1980. (a)

Jones, J. W. *The Staff Burnout Scale for health professionals*. Park Ridge, IL: London House Press, 1980. (b)

Jones, J. W. (Ed.). *The burnout syndrome*. Park Ridge, IL: London House Management Press, 1981. (a)

Jones, J. W. Diagnosing and treating staff burnout among health professionals. In J. W. Jones (Ed.), *The burnout syndrome*. Park Ridge, IL: London House Management Press, 1981. (b)

Jones, J. W. Staff burnout and employee counterproductivity. In J. W. Jones (Ed.), *The burnout syndrome*. Park Ridge, IL: London House Management Press, 1981. (c)

Jourard, S. *The transparent self* (2nd ed.). New York: Van Nostrand Reinhold, 1971.

Kadushin, A. Games people play in supervision. *Social Work*, 1968, *13*, 23-32.

Kadushin, A. Supervisor-supervisee: A survey. *Social Work*, 1974, *19*, 288-298.

Kadushin, A. *Supervision in social work*. New York: Columbia University Press, 1976.

Kafry, D. The research. Appendix in A.M. Pines & E. Aronson, *Burnout: From tedium to personal growth*. New York: Free Press, 1981.

Kafry, D., & Pines, A. The experience of tedium in life and work. *Human Relations*, 1980, *33*, 477-503.

Kahn, R. L. Job burnout: Prevention and remedies. *Public Welfare*, 1978, *16*, 61-63.

Kahn, G. S., Cohen, B., & Jason, H. The teaching of interpersonal skills in U.S. Medical Schools. *Journal of Medical Education*, January 1979.

Kahn, R. L., Wolfe, D. M., Quinn, R. P., Snoek, J. D., & Rosenthal, R. A. *Organizational stress: Studies in role conflict and ambiguity*. New York: John Wiley, 1964.

Kamis, E. *An epidemiological approach to staff burnout*. Paper presented at the 88th Annual Convention of the American Psychological Association, Montreal, September 1-5, 1980.

Kanner, A. D., Kafry, D., & Pines, A. Conspicuous in its absence: The lack of positive conditions as a source of stress. *Journal of Human Stress*, 1978, *4*, 33-39.

Kanter, R. M. *Men and women of the corporation*. New York: Basic Books, 1977.

Kaplan, R. D. *Job demands and worker health: Main effects and occupational differences*. Washington, DC: U.S. Department of Health, Education, and Welfare, 1975.

Kaplan, B. H., Cassel, J. C., and Gore, S. Social support and health. *Medical Care*, 1977, 25(5), Supplement, 47-58.

Kaplan, R. M., & Bush, J. W. Health-related quality of life measurement for evaluation research and policy analysis. *Health Psychology*, 1982, *1*(1), 61-80.

Katzell, R. A., Korman, A. K., & Levine, E. L. *Research report #1: Overview of the dynamics of worker job mobility*. National Study of Social Welfare and Rehabilitation Workers, Work, and Organizational Contexts. Washington, DC: HEW, Social and Rehabilitation Service (SRS), 72-05401, November 1971.

Kauss, D. R., Robbins, A. S., Abrass, I., Bakaitis, R. F., & Andersen, L. A. The long-term effectiveness of interpersonal skills training in medical schools. *Journal of Medical Education*, July 1980.

Keleman, S. *Living your dying*. New York: Random House, 1974.

Keleman, S. *Your body speaks its mind*. New York: Pocket Books, 1976.

Keniston, K. The medical student. *Journal of Biology and Medicine*, June 1967, *39*.

Kenny, D. A. Cross-lagged panel correlation: A test for spuriousness. *Psychological Bulletin*, 1975, *82*, 887-903.

Kermish, I., & Kushin, F. Why high turnover? Social staff losses in a county welfare agency. *Public Welfare*, 1969, *27*, 34-35.

Khalsa, G. S., & Briggs, G. *Stress away*. Toronto: Gage, 1979.

Kirschenbaum, H. *Advanced value clarification*. La Jolla, CA: University Associates, 1977.

Kolb, D. A., Rubin, I., & McIntyre, J. *Organization psychology: An experiential approach*. Englewood Cliffs, NJ: Prentice-Hall, 1971.

Kramer, M. *Reality Shock*. St. Louis: C. V. Mosby, 1974.

Kramer, M., & Schmalenberg, C. *Path to biculturalism*. Wakefield, MA: Contemporary, 1977.

Kryter, K. D. *The effects of noise on man*. New York: Academic Press, 1970.

Kutash, I. L., Schlesinger, L. B., & Associates. *Handbook on stress and anxiety*. San Francisco: Jossey-Bass, 1980.

Kutner, N. G. Medical students' orientation toward the chronically ill. *Journal of Medical Education*, February 1978, *53*.

Lakein, A. *How to get control of your time and your life*. New York: New American Library, 1973.

Lange, A., & Jakubowski, P. *Responsible assertive behavior*. Champaign, IL: Research Press, 1976.

Langner, T. A. A 22-item screening score of psychiatric symptoms indicating impairment. *Journal of Health and Human Behavior*, 1962, *3*, 269-276.

Lappe, F. M. *Diet for a small planet*. New York: Ballantine, 1975.

LaRocco, J. M., House, J. S., & French, J.R.P., Jr. Social support, occupational stress, and health. *Journal of Health and Social Behavior*, 1980, *21*, 202-218.

Larson, C. C., Gilbertson, D. L., & Powell, J. A. Therapist burnout: Perspectives on a critical issue. *Social Casework*, November 1978, *59*, 563-565.

Lasch, C. *The culture of narcissism: American life in an age of diminishing expectations*. New York: Norton, 1979.

Lawrence, P. R., & Lorsch, J. *Organization and environment*. Boston: Harvard Graduate School of Business Administration, 1967.

Lazaro, C., & Shinn, M. *Burnout and job performance*. Unpublished manuscript, 1981.

Lazarus, R. S. *Psychological stress and the coping process*. New York: McGraw-Hill, 1966.

Lazarus, R. S., & Launier, R. Stress-related transactions between person and environment. In L. A. Pervin & M. Lewis (Eds.), *Internal and external determinants of behavior*. New York: Plenum, 1978.

Lazarus, R. S., Opton, E. M., Norrikos, M. S., & Rankin, N. O. The principle of shortcircuiting of threat: Further evidence. *Journal of Personality*, 1965, *33*, 622-635.

Lefcourt, H. M. The function of the illusions of control and freedom. *American Psychologist*, *1973, 28*, 417-425.

Lenrow, P. B. Dilemmas of professional helping: Continuities and discontinuities with folk helping roles. In L. Wispe (Ed.), *Altruism, sympathy, and helping*. New York: Academic Press, 1978. (a)

Lenrow, P. B. The work of helping strangers. *American Journal of Community Psychology*, 1978, *6*, 555-571. (b)

Levin, A. Dental burn-out: Are you a candidate? *California Dental Association Journal*, April 1980, 37-45.

Levinson, H. *Executive stress*. New York: New American Library, 1975.

Lewin, K. *A dynamic theory of personality*. New York: McGraw-Hill, 1935.

Lewin, K. *Principles of topological psychology*. New York: McGraw-Hill, 1936.

Liddel, H. Some specific factors that modify tolerance for environmental stress. In H. G. Wolf et al. (Eds.), *Life stress and bodily disease*. Baltimore: Williams & Wilkins, 1950.

Lief, H. I., & Fox, R. C. Training for detached concern in medical students. In H. I. Lief, et al. (Eds.), *The psychological basis of medical practice*. New York: Harper & Row, 1963.

Lief, H. I., Lief, V., & Lief, N. R. (Eds.). *The psychological basis of medical practice*. New York: Harper & Row, 1963.

Likert, R. *Past and future perspectives on System 4*. Paper presented at the annual meeting of the American Academy of Management, Orlando, Florida, 1977.

Locke, E. The nature and the causes of job satisfaction. In M. D. Dunette (Ed.), *Handbook of industrial and organizational psychology*. Chicago: Rand McNally, 1976.

Luke, R. A., Jr., Block, P., Davey, J. M., & Averch, V. A structural approach to organizational change. *Journal of Applied Behavioral Science*, September 1973, *9*, 611-635.

Lynn, K. S. *The professions in America*. Boston: Houghton Mifflin, 1965.

MacNeill, D. H. The relationship of occupational stress to burnout. In J. W. Jones (Ed.), *The burnout syndrome*. Park Ridge, IL: London House Management Press, 1981.

Maluccio, A., & Marlow, W. The case for the contract. *Social Work*, 1974, *19*, 28-36.

Margulies, N. Perspectives on the marginality of the consultant's role. In W. W. Burke (Ed.), *The cutting edge*. La Jolla, CA: University Associates, 1978, 60-69.

Margulies, N., Wright, P. L., & Scholl, R. W. Organization development techniques: Their impact on change. *Group and Organization Studies*, December 1977, *2*, 428-448.

Marrow, A. J. (Ed.). *The failure of success*. New York: AMACOM, 1972.

Marshall, R. E., & Kasman, C. Burnout in the neonatal intensive care unit. *Pediatrics*, June 1980, *65*, 1161-1165.

Martin, M. P., & Klaus, S. *Worker burnout among child protective service workers*. Washington, DC: U.S. Department of Health, Education, and Welfare, 1979.

Maslach, C. *"Detached concern" in health and social service professions*. Paper presented at the annual convention of the American Psychological Association, Montreal, August 1973.

Maslach, C. Burned-out. *Human Behavior*, September 1976, *5*(9), 16-22.

Maslach, C. *Burnout: A social psychological analysis*. Paper presented at the meeting of the American Psychological Association, San Francisco, August 1977.

Maslach, C. The client role in staff burn-out. *Journal of Social Issues*, 1978, *34*, 111-124. (a)

Maslach, C. Job burn-out: How people cope. *Public Welfare*, 1978, *36* (4), 56-58. (b)

Maslach, C. The burn-out syndrome and patient care. In C. A. Garfield (Ed.), *Stress and survival: The emotional realities of life-threatening illness*. St. Louis: C. V. Mosby, 1979.

Maslach, C. Burnout: A social psychological analysis. In J. W. Jones (Ed.), *The burnout syndrome*. Park Ridge, IL: London House Management Press, 1981. (a)

Maslach, C. Understanding burnout: Problems, progress and promise. In W. S. Paine (Ed.), *Proceedings of the First National Conference on Burnout*, Philadelphia, November 1981. (b)

Maslach, C. *Burnout: The cost of caring*. Englewood Cliffs, NJ: Prentice-Hall, 1982.

Maslach, C., & Jackson, S. E. Lawyer burn-out. *Barrister*, 1978, *5*(2), 8, 52-54.

Maslach, C., & Jackson, S. E. Burned-out cops and their families. *Psychology Today*, 1979, *12*(12), 59-62.

Maslach, C., & Jackson, S. E. The measurement of experienced burnout. *Journal of Occupational Behaviour*, 1981, *2*, 99-113. (a)

Maslach, C., & Jackson, S. E. *The Maslach Burnout Inventory*. Palo Alto, CA: Consulting Psychologists Press, 1981. (b)

Maslach, C., & Jackson, S. E. Burnout in health professions: A social psychological analysis. In G. Sanders & J. Suls (Eds.), *Social psychology of health and illness*. Hillsdale, NJ: Lawrence Erlbaum, 1982.

Maslach, C., Jackson, S. E., & Barad, C. B. *Patterns of burnout among a national sample of public contact workers*. Unpublished manuscript, 1982.

Maslach, C., & Pines, A. The burn-out syndrome in the day care setting. *Child Care Quarterly*, 1977, *6*, 100-113. (a)

Maslach, C., & Pines, A. Burnout in mental health professionals. In *Proceedings of the Second Annual Conference on Child Abuse and Neglect*. Austin, TX: Resource Center on Child Abuse and Neglect, 1977. (b)

Maslach, C., & Pines, A. Burnout: The loss of human caring. In A. Pines & C. Maslach (Eds.), *Experiencing social psychology*. New York: Knopf, 1979.

Maslow, A. *Toward a psychology of being*. New York: Van Nostrand Reinhold, 1962.

Mattingly, M. A. Sources of stress and burnout in professional child care work. *Child Care Quarterly*, 1977, *6*(2), 127-137.

McConnell, E. A. (Ed.). *Burnout in the nursing profession*. St. Louis: C. V. Mosby, 1982.

McGregor, D. *The human side of enterprise*. New York: McGraw-Hill, 1960.

McKay, M., Davis, M., & Fanning, P. *Thoughts and feelings: The art of cognitive stress intervention*. Richmond, CA: New Harbinger, 1981.

McMichael, A. J. Personality, behavioral, and situational modifiers of work stressors. In C. L. Cooper & R. Payne (Eds.), *Stress at work*. New York: John Wiley, 1978, 127-147.

McQuade, W., & Aikman, A. *Stress*. New York: Bantam, 1975.

Mechanic, D. Social structure and personal adaptation: Some neglected dimensions. In G. V. Coelho et al. (Eds.) *Coping and adaptation*. New York: Basic Books, 1974.

Mehrabian, A. *Public spaces, private places*. New York: Basic Books, 1976.

Meichenbaum, D. (Ed.). *Cognitive behavior modification: An integrative approach*. New York: Plenum, 1977. (a)

Meichenbaum, D. Stress-inoculation training. In D. Meichenbaum (Ed.), *Cognitive behavior modification: An integrative approach*. New York: Plenum, 1977, 143-182. (b)

Merton, R. K., Reader, C. G., & Kendell, P. S. (Eds.). *The student physician*. Cambridge, MA: Harvard University Press, 1957. (a)

Merton, R. K. Some preliminaries to a sociology of medical education. In R. K. Merton et al. (Eds.), *The student physician*. Cambridge, MA: Harvard University Press, 1957, 71-79. (b)

Michigan Organizational Assessment Package. Ann Arbor: Institute for Social Research, 1975.

Miles, R. H. Organization boundary roles. In C. L. Cooper & R. Payne (Eds.), *Stress at work*. New York: John Wiley, 1978, 61-96.

Miller, G. J. *The laboratory approach to planned change in the public sector*. Unpublished doctoral dissertation, University of Georgia, 1979.

Miller, S., Nunnally, E. W., & Wackman, D. B. *Alive and aware: Improving communication in relationships*. Minneapolis: Interpersonal Communication Programs, 1975.

Minnehan, R. F., & Paine, W. S. Burning money: Analyzing some basic economic and legal consequences of burnout. In W. S. Paine (Ed.) *Proceedings of the First National Conference on Burnout*, Philadelphia, November 1981.

Mischel, W. *Personality and assessment*. New York: John Wiley, 1968.

Mischel, W. Toward a cognitive social learning: Reconceptualization of personality. *Psychological Review*, 1973, *80*, 252-283.

Mitchell, M. *Consultant burnout*. Presentation at the 1977 Meeting of the Organizational Development Network, San Diego, 1977.

Mobley, W. H., Griffeth, R. W., Hand, H. H., & Meglino, B. M. Review and conceptual analysis of the employee turnover process. *Psychological Bulletin,* 1979, *86,* 493-522.

Mobley, W. H., Horner, S. O., & Hollingsworth, A. T. An evaluation of precursors of hospital employee turnover. *Journal of Applied Psychology,* 1978, *63,* 408-414.

Moody, R. A. *Laugh after laugh: The healing power of humor.* Jacksonville, FL: Headwaters Press, 1978.

Moos, R. H. A social-ecological perspective on health. In G. Stone et al. (Eds.), *Health psychology.* San Francisco: Jossey-Bass, 1979.

Morrison, P. Evaluation in OD: A review and an assessment. *Group and Organization Studies,* March 1978, *3,* 42-70.

Moustakas, C. *Portraits of loneliness and love.* Englewood Cliffs, NJ: Prentice-Hall, 1974.

Mowrer, O. H. *The new group therapy.* Princeton, NJ: D. Van Nostrand, 1964.

Moynihan, D. P. *Maximum feasible misunderstanding: Community action in the war on poverty.* New York: Free Press, 1969.

Muchinsky, P. M., & Tuttle, M. L. Employee turnover: An empirical and methodological assessment. *Journal of Vocational Behavior.* 1979, *14,* 43-77.

Mudd, E. H., Freeman, C. H., & Rose, E. K. Premarital counseling in the Philadelphia Marriage Counsel. *Mental Hygiene,* 1941, *25.*

Mullahy, P. *Psychoanalysis and interpersonal psychiatry: The contributions of Harry Stack Sullivan.* New York: Science House, 1970.

Nadler, D. A. *Feedback and organization development.* Reading, MA: Addison-Wesley, 1977.

Naismith, D. *Stress among managers as a function of organizational change.* Unpublished doctoral dissertation, George Washington University, 1975.

Newman, J. E., & Beehr, T. A. Personal and organizational strategies for handling job stress: A review of research and opinion. *Personnel Psychology,* 1979, *32,* 1-43.

Nollen, S. D. Does flexitime improve productivity? *Harvard Business Review,* September 1979, *57,* 16-18; 76; 80.

Norfolk, D. *The stress factor.* New York: Simon & Schuster, 1977.

Oppenheimer, M. The unionization of the professional. *Social Policy,* January/February 1975, *5,* 34-40.

Ottenberg, D. J., & Madden, E. E. (Eds.). *Proceedings of the 12th Annual Eagleville Conference: Ethical issues in substance abuse treatment.* Eagleville, PA: Eagleville Hospital and Rehabilitation Center, 1980.

Pacoe, L. V., Narr, R., Guyett, I. P. R., & Wells, R. Training medical students in interpersonal relationship skills. *Journal of Medical Education,* September 1976.

Paine, W. S. Burnout in context. In J. W. Jones (Ed.), *The burnout syndrome.* Park Ridge, IL: London House Management Press, 1981. (a)

Paine, W. S. (Ed.). *Proceedings of the First National Conference on Burnout,* Philadelphia, November 1981. (b)

Paine, W. S. Burnout, decision makers and the First National Conference. In W. S. Paine (Ed.), *Proceedings of the First National Conference on Burnout,* Philadelphia, November 1981. (c)

Paine, W. S. *Burnout as kaleidoscope or calliope: Area and disciplinary insights into a generic process.* Paper presented at the annual conference of the American Psychological Association, Los Angeles, August 1981. (d)

Paine, W. S. *Burnout interventions: Personal and organizational considerations.* Paper presented at the meeting of the New Jersey Association of Mental Health Agencies, Tinton Falls, New Jersey, March 30, 1982.

Paine, W. S., & O'Brian, C. Critical care nursing and the burnout stress syndrome. *Critical Care Nursing*, in press.

Patrick, P.K.S. Burnout: Job hazard for health workers. *Hospitals*. November, 1979, *54*, 87-89.

Payne, R. Organization stress and social support. In C. L. Cooper & R. Payne (Eds.), *Current concerns in occupational stress*. New York: John Wiley, 1980, 269-298.

Pearlin, L. I., & Schooler, C. The structure of coping. *Journal of Health and Social Behavior*, 1978, *19*, 2-21.

Pellegrino, E. D. Educating the humanist physician: An ancient ideal reconsidered. *Journal of the American Medical Association*, 1974, *227*(11).

Pelz, D. C., & Andrews, F. M. Detecting causal priorities in panel study data. *American Sociological Review*, 1964, *29*, 56-68.

Percarich, F. Hidden agendas and consultant burnout. *OD Practitioner*, 1974, *6*, 3.

Perlman, B., & Hartman, E. A. Burnout: Summary and future research. *Human Relations*, in press.

Perrow, C. *Organizational analysis*. Monterey, CA: Brooks/Cole, 1970.

Pervin, L. A., & Lewis, M. (Eds.). *Internal and external determinants of behavior*. New York: Plenum, 1978.

Pfifferling, J. H., Blum, J. C., & Wood, A. M. Physician impairment: Some criteria for prevention. *Journal of the Kansas Medical Society*, 1981, *82*(11), 509-515; 520.

Phelps, S., & Austin, N. *The assertive woman*. San Luis Opispo, CA: Impact Press, 1975.

Pines, A. Burnout: A current problem in pediatrics. *Current Problems in Pediatrics*, July 1981. (a)

Pines, A. The impossible goal? A work environment without burnout. In W. S. Paine (Ed.), *Proceedings of the First National Conference on Burnout*, Philadelphia, November 1981. (b)

Pines, A. *The burnout measure*. Paper presented at the First National Conference on Burnout, Philadelphia, November 1981. (c)

Pines, A. Helpers' motivation and the burnout syndrome. In T. A. Wills (Ed.), *Basic processes in helping relationships*. New York: Academic Press, 1982. (a)

Pines, A. On burnout and the buffering effects of social support. In B. Farber (Ed.), *Stress and burnout in human service professions*. New York: Pergamon, 1982. (b)

Pines, A., & Aronson, E. *Burnout*. Schiller Park, IL: MTI Teleprograms, 1980.

Pines, A., & Aronson, E. Combatting burnout. *Children and Youth Services Review*, 1981.

Pines, A., Aronson, E., with Kafry, D. *Burnout: From tedium to personal growth*. New York: Free Press, 1981.

Pines, A., & Kafry, D. Occupational tedium in social service professionals. *Social Work*, November 1978, *23*, 499-507.

Pines, A., & Kafry, D. Tedium in the life and work of professional women as compared with men. *Sex Roles*, 1981. (a)

Pines, A., & Kafry, D. Coping with burnout. In J. W. Jones (Ed.), *The burnout syndrome*. Park Ridge, IL: London House Management Press, 1981. (b)

Pines, A., Kafry, D. The experience of life tedium in three generations of professional women. *Sex Roles*, 1981 *7*(2), 117-134. (c)

Pines, A., Kafry, D., & Etzion, D. Job stress from a cross cultural perspective. In K. Reid (Ed.), *Burnout in the helping professions*. Kalamazoo: College of Health and Human Services, Western Michigan University, 1980.

Pines, A., & Kanner, A. Nurse's burnout: Lack of positive conditions and presence of negative conditions as two independent sources of stress. In E. A. McConnell (Ed.), *Burnout in the nursing profession*. St. Louis: C. V. Mosby, 1982.

Pines, A., & Maslach, C. Characteristics of staff burnout in mental health settings. *Hospital and Community Psychiatry*, 1978, *29*, 233-237.

Pines, A., & Maslach, C. (Eds.). *Experiencing social psychology*. New York: Knopf, 1979.

Pines, A., & Maslach, C. Combatting staff burn-out in a day care center: A case study. *Child Care Quarterly*, 1980 *9*(1), 5-16.

Plutchik, R. *The emotions: Facts, theories and a new model*. New York: Random House, 1962.

Plutchik, R. *Emotion: A psychoevolutionary synthesis*. New York: Harper & Row, 1980.

Podell, L. Attrition of first line social service staff. *Welfare Review*, 1967, *5*, 9-14.

Porras, J. I. The comparative impact of different OD techniques and intervention intensities. *Journal of Applied Behavioral Science*, April 1979, *15*, 156-178.

Porter, L. W., & Steers, R. M. Organizational, work, and personal factors in employee turnover and absenteeism. *Psychological Bulletin*, 1973, *80*, 151-176.

Powell, J. *Why am I afraid to tell you who I am?* Niles, IL: Argus, 1969.

Proehl, C.W., Jr. *Planned organizational change*. Unpublished doctoral dissertation, University of Georgia, 1980.

Prottas, J. M. *People-processing: The street-level bureaucrat in public service bureaucracies*. Lexington, MA: D. C. Health, 1979.

Public Health Service Task Force on Cost of Illness Studies. *Guidelines for cost of illness studies in the public health service*. May 31, 1979. (Mimeo)

Reddin, W. J. Confessions of an organizational change agent. *Group and Organization Studies*, March 1977, *2*, 33-41.

Reed, S. What you can do to prevent teacher burnout. *National Elementary Principal*, 1979, *58*, 67-70.

Reid, K. (Ed.). *Burnout in the helping professions*. Kalamazoo: College of Health and Human Services, Western Michigan University, 1980.

Rice, B. Can companies kill? *Psychology Today*, 1981, *151*(6), 3.

Robbins, A. S., Kauss, D. R., Heinrich, R., Abrass, I., Dryer, J., & Clyman, B. Interpersonal skills training: Evaluation in an internal medicine residency. *Journal of Medical Education*, November 1979.

Robinson, P. E. *Work climate and satisfaction in human service and other professions*. Paper presented at the meeting of the American Psychological Association, Montreal, September 1-5, 1980.

Rogers, C. R. The necessary and sufficient conditions of therapeutic personality change. *Journal of Counseling Psychology*, 1957, *121*(2), 95-103.

Rogers, C. R. *On becoming a person*. Boston: Houghton Mifflin, 1961.

Rogosa, D. A. Critique of cross-lagged correlation. *Psychological Bulletin*, 1980, *88*, 245-258.

Ronen, S. *Flexible working hours*. New York: McGraw-Hill, 1981.

Rose, B. K., & Osterud, H. T. Humanistic geriatric health care: An innovation in medical education. *Journal of Medical Education*, November 1980, *55*.

Rose, R. M., Jenkins, C. D., & Hurst, M. W. *Air traffic controller health change study*. Boston: Boston University School of Medicine, 1978.

Rothman, D. J. The state as parent: Social policy in the progressive era. In W. Gaylin et al., *Doing good: The limits of benevolence*. New York: Pantheon, 1978.

Rubin, T. *The angry book*. New York: Macmillan, 1969.

Ryan, W. *Blaming the victim*. New York: Pantheon, 1971.

Ryerson, D. M. *The burn out blues*. n.d. (Mimeo)

Ryerson, D. M., & Marks, N. *Career burnout in the human services: Strategies for intervention*. n.d. (Mimeo)

Samuels, M., & Samuels, N. *Seeing with the mind's eye*. New York: Random House, 1975.

Sanders, G., & Suls, J. (Eds.). *Social psychology of health and illness*. Hillsdale, NJ: Lawrence Erlbaum, 1982.

Sandler, I. N. Life stress events and community psychology. In I. G. Sarason & C. D. Spielberger (Eds.), *Stress and anxiety*. New York: Halstead, 1979, 213-234.

Sarason, S. B. *The creation of settings and the future societies*. San Francisco: Jossey-Bass, 1972.

Sarason, I. G., & Spielberger, C. D. (Eds.). *Stress and anxiety*. New York: Halstead, 1979.

Satir, V. *Self-esteem*. Millbrae, CA: Celestial Arts, 1975.

Sayles, L. R., & Chandler, R. *Managing large systems*. New York: Harper & Row, 1971.

Schein, E. H. *Process consultation*. Reading, MA: Addison-Wesley, 1969.

Schein, E. H. *Professional education: Some new directions*. New York: McGraw-Hill, 1972.

Scholz, N. T., Prince, J. S., & Miller, G. P. *How to decide: A guide for women*. New York: College Entrance Examination Board, 1975.

Schumm, W. R., & Denton, W. Trends in premarital counseling. *Journal of Marital and Family Therapy*, October 1979.

Scott, D. *How to put more time in your life*. New York: New American Library, 1980.

Seashore, S. E., & Bowers, D. G. Durability of organizational change. *American Psychologist*, January 1970, *25*, 232-235.

Seashore, S. E., Lawler, E. E. III, Mervis, P. H., & Cammon, C. (Eds.). *Observing and measuring organizational change: A guide to field practice*. New York: Wiley-Interscience, in press.

Sehnert, K. W. *Stress/unstress*. Minneapolis: Augsburg, 1981.

Seligman, M.E.P. *Helplessness: On depression, development and death*. San Francisco: W. H. Freeman, 1975.

Selltiz, C. Wrightsman, L. S., & Cook, S. W. *Research methods in social relations* (3rd ed.). New York: Holt, Rinehart Winston, 1976.

Selye, H. *Stress without distress*. Philadelphia: Lippincott, 1974.

Selye, H. *The stress of life* (2nd ed.). New York: McGraw-Hill, 1976.

Seybolt, J. W. Career development. *Training Directors Journal*, April 1979, *33*, 16-21.

Shaffer, C. R. The organization doctors: Some surprising remedies for ailing human systems. *San Francisco Examiner and Chronicle, Sunday Magazine Section*, January 25, 1981. (Reprinted in *OD Practitioner*, May 1981, *13*, 1-5)

Shannon, C., & Saleebey, D. Training child welfare workers to cope with burnout. *Child Welfare*, 1980, *59*, 463-468.

Shapiro, C. H. *The use of assertive training to enhance interpersonal communication between students and field instructors*. Paper presented at the annual program meeting of the Council on Social Work Education, 1981. (a)

Shapiro, C. H. Creative supervision: An antidote for burnout. In W. S. Paine (Ed.), *Proceedings of the First National Conference on Burnout*, Philadelphia, November 1981. (b)

Sharpe, R., & Lewis, D. *Thrive on stress*. New York: Warner Books, 1977.

Shealy, C. N. *90 days to self-health*. New York: Dial, 1977.

Shepard, H. A. Rules of thumb for change agents. *OD Practitioner*, November 1975, *7*, 1-5.

Shepard, H. A., & Hawley, J. A. *Life planning: Personal and organizational*. Washington, DC: National Training and Development Service, 1974.

Shinn, M. Evaluation of a survey-guided development process in group homes for youths (Doctoral dissertation, University of Michigan, 1978). *Dissertation Abstracts International,* 1979, *39,* 5154B.

Shinn, M. Burnout in human service agencies: Patterns of job stress, psychological strain, and coping responses. In K. Reid (Ed.), *Burnout in the helping professions.* Kalamazoo: College of Health and Human Services, Western Michigan University, 1980.

Shinn, M. Caveat emptor: Potential problems in using information on burnout. In W. S. Paine (Ed.), *Proceedings of the First National Conference on Burnout,* Philadelphia, November 1981.

Shinn, M., & Mørch, H. A tripartite model of coping with burnout. In B. Farber (Ed.), *Stress and burnout in human service professions.* New York: Pergamon, 1982.

Shinn, M., Perkins, D.N.T., & Cherniss, C. Using survey-guided development to improve social climates: An experimental evaluation in group homes for youths. In *Optimizing environments: Research, practice, and policy.* Washington, DC: EDRA, 1980.

Shinn, M., Rosario, M., Mørch, H., & Chestnut, D. E. *Coping with job stress and burnout.* Unpublished manuscript, 1981.

Shorr, J. *Go see the movie in your head.* New York: Popular Library, 1977.

Shriescheim, C., & Bird, B. *Social desirability response bias as a confounding factor in organizational surveys: A closer look.* Paper presented at the annual meeting of the Academy of Management, San Diego, August 2-5, 1981.

Simon, S. B. *Meeting yourself half-way: 31 value clarification strategies for daily living.* Niles, IL: Argus, 1974.

Simon, S. B., Howe, L., & Kirschenbaum, H. *Values clarification: A handbook of practical strategies for teachers and students.* New York: Hart, 1972.

Singer, J. D., & Glass, D. C. Making your world more livable. In *Stress.* Chicago: Blue Cross, 1974.

Slote, A. *Termination.* Indianapolis: Bobbs-Merrill, 1977.

Smith, K. K. What constraints limit feedback and disclosure? In R. T. Golembiewski (Ed.), *Approaches to planned change,* Part 2. New York: Marcel Dekker, 1979, 397-408.

Smith, P. C., Kendall, L. M., & Blood, C. L. *The measurement of satisfaction in work and retirement.* Chicago: Rand McNally, 1969.

Smith, R. E., Johnson, J. H., & Sarason, I. G. Life change, the sensation seeking motive, and psychological distress. *Journal of Consulting and Clinical Psychology,* 1978, *46,* 348-349.

Snow, D. L., & Newton, P. M. Task, social structure, and social process in the community mental health center movement. *American Psychologist,* 1976, *31,* 582-594.

Solo, R., & Anderson, C. H. (Eds.). *Value judgments and income distribution.* New York: Praeger, in press.

Speiser, S. M. *Recovery for Wrongful Death: Economic Handbook.* Rochester, NY: Bancroft Whitney, 1979.

Stiles, E. Supervision in perspective. *Social Casework,* 1963, *44,* 19-25.

Stokols, D. A congruence analysis of human stress. In I. G. Sarason & C. D. Spielberger (Eds.), *Stress and anxiety.* New York: Halstead, 1979, 27-53.

Stone, G., Cohen, F., & Adler, N. (Eds.). *Health psychology.* San Francisco: Jossey-Bass, 1979.

Stumpf, S. A. Using integrators to manage conflict in a research organization. *Journal of Applied Behavioral Science,* October 1977, *13,* 507-517.

Sue, S. Community mental health services to minority groups: Some optimism, some pessimism. *American Psychologist,* 1977, *32,* 616-624.

Suedfeld, P. Stressful levels of environmental stimulation. In I. G. Sarason & C. D. Spielberger (Eds.), *Stress and anxiety*. New York: Halstead, 1979, 109-127.

Sullivan, H. S. *Personal psychopathology*. Washington, DC: William Alanson White Psychiatric Foundation, 1965.

Sweeney, D. Burnout: Is it really a stress syndrome? In W. S. Paine (Ed.), *Proceedings of the First National Conference on Burnout*, Philadelphia, November 1981.

Taber, T. D., Walsh, J. T., & Cooke, R. A. Developing a community-based program for reducing the social impact of a plant closing. *Journal of Applied Behavioral Science*, April 1979, *15*, 133-155.

Tannenbaum, A. S., Kavčič, B., Rosener, M., Vianello, M., & Weiser, G. *Hierarchy in organizations: An international comparison*. San Francisco: Jossey-Bass, 1974.

Tavernier, G. How America can manage its flexible benefits program. *Management Review*, August 1980, 8-12.

Thamhain, H. J., & Wilemon, D. L. Conflict management in project life cycles. *Sloan Management Review*, July 1975, *16*, 31-50.

Tournier, P. *The meaning of persons*. New York: Harper & Row, 1957.

Tournier, P. *To resist or surrender?* Atlanta: John Knox, 1962.

Townsend, R. *Up the organization: How to stop the corporation from stifling people and strangling profits*. New York: Fawcett, 1970.

Triplett, N. The dynamogenic factors in pacemaking and competition. *American Journal of Psychology*, 1898, *9*, 597-533.

Tubesing, D. A. *Wholistic health: A whole person approach to primary health care*. New York: Human Sciences Press, 1979. (a)

Tubesing, D. A. *Stress skills participant workbook*. Duluth, MN: Whole Person Associates, 1979. (b)

Tubesing, D. A. *Kicking your stress habits: A do-it-yourself guide for coping with stress*. Duluth, MN: Whole Person Associates, 1981.

Tubesing, D. A., & Strosahl, S. G. *Wholistic health centers: Survey research report*. Hinsdale, IL: Society for Wholistic Medicine, 1976.

Tubesing, D. A., & Tubesing, N. L. *Tune in: Empathy training workshop*. Duluth, MN: Listening Group, 1974.

Tubesing, D. A., Tubesing, N. L., & Sippel, M. O. *Rx for BURNOUT: A structured strategy for promoting vitality and preventing burnout in the care-giving professions*. Duluth, MN: Whole Person Associates, 1981.

Tubesing, N. L., & Tubesing, D. A. The treatment of choice: Selecting stress skills to suit the individual and the situation. In W. S. Paine (Ed.), *Proceedings of the First National Conference on Burnout*, Philadelphia, November 1981.

Vash, C. L. *The burnt-out administrator*. New York: Springer, 1980.

Veninga, R. L., & Spradley, J. P. *Work/stress connection: How to cope with job burnout*. Boston: Little, Brown, 1981.

Veysey, L. Who's a professional? Who cares? (Review of *Advocacy and objectivity: A crisis in the professionalization of American social science, 1865-1905*, by M. O. Furner). *Reviews in American History*, 1975, *3*(4), 419-423.

Virshup, B. *Coping in medical school*. Chapel Hill, NC: Health Sciences Consortium, 1982.

Wade, C. *Natural way to health through controlled fasting*. New York: Arc Books, 1970.

Wahlund, I., & Nerell, G. Stress factors in the working environment of white collar workers. In *Reducing occupational stress: Proceedings of the National Institute for Occupational Safety and Health*, White Plains, New York, May 1977, 62-72.

Walsh, D. Classroom stress and teacher burnout. *Phi Delta Kappan,* 1979, *61,* 253.

Walton, R. E. *Interpersonal peacemaking.* Reading, MA: Addison-Wesley, 1969.

Walton, R. E. Work innovations at Topeka. *Journal of Applied Behavioral Science,* July 1977, *13,* 422-433.

Walton, R. E., & Warwick, D. P. The ethics of organization development. *Journal of Applied Behavioral Science,* November 1973, *9,* 681-699.

Wanous, J. P. Organizational entry: Newcomers moving from outside to inside. *Psychological Bulletin,* 1977, *84,* 601-618.

Ward, L. M., & Suedfeld, P. Human response to highway noise. *Environmental Research,* 1973, *6,* 306-326.

Warnath, C. F. Counselor burnout: Existential crisis or a problem for the profession? *Personnel and Guidance Journal,* 1979, *57,* 325-328.

Warrick, D. D. Managing the stress of organization development. *Training and Development Journal,* April 1981, *35,* 36-41.

Watson, D. The manpower team in a child welfare setting. *Child Welfare,* 1968, *47,* 446-454.

Watson, K. Differential supervision. *Social Work,* 1973, *18,* 80-88.

Webb, E. J., Campbell, D. T., Schwartz, R. D., & Sechrest, L. *Unobtrusive measures: Non-reactive research in the social sciences.* Chicago: Rand McNally, 1966.

Weinberg, S., Edwards, G., & Garove, W. E. *Burnout among employees of residential facilities serving developmentally disabled persons.* Birmingham: University of Alabama, Management Training Program, 1979.

Weinberger, J. Job burnout. *Omnibus,* December 1980, *3,* 2-3.

Weinberger, P. *Job satisfaction and staff retention in social work.* San Diego: San Diego State College School of Social Work, 1970.

Weisbord, M. The Wizard of OD. *OD Practitioner,* Summer 1978, *10,* 1-4.

Weiss, J. M. Effects of coping behavior in different warning signal conditions on stress pathology in rats. *Journal of Comparative and Physiological Psychology,* 1970, *77,* 1-13.

Welch, I. D., Medeiros, D. C., & Tate, G. A. *Beyond burnout: How to enjoy your job again when you've just about had enough.* Englewood Cliffs, Prentice-Hall, 1982.

Westberg, G. *Good grief.* Philadelphia: Fortress Press, 1962.

White, J., & Fadiman, J. *Relax.* New York: Dell, 1976.

White, W. L. *Incest in the organizational family: The unspoken issues in staff and program burn-out.* Rockville, MD: HCS, 1978. (a)

White, W. L. *A systems response to staff burnout.* Rockville, MD; HCS, 1978. (b)

White, W. L. *Relapse as a phenomenon of staff burn-out among recovering substance abusers.* Rockville, MD: HCS, 1978. (c)

White, W. L. The organizational context of staff burn-out. In D. J. Ottenberg & E. E. Madden (Eds.), *Proceedings of the 12th Annual Eagleville Conference: Ethical issues in substance abuse treatment.* Eagle Eagleville, PA: Eagleville Hospital and Rehabilitation Center, 1980, 186-195.

White, W. L. *Organizational responses to victims of professional burn-out: A conceptual schema.* Unpublished manuscript, 1981. (Available from William L. White, HCS, Inc., 11325 Seven Locks Rd., Suite 231, Potomac, MD 20854.) [a]

White, W. L. *Managing personal and organizational stress in health and human service agencies: A workshop for the Montgomery County Health Department.* Unpublished manuscript, 1981. (Available from William L. White, HCS, Inc., 11325 Seven Locks Rd., Suite 231, Potomac, MD 20854.) [b]

Wilder, J., & Plutchik, R. Preparing the professional: Building prevention into professional training. In W. S. Paine (Ed.) *Proceedings of the First National Conference on Burnout,* Philadelphia, November 1981.

Wilensky, H. L. The professionalization of everyone? *American Journal of Sociology,* 1964, *70,* 137-158.

Wiley, D. B. They used to call it depression; now it's known as "burnout." *Philadelphia Bulletin,* April 26, 1981, 1D-2D.

Williams, G. Personal growth overkill. *OD Practitioner,* May 1981, pp. 9-10.

Wills, T. A. (Ed.). *Basic processes in helping relationships.* New York: Academic Press, 1982.

Winn, A. *The laboratory approach to organization development.* Paper presented at the 1968 Annual Conference of the British Psychological Association, Oxford, 1968.

Winston, S. *Getting organized: The easy way to put your life in order.* New York: Norton, 1978.

Wispe, L. (Ed.). *Altruism, sympathy, and helping.* New York: Academic Press, 1978.

Wolf, H. G., Wolf, S. G., Jr., & Hare, C. C. (Eds.). *Life stress and bodily disease.* Baltimore: Williams & Wilkins, 1950.

Worthy, J. *Big business and free men.* New York: Harper & Brothers, 1959.

Yates, J. E. *Managing stress: A business person's guide.* New York: ANACOM, 1979.

Ziller, R. G., Stark, B. J., & Pruder, H. O. Marginality and integrative management positions. *Academy of Management Journal,* December 1969, *12,* 487-493.

Zimring, C. M. Stress and the designed environment. *Journal of Social Issues,* 1981, *37,* 145-171.

Zola, I. K. In the name of health and illness: On some socio-political consequences of medical influence. *Social Science and Medicine,* 1975, *9,* 83-87.

Zunin, L., & Zunin, N. *Contact: The first four minutes.* New York: Ballantine, 1972.

Index

About the Authors

ARCHIE BRODSKY, a professional writer, has co-authored two books with Jerry Edelwich as well as *Love and Addiction* and *Medical Choices, Medical Chances.*

JEROME F. X. CARROLL, Ph.D., is Associate Director of Inpatient Services and Director of Psychological Services, Eagleville Hospital. Dr. Carroll served as consultant to the National Drug Abuse Center for Training and Resources Development on Burnout. He has conducted numerous workshops on burnout and alcohol and drug abuse, as well as written extensively in the field.

CARY CHERNISS, Ph.D., is a Research Scientist for the Illinois Institute for Developmental Disabilities. Dr. Cherniss is a Research Psychologist whose books include *Professional Burnout in Human Service Organizations* and *Staff Burnout: Job Stress in the Human Services.*

FRED M. ECKEL, R.Ph., M.S., is Chairman of the Division of Pharmacy Practice at the University of North Carolina School of Pharmacy. He is past president of the American Society of Hospital Pharmacists, and Membership Director of the Center for the Well-Being of Health Professionals.

JERRY EDELWICH, M.S.W., lecturer and consultant in human services and certified reality therapist, conducts nationwide workshops and training courses in such areas as burnout, human sexuality, substance abuse, counseling skills, and staff development. He is the author (with Archie Brodsky) of *Burnout: Stages of Disillusionment in the Helping Professions* and the forthcoming *Sexual Dilemmas for the Helping Professional.*

HERBERT J. FREUDENBERGER, Ph.D., is a psychoanalyst in independent practice. He is a consultant on burnout to agencies and corporations and the author of *Burnout: How to Beat the High Cost of Success* (New York, Bantam Books, 1982) and *Situational Anxiety* (Garden City, New York, Doubleday, 1982).

ROBERT T. GOLEMBIEWSKI is Research Professor of Political Science and Management at the University of Georgia and Distinguished Visiting Scholar at the University of Calgary. He is an active consultant and the author or editor of forty books.

CHRISTINA MASLACH, Ph.D., is an Associate Professor of Psychology at the University of California, Berkeley. She is one of the leading researchers on burnout and her measure, the Maslach Burnout Inventory, is the most widely used instrument in the field. She is the author of *Burnout: The Cost of Caring* and numerous scientific publications.

ROBERT F. MINNEHAN, Ph.D., is President of Program Evaluation and Planning Services, Inc., and is author of numerous technical papers and monographs on the economic analysis of social programs and program evaluation.

WHITON STEWART PAINE, Ph.D., is Director of Human Services at Mercy Catholic Medical Center in Philadelphia, Pennsylvania. A psychologist and specialist in the evaluation and administration of human services programs, he served as Program Chair for the First National Conference on Burnout, November 1981. Dr. Paine was formerly Associate Professor in the Department of Human Service Studies at Cornell University.

JOHN-HENRY PFIFFERLING is Director of the Center for the Well-Being of Health Professionals, Durham, North Carolina; Clinical Associate Professor at the University of North Carolina School of Pharmacy; and consultant to state medical, dental, and pharmacy societies on the prevention of burnout. He has published widely on the cultural values of health professionals and has conducted research on risk factors for impairment among health professionals. He lectures on the prevention of impairment and on the promotion of well-being for professionals.

AYALA M. PINES, Ph.D., is a Research Associate, Department of Psychology, University of California, Berkeley. Dr. Pines, a noted researcher, lecturer, and educator, has conducted workshops on burnout all over the United States and abroad, and has published eight book chapters as well as numerous scientific articles on the subject. Her most recent book is *Burnout: From Tedium to Personal Growth* (co-authored with Aronson and Kafry, 1981).

ROBERT PLUTCHIK, Ph.D., is Professor of Psychiatry and Psychology, Albert Einstein College of Medicine. Dr. Plutchik has written and lectured widely. Two of his recent books are *Emotion: A Psychoevolutionary Synthesis* and *Foundations of Experimental Research*.

CONSTANCE HOENK SHAPIRO, Ph.D., is Associate Professor, Department of Human Service Studies, Cornell University. Dr. Shapiro has specialized in staff training of professional social workers and has conducted numerous staff training workshops with social service and other workers.

MARYBETH SHINN, Ph.D., is Assistant Professor, Community Psychology Program, New York University. Dr. Shinn currently serves on the editorial board of the American Journal of Community Psychology. Her research is in the area of job stress and coping.

DONALD A. TUBESING holds a doctorate in psychology from Ohio University and a master's in divinity degree from Concordia Seminary. He has held a medical school faculty appointment; has written extensively in the fields of counseling skills, stress management, and interdisciplinary approaches to holistic health care; and is the author of *Kicking Your Stress Habits*.

NANCY LOVING TUBESING received her doctorate in counselor education/marriage and family counseling from Northern Illinois University. She has held a medical school faculty appointment and has written extensively in the field of counseling skills, stress management, and interdisciplinary approaches to holistic health care.

WILLIAM L. WHITE, M.A., is Senior Research Associate, HCS, Inc. Mr. White is a researcher, author, and lecturer and has written numerous articles on burnout and related areas.

JACK F. WILDER, M.D., is Associate Dean for Planning and Operations, Albert Einstein College of Medicine. Dr. Wilder, a psychiatrist, has had extensive experience in clinical administration, program planning, and teaching. He has written numerous articles for professional journals in psychiatry and mental health.